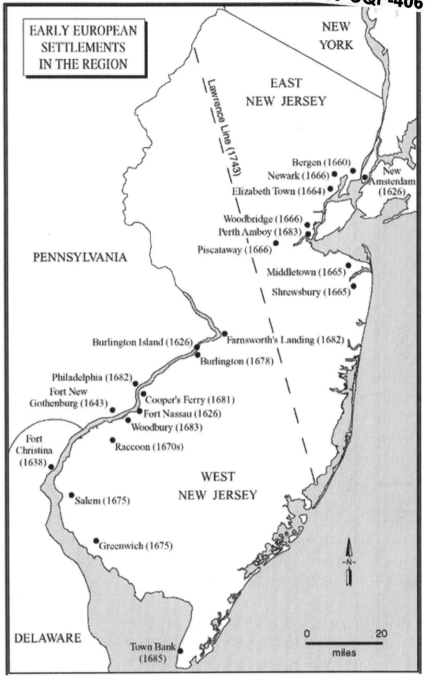

EARLY EUROPEAN
SETTLEMENTS
IN THE REGION

NEW
YORK

EAST
NEW JERSEY

Lawrence Line (1743)

Bergen (1660)
Newark (1666)
Elizabeth Town (1664)

New
Amsterdam
(1626)

Woodbridge (1666)
Perth Amboy (1683)
Piscataway (1666)

PENNSYLVANIA

Middletown (1665)
Shrewsbury (1665)

Burlington Island (1626)
Farnsworth's Landing (1682)
Burlington (1678)

Philadelphia (1682)
Fort New
Gothenburg (1643)
Cooper's Ferry (1681)
Fort Nassau (1626)
Woodbury (1683)
Raccoon (1670s)

Fort
Christina
(1638)

WEST
NEW JERSEY

Salem (1675)

Greenwich (1675)

-N-

DELAWARE

Town Bank
(1685)

0   20
miles

CREDIT: HTTP://WHAT-WHEN-HOW.COM/NEW-JERSEY/HISTORIC-
SPEEDWELL-TO-HISTORIOGRAPHY-NEW-JERSEY/

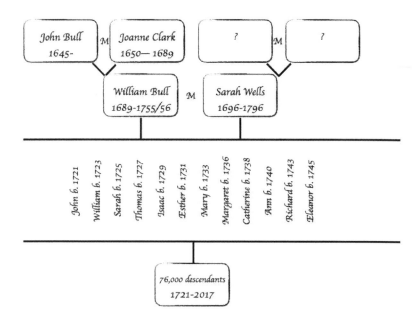

Sarah
An American Pioneer

The Circumstantial and Documented
Evidence of the
Courageous Life of
Sarah Wells Bull

By Julie Boyd Cole

With Sarah Brownell

Julie Boyd Cole, with Sarah Brownell

ISBN:13:978-1981483334
ISBN-10:1981483330

A non-fiction work.

DEDICATION

This work is dedicated to my children, Henry and Campbell Cole, my niece, Samantha Boyd, and nephews, William Boyd and Damon Fredlund. May they continue to love their heritage as much as I do and continue to hand it down;

To all the Bull family members who have made it their passion to dig among the ancient records and build family trees. We've seen your work all on the internet in shared family trees and histories and we are incredibly impressed with your commitment to documenting our heritage;

To the past, current, and future descendants of Sarah Wells Bull. You are all part of the incredible legacy created by the first tentative steps of a teenage girl, made in the earliest days of our country. You are from courageous stock, and from a special family.

My hope is that each generation will rise to great heights despite any odds, just like Sarah.

Sincerely,
Julie Boyd Cole

My work on this book is dedicated to my husband Jim Brownell who has supported every new endeavor I have had the opportunity to pursue;

To my children, the 10th generation, Pierson, Emily and Tucker Brownell. Your support of my efforts on the Association Board, and your willingness to pitch in at Bull Picnic to my every possible request, makes me very proud of the genuine Bull people you have become;

To my mother Mary Jane Bull Sorrell. Your legacy in the Bull family history gives me great pride. I will treasure forever our Sunday drives around Orange County as we strove to uncover and remember our family's stories.

To my cousin Julie Boyd Cole. The time we've spent together during this research has been a true experience of love. Your support and encouragement of me as I continue to learn what I am capable of has been immeasurable.

Sincerely,
Sarah J. Brownell

CONTENTS

ACKNOWLEDGMENTS

We would like to thank the many people who have helped with this project. We have spent the last year with our noses buried in ancient books, scrolling through thousands of Google pages, walking through acres of headstones, and talking to dedicated folks who work equally hard to understand the lineage of so many American families.

Our cousin, Michael Brown, our longest Bull Stone House caretaker, has given his life to understanding the stories of thousands of distant cousins who all can say they descend from Sarah and William Bull. We have heard so many stories from people who started on the path of learning about their past by hearing Michael say: "Welcome home!"

No matter the circumstances within his own life, he always greeted the strangers at the door as family. We were lucky enough to grow up knowing Michael. To us, he is a close cousin. He has been there with us during the happiness of marriage and the sadness of death more than once. He was there with us during this project as well. He spent many hours going over details and sharing his knowledge on the story of Sarah. He also helped us analyze our hypothesis, and we are forever grateful. The Bull Family is so lucky to have Michael Brown!

Melanie Brown Latimer opened her home, the Bull Stone House, to us more than once so we could search through records or just wander the homestead. We love you, Melanie!

Mary Jane Sorrell read the book and checked us on details of Sarah's story. Her love, support and encouragement has meant the world to us. Her information has been invaluable.

Several historians and amateur genealogists have been kind enough to offer their help, advice, and information. We are grateful to Judy Wood, our current keeper of the genealogy of the Bull Family. Thank you for your information and daily work.

We're grateful for Al and Linda Bull, John Pennings, Frank Gillespie, Emily Brownell, Henry Z. Jones, Sherry White, Campbell Cole, Henry Cole, Nancy Boyd, Denver Fredlund, Rosa Boyd, Lyle Shute, and the many librarians and their assistants who offered their help without giving their names.

We are grateful to our editor, Eileen Spiegler, for her careful review of this work.

We would also like to thank our dear, departed ancestors who instilled in us the need to know about our heritage and the passion to dig deeper. We especially want to remember our grandfather, Henry Pierson Bull. He was an amazing teacher and loving man. Virginia Bull, his daughter, Julie's mother and Sarah's aunt, would love this project if she were alive. We know that she is with us, and has been, every step of the way.

Over the last year, we have come to know truly, for the first time, two incredible ancestors: Peter Bull and Sarah Wells Bull. This book tells Sarah's story, thanks to her grandson, Peter Bull. Peter was this family's first historian and genealogist. Without his foresight two centuries ago, we might not know as much as we do about Sarah's journey into the land known as the Wawayanda Patent. We often wished that we knew both of these people, that we could ask questions or just have dinner with either of them. In the end, we got to know them both pretty well. We hope through this work, you will come to know and care about them, too.

To the native people, African people and indentured servants, we would like to give a special acknowledgement. We found that Sarah Wells Bull, and many of her children and grandchildren, received a good deal of aid from the indigenous people of New York. We will address that more in the book. We found that Sarah, once owned herself, also own African people, a man and woman. It is very hard to reconcile that there was a time when it was acceptable to actually own another human being.

We tried to dig into who they were, but we could find only that they were most likely buried in the family cemetery in unmarked graves. We known that Sarah's accomplishments and survival depended on the help of other people, especially the native family of Munsee people who lived on the Otter Kill tributary of Moodna Creek, and the enslaved population among them.

This book does not dig into the horrors of genocide and enslavement, or the bigotry associated with them, but we don't mean to imply it is not an important part of Sarah's story. We must never forget from whence we have come, even those parts that break our hearts.

A Note About Spelling

Readers will notice that names throughout our work may be spelled multiple ways. For example, Christopher Denne's last name was spelled many ways throughout the record, as Den, Denn, Dean and Denne. Spelling became standardized in the 19th century. Prior to that time, spelling was more art than science and at the discretion of the scribe. As a result, we used different spelling based on where we found the record. However, we only assumed someone with two different spelled names was the same person when we could cross reference it with other data.

FOREWARD

Sarah, Sarah who? Sarah Wells, most commonly referred to in her position as female progenitor, or matriarch, of the Orange County, NY, Bull family. The mystery of her biological parents has haunted the minds of her descendants and others since her demise more than 100 years old.

Over the years and generations, many intrigued by this uniquely sturdy courageous woman, have attempted to locate her birth parents without success. That is, until now when two Bull, first cousins of the ninth generation, by heritage, education, and personal life experience have delved into a quest to uncover the mystery. It is a true labor of love, at their own expense of time and money, to record for us, the readers, a compelling discourse leaving no stone available to them uncovered. Thank you for your honest, fair presentation to help us all understand the ending.

Your cousin, with deep appreciation,

Michael K.Brown,
Line of John, Thomas and William
eighth generation
& 60-year Bull Stone Homestead resident caretaker

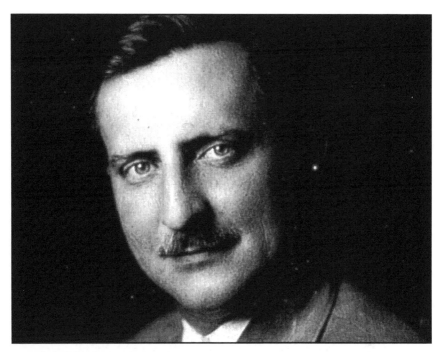

SARAH BROWNELL COLLECTION. HENRY PIERSON BULL, 1901-1985, LINE OF JOHN, THOMAS AND WILLIAM.

PREFACE

My first memory of my grandfather, Henry Pierson Bull, was solidified by an eight-millimeter movie camera my mother used often when I was young. She captured her parents' visit to our home in Oregon and my reaction to their arrival on an airplane in a home movie I've now seen dozens of times.

It was the 1960s, at a time when people dressed up to fly or receive visitors. As we waited at the Portland airport for their plane to arrive, my brother and I danced around happily on the tarmac in our fancy new outfits bought for the occasion, in front of my mother's rolling camera.

I don't remember the plane landing, but I do remember that they descended the aircraft on stairs pushed up to the door like they were heads of state. They walked across the runway to where we stood waving.

My grandfather was giant, over six feet tall. His size was immediately intimidating to me, a tiny little girl, and I stopped dancing around and retreated behind my mother's leg.

PHOTO CREDIT: UNKNOWN. BULL FAMILY COLLECTION. AUGUST 1968, BULL FAMILY PICNIC. VIRGINIA BULL (BOYD) MEATH, LEFT, IS AWARDED THE RIBBON FOR FURTHEST TRAVELLED. HENRY P. BULL, TREASURER, HER FATHER, RIGHT, NANCY BOYD, HER DAUGHTER.

My grandmother, Mary Elizabeth Cocks Bull, was much smaller and not the least bit frightening. She walked over to my mother, gave her a hug and patted me on the head. My grandfather was talking to my father and brother, who didn't seem at all afraid of the giant. I stared in amazement.

He stood with ease, laughing and smiling as he spoke. Grandpa, as I would always call him, turned and caught my eye. He held my gaze for just a minute, then his easy smile grew broad. He winked, and I smiled.

My mother took my hand and walked me over to her father, whom she loved with all her heart.

He bent over and took my hand. My tiny fingers and palm disappeared in his great, warm, and gentle grip.

"Well hello, Julie. How nice to see you," my grandfather said as he lovingly looked in my eyes. He bent down further and gathered me in his big arms, giving me a warm bear hug. "I'm your grandfather!"

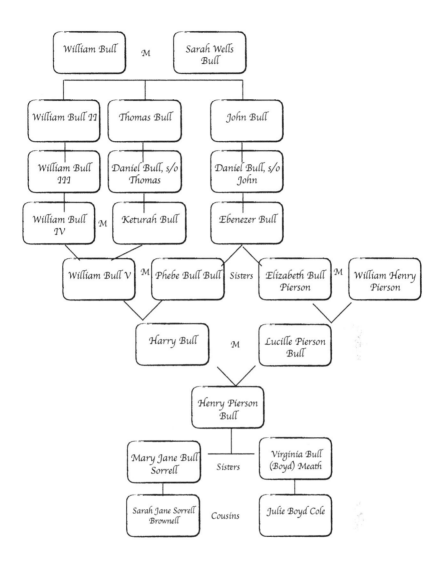

Every time I saw him in the decades that followed that first memory, my grandfather greeted me that same way. First a serious and official handshake, as if we were peers, then a grandfatherly hug that made me feel loved and important. He did that until finally he could no longer stand from the cancer that eventually took his life.

The jumpy, silent film cementing that first memory goes on to show my brother and I dancing around my grandfather, running circles around the happy-go-lucky man with the broad smile as he tried to catch us.

I am my grandfather's sixth grandchild, second granddaughter, and a child of his third daughter.

We eventually moved back to my parents home, Orange County, New York, and were lucky enough to grow up with not just my grandparents, but our enormous, extended family on my mother's side – the Bull family.

Sarah Brownell and I are Sarah and William Bull's great-great-great-great-great-great-granddaughters. Over the years, we made many memories with my grandparents, aunts, uncles and cousins. As a child, I thought everyone had annual family reunions with hundreds of relatives and were lucky enough to walk through an old stone house built by their ancestors. I had no idea that was so special and unusual.

I took for granted the many rides in my grandfather's Ford Galaxy sedan around the backroads of Orange County and his tales about stone houses, ancient farms, and the mark our ancestors' made on the New York community. From him, I learned about his father, Harry Bull, and his late sister, Keturah, who died when she was just 18. His mother and Keturah were victims of the tuberculosis and influenza outbreaks of the early 20th century. I learned the story of Sarah Wells and William Bull, and how our family got started in Orange County 300 years ago.

My grandparents' home was filled with newspaper clippings of family members' accomplishments and obituaries. My grandfather kept up on the comings and goings of every Bull he knew, and he often shared that information with me. Somehow, his tales about this person or that didn't bore the teenager in me enough to tune it all out. Instead, I developed a love of history in general, and spent much of my adult life researching all kinds of topics in my various careers.

I saw my grandfather as our patriarch, the caretaker in our lives. I watched my grandmother, his three daughters and nine grandchildren turn to him again and again for advice in managing daily life. My childhood had its share of traumas and was far from perfect, but it seemed like my grandfather was always there to offer love and optimism no matter the situation.

It wasn't until his death that I realized he was a source of support and strength to other families as well. Hundreds of strangers attended my grandfather's funeral and told us stories of his kindness and understanding; it was wonderful and overwhelming. I realized then how lucky I was to have him as a grandfather and the Bull family as my heritage.

He wasn't the only Bull who made an indelible mark on my life. Of course, longtime Stone House resident Michael Brown and his wife, Betty, and children were part of my countless family memories. Michael's great-grandmother, and our great-great-grandmother, Phebe Bull, lived in the Stone House with her parents, who owned it then. Michael first lived in the house as a child with his siblings and parents, who served as the resident caretakers of the property soon after the corporation bought it. They moved into the house a few years after Michael's great-great-uncle, Ebenezer Bull, line of John, turned the house over to all 12 lines of the Bull family in 1920.

Later, Michael moved into the house again as an adult, and raised his seven children there.

Sarah and I would spend the night with the Brown girls and our sisters after the annual Bull Family Reunion and Picnic days. Michael, despite being exhausted after hosting hundreds of people on his lawn, played a game with us we called "The Ghost of William Bull." At dusk, we girls would walk down the long, tree-lined lane to collect Saturday's mail. We would take the path through the cemetery and the woods on our way back, giggling and goading each other the whole way. We knew what was coming, but it never diluted the surprise. Michael would jump out from behind a tree or brush-covered knoll and shout "I AM THE GHOST OF WILLIAM BULL!" Our collective, high-pitched scream and terrified, tangled sprint back to the house was mixed with the memories of the bats scattering out of the barn and Michael in hysterics.

There were many, many Bull elders who mattered to me back then. My great-aunt Marge Bull Jackson was a wonderful woman who shared her brother Henry's optimism and joy.

Michael's parents, Corinne "Jo" and Lou Brown, were always kind and loving to me whenever I saw them. The elder Browns and my family all lived in Montgomery, New York, and I will never forget my visits with them and Jo's long, braided grey hair. She seemed to always have it tied up in a bun around her head. Her smile was infectious and a bit sly.

I remember "W.B.," who was a cousin to both my grandmother and grandfather, and the oldest man I ever knew. And any Bull back then knew cousin Amy Bull Crist, who was an inspiring, independent woman who fought hard for the Bull legacy around Orange County and kept her family accountable. The list of elders in my life is long, and until I was older, I had no idea how remarkable that is. I thought everyone had the same.

It is now, after raising children, that I understand how lucky I was to be raised in such an incredible family. I named both my children after my beloved mother and grandfather because they meant so much to me. It is now, as my nest has emptied and my career is winding down, that I turned my attention and curiosity to how my wonderful family got started. The words of my elders, and my sweet grandfather, Henry, echo in my mind, and I hear his voice encouraging me to uncover more pieces of our history. He would love that two of his granddaughters are now delving into the same past, and searching for more of the same clues, along the winding roads of Orange County we travelled with him for hours on end.

— Julie Boyd Cole

When I was growing up in Orange County, NY, I knew that I was part of a well-known family. I was named Sarah for *the* Sarah Wells, but I never really appreciated the legacy I was given along with her name. When my mother would introduce me to everyone as "Sarah Jane," using my middle name, I usually cringed. I didn't like it when she used both my first and middle name. Her name is Mary Jane Bull Sorrell. She was always Mary and Jane, and she has always made sure people knew that. It wasn't until later that I realized that maybe she was distinguishing herself from her mother who was Mary Elizabeth Cocks Bull. As an adolescent struggling to understand who I was and trying to separate myself from my mother in those angsty times, I think it was the Jane thing that kept me from feeling fully prideful about my name as a whole.

I moved back to Orange County in 2004 from California, where I had lived for 20 years. After the passage of time and, perhaps, with a bit of the maturity that comes from marriage and child-rearing, I began to see the significance of my ancestry and my name. As I met new people and reconnected with old friends, I realized that my name and my Bull heritage meant something in Orange County. My name became a strong source of pride.

Soon after moving back to Orange County, I got involved with the William Bull and Sarah Wells Stone House Association — very involved. I took many a drive back and forth from my house in Goshen along Ridge Road down to Purgatory Road or County Route 51 to the Bull Stone House. I delivered newsletters for my cousin Michael Brown, the Bull Stone House resident and board vice-president. "Eagle Eye," Michael's loving and appropriate nickname, would review my work. It didn't stop there. I picked up Bull family goods for presentations, ran my kids back and forth to help set up for the Bull Family annual reunion, or I'd work on some other project or board detail. It was during those drives that I began to feel a pull or energy, connecting me to Sarah, the Sarah. So many times, as I drove the country roads, I imagined Sarah riding her horse along the same routes.

In my earlier life in Orange County, I was once a young Girl Scout. The Girl Scout Council in Orange County used to be called "The Sarah Wells Girl Scout Council." I still have my Girl Scout uniform sash with the Sarah Wells Council patch hand sewn at the top. My troop once performed a pageant about Sarah Wells and because of who I was, I got to play her character in the presentation.

Soon after I returned to the area, I was disheartened to hear that the "Sarah Wells" part was removed from the council's name during the restructuring of the organization. In 2010, the Goshen Area Girl Scouts' Service unit manager, Lisa Forst, reached out to the William Bull and Sarah Wells Stone House Association to enlist some support in getting the Sarah Wells name back and using it for the Goshen Area Scouts. Lisa worked tirelessly to get permission from the council; writing letter after letter, making phone calls and sending emails. She persisted in making the point that Sarah was a clear example of a Girl Scout. Finally, the Goshen Area Girl Scouts were awarded the name. The Bull association and I were elated. Lisa and I became very good friends and eventually, we co-chaired a year-long celebration of the tricentennial of Sarah Wells' arrival in Orange County. Through the lens of this staunch supporter of Sarah Wells, someone who wasn't a descendant, and the time we spent creating several large community events in Sarah's name, the impact of Sarah's legacy became more clear. I decided I should wear her name more proudly.

Working on this book, the experience of traveling to so many places where our family once tread and discovering about Sarah's world in the 1700s continues to add to my sense of pride. I got to know my cousin Julie Boyd Cole, who I have known for most of my life, in a new way and have come to know her as an amazing investigative journalist, writer, and mentor. There are so many other touchstones in my life that I now recognize have helped me to cherish my name in a much deeper way — and the woman from whence it came, my ancestor Sarah.

— Sarah Brownell

VIRGINIA BULL COLLECTION. CIRCA 1976. BULL FAMILY PICNIC. FROM LEFT, MARGE JACKSON, OUR GREAT AUNT, MELANIE BROWN LATIMER, LISA BROWN RYAN, NANCY BOYD, JULIE BOYD COLE.

PHOTO CREDIT: JULIE BOYD COLE, 2017. DESCENDANTS OF SARAH AND WILLIAM BULL GATHERED AT THE BULL FAMILY REUNION, AUGUST 2017.

PART I
CHAPTER 1
BULLS IN AMERICA

The United States of America was formed centuries ago with the singular vision that "all men are created equal." Jamestown, Virginia was settled in 1607 and Plymouth, Massachusetts was settled in 1620. America is now home to 323 million people of all ethnic backgrounds, nations and creeds. Dozens of languages are spoken, hundreds of religions are practiced, a multitude of occupations worked, and many family types celebrated. We are an extremely diverse country and have been since the first European explorers arrived on our shores five centuries ago, altering this continent's trajectory and forever changing its population.

Millions of citizens have deep-rooted family trees in America because of a single, wide-eyed and hopeful progenitor disembarking onto our shores off a ship from a faraway land. Over centuries, those people navigated hardships, relationship dynamics and unthinkable mistakes to forge one of the longest and most successful democracies in the world.

But what makes this story of Sarah Wells, of Orange County, New York, so noteworthy among all the other remarkable immigrant stories?

For starters, in 1712, Sarah Wells, as a teenager, became the first European settler in Goshen, New York. At a time when even the indigenous population was sparse, Sarah left the small, developing hamlet of Manhattan and entered the wilderness, where she built a life that lasted a century. Sarah did what most people, even then, thought was treacherous, yet she thrived.

She was not the only settler along the Hudson River between Albany and Manhattan, or even the first in what is now Orange County. Of course, she wasn't the last. Thousands of families soon followed Sarah into the New York frontier and carved out homesteads for their families. Within her lifetime, the European population of the county grew from about 300 people to nearly 30,000.

Names of those early families still populate all corners of the area today.

However, few of those earlier settlers accomplished the same outcome of the Bulls of Orange County – a celebrated history and family traditions handed down through the generations.

Though it is clear by what Sarah and William left behind that they focused their efforts on developing the wilderness and survival, their immediate descendants saw something in their matriarch and patriarch much greater than a stone house or a large family tree. Those descendants had the forethought to take on the task of preserving what they saw for generations to come.

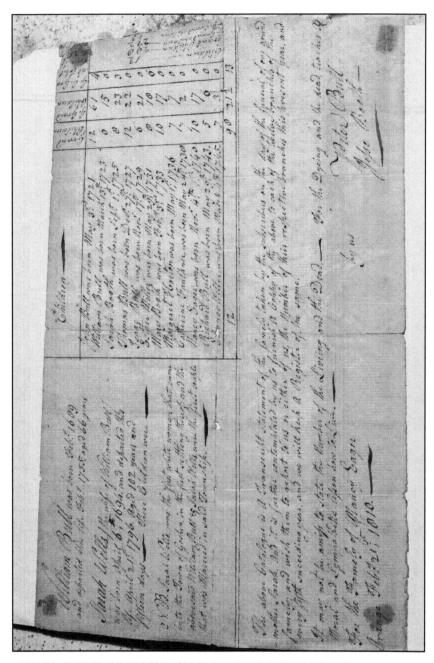

PHOTO CREDIT: JULIE BOYD COLE, 2017. BULL STONE HOUSE
COLLECTION. ORIGINAL 1810 BULL FAMILY GENEALOGY RECORD
CREATED BY PETER BULL AND JESSE BOOTH TO LIST THE
DESCENDANTS OF WILLIAM AND SARAH BULL.

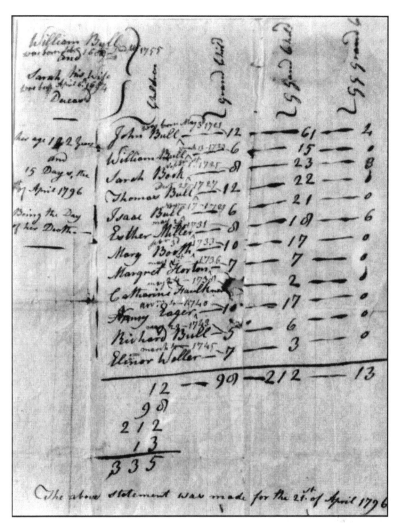

PHOTO CREDIT: MELANIE BROWN LATIMER, 2017. BULL STONE HOUSE
COLLECTION. ANOTHER DOCUMENT OF THE GENEALOGY RECORD
CREATED BY PETER BULL AND JESSE BOOTH IN 1796.

CHAPTER 2
COUNTING DESCENDANTS

Sarah and William's grandsons, Peter Bull and Jesse Booth, were the first known descendants to document the Bull family of Orange County, New York. Who knows if they were aware of what they started, or that their work was destined to continue for more than 200 years.

In the Spring of 1796, on the day of Sarah Wells Bull's funeral, Peter, 43, and Jesse, 31, wrote down all the names of Sarah's descendants and shared that list with the family. Peter and Jesse calculated that the family had already grown to 335 descendants, including great-great-grandchildren of Sarah at the time of her death. Peter and Jesse continued counting new additions until at least 1810, and shared those lists with their cousins.

Peter was the son of William and Sarah's fourth son, Isaac Bull. Isaac was married to Sarah Mulliner, of Little Britain, New York. Isaac and Sarah raised their family on a farm next door to his parents' homestead, surrounded by a swamp the locals named Purgatory Swamp. The wetland earned the colorful name during the French and Indian War, when a messenger lost his way to the Stone House and ended up in the mud. He spent the night struggling to get out of the swamp and finally showed up the next morning at the door of the Stone House covered in muck, proclaiming he had spent the night in "Purgatory," according to family historians and authors. Witty Peter Bull later gave his home site, so close to the swampy landscape a new nickname: he called it Paradise as a bit of a joke.

Peter Bull knew his grandmother Sarah Wells, having lived 43 years of his life overlapping hers. He became the source of a good deal of the family history for various publications in the 19th century, including the work of his cousin, Samuel W. Eager. Many of Peter's papers are stored at the Stone House today.

Peter's first cousin and genealogy partner, Jesse Booth, was born in 1765 in Wallkill, NY. He was the son of Mary Bull, William and Sarah's seventh child, and her husband Benjamin Booth. During the American Revolution, Benjamin was a known loyalist of King George. According to the family lore retold in The History and Genealogy of The William Bull and Sarah Wells Family of Orange County, New York (page 125, published in 1974, lovingly known as the "Blue Book"), Benjamin Booth was chased out of Orange County in the dead of night by those who supported the American Revolution. He narrowly escaped to Canada with the help of Bull family members, both revolutionaries and loyalists among them.

Mary (Bull) Booth was herself a rebel, and supported the American patriots. She stayed in Orange County, raised her many children and maintained their farm alone throughout the rest of her life. It is not clear if Jesse ever saw his father again.

These two grandsons, Peter and Jesse, wrote several family genealogies through the years and shared them with each of the 12 lines of Sarah and William. Those written genealogies became the basis of all Bull family genealogies today.

In 1840, one of the many of Sarah and William's great-great grandsons renewed the effort of keeping track of the now-enormous Bull family. New York University Professor Dr. Richard H. Bull was born in Goshen in 1817, the son of Benjamin and Eliza Wade Bull, in the line of William and Sarah's son, John. He was an accomplished and revered college professor, mathematician, and theologist. Professor Bull lived most of his life in Manhattan, where he served for a time as the president of New York Savings Bank, and in Poughkeepsie, New York.

"His students long remembered the imposing looking gentleman with the white whiskers who explained God's secrets as revealed by mathematics," is the description of Professor Bull printed in New York University 1832-1932 by Theodore Francis Jones, published by New York University Press in1933.

Professor Bull married Mary Ann Schouten and the two raised a family; he frequently organized and attended the Bull family picnics of the 19th century. Richard was as dedicated to his heritage as Peter and Jesse, because he continued his work on the genealogy for decades. He was often in the Bull family picnic meeting minutes as an organizer and presenter of the history. According to the recorded minutes of the 1869 Bull family picnic: "The names of many present were registered in a large book presented for the purpose of Prof. Richard H. Bull."

He and Mary Ann had several children, including J. Eager Bull. Eager Bull married the great-granddaughter of President John Adams and had an accomplished career practicing law in New York City. Prof. Samuel W. Eager, the famous Bull cousin, was 28 years older than Richard and enjoyed exploring the family history just as much.

When Professor Bull died in 1892, the records he collected for decades on the family genealogy were passed to Sarah and William's great-great-great-grandson, Stevenson H. Walsh (Blue Book, page 726) of Philadelphia. He was the son of George Walsh, in the line of William.

Stevenson H. Walsh, and was a home insurance agent in Philadelphia and a director of the Historic Society of Pennsylvania.

He and his wife were listed in the Philadelphia Social Register in 1919 and 1922, and he was a witness to several patents in the late 1800s. One patent was for a "better, more efficient" candlestick.

In the minutes of the Aug. 29, 1894 Bull picnic, the family secretary wrote: "Mr. Stevenson H. Walsh of Philadelphia is compiling a list of the names and families, dates of their births, marriages and deaths, which he expects to have published."

When he died in 1924, Walsh willed his documents to the Newburgh Historical Society (Blue Book, page 726). He also passed on this work to descendant Dolly W. Booth, William and Sarah's great-great-great-granddaughter in the line of Ann.

Dolly continued as the family genealogist for 30 years. Luckily, several copies of Walsh's genealogy are stored at the Stone House and were used extensively by the team created in 1965 to research the Blue Book. Though we do not know if Stevenson Walsh ever published a manuscript on the

Bull Family genealogy, we are fortunate to have record of some of his work.

In 1965, this team of nearly two dozen Bull cousins, led by Dolly, and descendants Emma McWhorter and Philip Seaman, researched the history and the genealogy further. In 1974, they eventually published The History and Genealogy of the William Bull and Sarah Wells Family of Orange County, New York: The First Six Generations in America and Canada. They conducted an amazing effort compiling documents and family trees of more than 4,000 descendants from around the country, Canada, and Great Britain.

These amateur researchers and genealogists did this work decades before the internet or even cheap long distance telephone service was available. They wrote letters and traveled to meet historians and distant family members. They gathered information that eventually filled more than 1,000 pages and covered the first six generations, and part of the seventh, of Bulls in America. Their hard work holds up today with little need of correction and is a must-read for any Bull descendant interested in the history and the people that make up their ancestors.

According to the notes stored in the Stone House and compiled for the Blue Book, those on the team were: Wesley L. Baker, of Douglaston, NY; Dolly W. Booth, of Warwick; Corinne Brown, of the Stone House in Hamptonburgh; Henry P. Bull, of Middletown; Jean Garbe of Schenectady; Margery Bull Jackson, of Middletown; William H. Lodge, of Woodstown, NJ; Emma J. McWorter, of Highland Mills; Margaret L. Moon, of Middletown; Dorothy Radzinsky, of Middletown; Philip H. Seaman, of Kingston; and Mary Shoemaker, of Middletown.

Each person on the team was responsible for researching at least one of the 12 lines of the Bull family of Orange County. Each line began with one of Sarah and William Bull's 12 children:

- Line of John: Researched by Emerson Bull of Binghamton; Emma McWhorter; Mrs. Joseph Post of Binghamton; Olive Nozell; Margery Bull Jackson of Middletown; S. Carlyle Bradley of Aurora; and Beatrice Bull of Monroe;
- Line of William: Researched by Margaret Moon;
- Line of Sarah: Researched by __ Mills;
- Line of Thomas: Researched by Henry P. Bull of Middletown;
- Line of Isaac: Researched by Elise Newman (possibly);
- Line of Esther: Researched by Jane Allen and Elise Newman;
- Line of Mary: Researched by Dolly Booth;
- Line of Margaret: Researched by Philip Seaman;
- Line of Catherine: Researched by Mrs. LeRoy Miller and Col. Lionel Faulkner;

- Line of Ann: Researched by Mrs. Chas. Radzinsky and Jean Garbe;
- Line of Richard: Mrs. Karl Beyea of Nauwigewauk, N. B., Canada (was asked);
- Line of Eleanor: Researched by Dolly Booth with corrections by Wesley Baker.

This list of family members researched up to seven generations of Bulls descended from William and Sarah. They began the joint effort in 1965 and worked for almost 10 years before the Blue Book was finally published.

Henry P. Bull, our grandfather, continued the genealogy work until his death in 1985. He and our grandmother even traveled to Wolverhampton, England, to view the baptism records of William Bull. It is likely that the rest of the team kept up their research as well.

Since then, several descendants have added and managed the genealogy through computer programs, such as Family Tree Maker and ancestry.com, and investigated distant branches lost over time. Their work continues today, and the number of descendants of William and Sarah counted is more than 76,000, and up to 13 generations.

PHOTO CREDIT: JULIE BOYD COLE, 2017. COLLECTION OF SKETCHES DRAWN AT 1893 BULL FAMILY REUNION OWNED BY HOWARD PROTTER. LEWIS HAWKINS WAS MARRIED TO SARAH BULL, DAUGHTER OF EBENEZER, WHO OWNED AND LIVED IN THE BULL STONE HOUSE IN THE 19TH CENTURY (HAWKINS IS PICTURED IN CHAPTER 5.)

CHAPTER 3
ANNUAL BULL FAMILY REUNIONS

Another early family tradition reached a milestone in 2017, when the descendants met in August for the 150th annual family reunion. Though many families around the world share the annual tradition of reuniting, the descendants of Sarah and William are unique in America as they have gathered together every summer since 1867.

The first gathering was actually just a planning meeting to erect a monument to honor Sarah and William on Burying Hill, the family cemetery. The daughters of Ebenezer Bull, son of Daniel, and owner of the Stone House, realized they so enjoyed gathering that they wanted to do it again. They organized the first family reunion and the Bulls have met every year since. Sometimes with as many as 1,000 people from all over the Northern Hemisphere have attended. The reunion picnic has been held at several locations in Orange County. Please read the book 50 Years of the Bull Family Picnics to learn more about the incredible stories. In the 1920s, the picnic moved permanently to the Stone House.

The picnic gains attention in Orange County every year as it is one of the largest and longest running family reunion in the country. One year, then-President Grover Cleveland sent his note of regret for not being able to make the picnic. The United States president served two nonconsecutive terms in the late 1800s. One of his more famous quotes: "A truly American sentiment recognizes the dignity of labor and the fact that honor lies in honest toil."

We don't know who among the Bull family invited Cleveland, but maybe the president was impressed by the honest toil of the Bull family.

VIRGINIA BULL COLLECTION. BULL FAMILY REUNION CIRCA 1967. CENTER IS SARAH BROWNELL WEARING FEATHER HEADBAND.

VIRGINIA BULL COLLECTION. BULL PICNIC, UNDATED, IN THE MID 1900S. FROM LEFT; RAYMOND ACKERLY, JOHN JACKSON (OUR GREAT-UNCLE), LOUIS BROWN (RESIDENT OF THE STONE HOUSE AT THE TIME OF THE PHOTO), HERMAN SCHUERHOLZ, WILLIAM BULL, MARK ROE, JIM MCCLUNG.)

VIRGINIA BULL COLLECTION. BULL STONE HOUSE. HANNAH BULL (1820-1907), DAUGHTER OF EBENEZER BULL IS ON THE FRONT PORCH.

CHAPTER 4
THE BULL STONE HOUSE

One of the most unique traditions, still held dear by the Bull descendants today, is the ownership and occupancy of the Bull Stone House in Hamptonburgh, New York. Few pre-colonial homes in America are still standing, let alone in the hands of the family who built them. William set this in motion by his 1755 last will and testament:

> "And I give and devise to my eldest son John, his heirs and assigns FOREVER, after the decease of my wife, my dwelling house and all that part of the hundred acres whereon I live..."

John took possession of the four-story Stone House after his father's death and likely when his mother remarried, sometime around 1760. John continued the tradition set by his father when he willed in 1795 the property in the same manner to his namesake John Junior:

> "And to my son John Bull and to his heirs and assigns FOREVER, my farm on which I now live..."

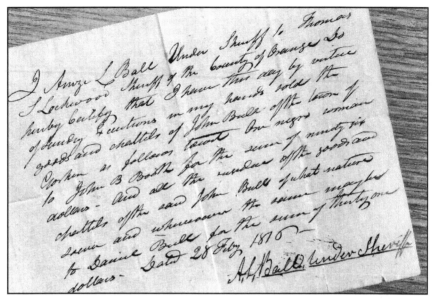

PHOTO CREDIT: JULIE BOYD COLE, 2017. RECORD IN GOSHEN PUBLIC LIBRARY LOCAL HISTORY ROOM. SHERIFF CERTIFICATE OF THE SALE OF JOHN BULL'S "GOODS AND CHATTELS," INCLUDING ONE "NEGRO WOMAN." DATED 1810. BELOW, AN 1872 ARTICLE FROM THE PORT JERVIS EVENING GAZETTE.

—A Goshen correspondent of the Newburgh *Telegraph* in giving reminiscences of the settlement of Wm. Bull and Sarah Wells on the Otterkill, near Hamptonburgh says, "the Bull stone house was the first stone house built in Orange county. The old house stands intact to-day, and although nearly one hundred and fifty years have elapsed, is still retained by the Bull family, a monument to the sturdy integrity of the man who built it, as undying as the more pretentious marble monuments that handed down the names of others much less worthy of note."

And so the Bull Stone House has now been the home of a Bull descendant continuously from about 1732 until 2017, nearly 300 years. The house had been out of the possession of a Bull for just a few hours around 1810, when the Orange County sheriff sold the home at public auction to satisfy John Junior's unpaid debts. Just a few hours later, John Junior's brother Daniel, our great-great-great-great-grandfather, believing that the home needed to stay in the family, bought the house from the highest bidder and prevented anyone unrelated to the Bull family from owning the house for more than a few hours, according to family lore.

We did find an interesting record in the Goshen Public Library Local History Room that appears to show Daniel buying at least part of John's estate directly from the sheriff. We did not investigate every aspect of these transactions, but they are interesting.

Daniel then gave the home to his son, Ebenezer, our great-great-great-grandfather, but allowed his brother, John Junior, to live out his life in the homestead. Ebenezer eventually moved into the Stone House and raised his family there. He willed the property to his son, Ebenezer II.

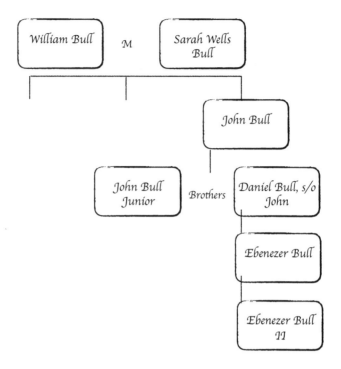

Ebenezer II didn't have any children. Toward the end of his life, he suggested to his immediate family they form an association of descendants to take possession of the estate and thereby keep the homestead in the possession of all of Sarah and William's descendants. The idea was then proposed to all the other lines of descendants.

In 1920, the family incorporated and bought the Stone House and the 100-acre estate for just $20,000 (about a quarter of what it was likely worth, by standard inflation calculations) from Ebenezer, and it has been held by the membership of descendants ever since. In 1920, they called it a tribute to the many fallen Bull World War I soldiers (Blue Book notes).

Ebenezer Bull I must have truly taught his children a love of the family because his son gave the house to all lines of the Sarah and William and his daughters organized the first Bull Family reunion.

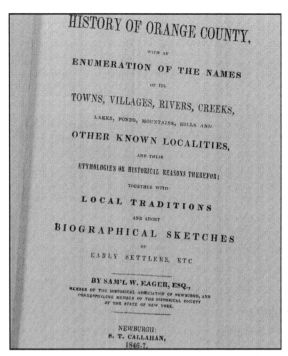

PHOTO CREDIT: JULIE BOYD COLE, 2017. TITLE PAGE OF SAMUEL W. EAGER'S WRITTEN HISTORY OF ORANGE COUNTY, NEW YORK. EAGER WAS THE GREAT-GRANDSON OF WILLIAM AND SARAH BULL.

CHAPTER 5
THE WRITTEN HISTORY

For generations, fathers, mothers, grandfathers, grandmothers, aunts and uncles have been telling their children the stories about Sarah and William Bull. Whenever my cousin and co-author, Sarah, and I were invited to go for a ride in Grandfather Henry P. Bull's giant Ford Galaxy, we knew we were about to get a family history lesson that lasted the duration of the journey.

He would point out every house that belonged to or was associated with a cousin and talked the entire time about the Bulls. But when I had the idea to give my grandfather a blank journal to fill with his memories, he never entered a single word. Instead, he stuffed it full of newspaper clippings he and my grandmother cut daily out of the Times Herald Record and other publications. The written word was apparently not his thing.

Thankfully, the Bull Family does have its share of excellent writers and historians. Many believe that if it weren't for the written work of one of the family historians, Samuel W. Eager, who was mentioned earlier, William and Sarah's story might not have gotten such early acclaim.

Eager wrote the first known published account of his great grandparents in the Outline History of Orange County, in 1846-47. Samuel was an attorney, bank president and U.S. congressman. He was responsible for highlighting Sarah's early achievements in such a way that brought more widespread, and even national, attention.

Eager wrote poetic passages of the family matriarch's journey into the wilderness. He was amazed that a teenage woman could pull off such a feat. In Eager's time, the American culture looked upon women as the more "delicate gender." Eager's romanticized version of Sarah's expedition into undeveloped Orange County seems to expose his similar attitudes about women in general. Eager wrote in his publication about Orange County:

> "...woman is a finer and more delicately strung instrument than man. Her whole nature vibrates with less force. She is more a creature of feeling and impulse rather than reason. Her perceptions are quicker, and of right and wrong almost unerring. She knows a thing because she feels it. ... She believes without a reason ... and acts accordingly." (Source page 26)

Eager met his great-grandmother when he was just a young boy. She died when he was 6 years old. He wrote:

> "We (referring to himself) admire thy maiden intrepidity in traversing the dark bosom of the Wawayanda, when in dutiful obedience to unkind authority, the red men of the forest led thy footsteps through the wild wood ... Sarah Wells was less than the majority of her sex, yet though light and fragile, she was active and capable of remarkable exercise and endurance ... (her childhood on the water) only hardened and compacted a constitution otherwise delicate ..." (page 456)

Sarah's journey and accomplishments are certainly noteworthy, but her expedition from Manhattan to Goshen is hardly filled with cliffhangers and a dramatic plot to earn such poetry from Eager. Sarah's journey to Goshen took just three days. The expedition resulted in no injury or Indian attacks. Sarah was not alone for a single night. She spent the first nights with Native Americans and hired hands, and after one night in Orange County, her employers, Christopher and Elizabeth Denne, arrived and remained for years.

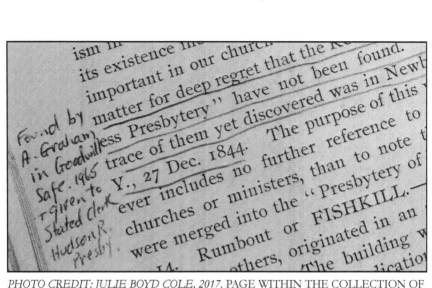

PHOTO CREDIT: JULIE BOYD COLE, 2017. PAGE WITHIN THE COLLECTION OF TOWN OF MONTGOMERY HISTORIAN JOHN PENNINGS. HE IS A MEMBER OF THE GOODWILL CHURCH.

Nevertheless, Eager's story got national attention when it was picked up repeatedly by future authors and writers. Of course, Sarah's expedition opened what had been a closed country to a flood of settlers, who developed acres of land by the thousands in less than a generation. Many

of those settlers went on to help create the United States of America. The history of the county was destined to be written. But if it were not for Eager's published account of Sarah's first days in Goshen and how she got there, we may not have known the story of a teenager settling a community.

Eager did not name his source for what he said was a firsthand account of Sarah's 1712 expedition. Instead, he wrote:

> "(My) remarks on this article are based chiefly on some notes made by an old and intelligent individual many years since, from his own knowledge, traditionary statements, and information received from Mrs. William Bull (previously Sarah Wells), of whom he was a descendant, and therefore, doubtless, very accurate. Personally, we know but little of these old matters, and are compelled to glean up and take the facts as we find them, scatter along a strong stream of tradition and verified by the direct testimony of Sarah Wells."

More than a century later, in 1965, the notes that were Eager's source were found in the records safe at the Goodwill Church in Montgomery, New York, and donated to the association of the Bull descendants. Records stored at the Stone House document this exchange. By happenstance, we got an extra bonus in our research. While sitting in the lovely home of John Pennings, the former historian of the Goodwill Church, he remembered

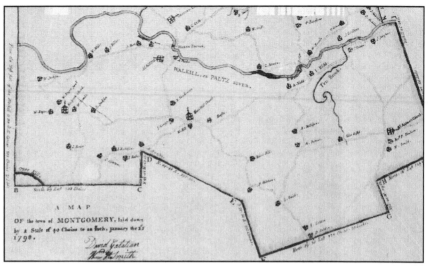

PHOTO CREDIT: JULIE BOYD COLE, 2017. 1798 MAP OF MONTGOMERY, N.Y., HANGING IN THE TOWNHALL OF MONTGOMERY. WILLIAM MILLER, GRANDSON OF WILLIAM AND SARAH BULL, LIVED IN HIS GRANDFATHER'S HOME. IT IS MARKED AS W. MILLER ON THE TOP, LEFT. HIS BROTHER, JOHANNES MILLER LIVED NEXT DOOR. HIS HOUSE STILL STANDS TODAY.

seeing a tiny notation in one of his collections that he was sure we had to see. He dug up the book among his hundreds and opened to a page where someone had documented in the margin the effort in 1965 at the church to clean out their safe and distribute all the important records. Apparently, the Bull family was just one of the recipients of their good deed.

The former Bull Stone House resident and Bull descendant Corinne "Jo" Bull Brown, line of John, Thomas and William, received the notes, transcribed them, and shared them with the rest of the family. The team of researchers for the Blue Book named them "The Goodwill Notes." The 40 pages of parchment paper handwritten in quill and ink have been stored at the Stone House among the other historical documents ever since.

The researchers of the Blue Book speculated that Johannes Miller III, born in 1760, another grandson of Sarah and William and son of Esther Bull Miller, wrote the notes. They based this on two pieces of data: Samuel Eager admired Johannes Miller III; and they believed that Miller had a unique access to Sarah during their overlapping lives.

Johannes Miller III was Sarah and William Bull's grandson; the son of Esther and Johannes "John" Miller II. They lived in the town of Montgomery on the Wallkill River, a piece of land that is now the Orange County Airport. John's father, Johannes Miller I, born in about 1690, was the first settler of Montgomery and a German immigrant. Johannes III married his first wife, Jacomyntie Schoonmaker, on Sept. 22, 1726, in

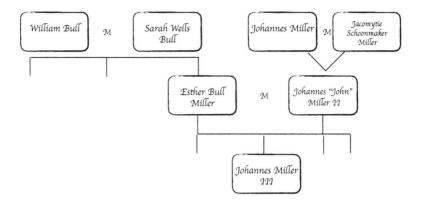

Kingston, NY, according to the church records at the Dutch Reformed Church.

The two moved to Montgomery and raised just one child, John. Jacomyntie and Johannes III were active leaders in the Harrison Meeting/ Hebron Lutheran Church, which was located in Montgomery near their home. A cemetery and marker remain at the corner of routes 211 and

416 where the church once stood; the records are kept in Salt Lake City by the Mormon Church.

In those church records, Jacomyntie and Johannes III were listed as witnesses to a baptism in 1755. The Blue Book researchers speculated that Jacomyntie died between 1760 and 1764, but they did not give any record of this nor could we find a record of her death. We also could not find a record of a wedding between Johannes Miller I and Sarah Bull. We did find two new records of their "divorce" in 1770; we will discuss the divorce in subsequent chapters. But, since we now have third party record of a marriage between Sarah Wells Bull and Johannes Miller, we can piece together the timeline of Sarah's overlapping life with her grandson.

Johannes III was just 10 years old when his grandparents divorced and Sarah left Montgomery. The new information doesn't rule out that Sarah might have shared stories about her life with her grandson, but the weight given to their theory that the young man wrote the Goodwill Notes because he had spent more time than most with his grandmother due to the marriage no longer holds up.

We found some interesting references in the Goodwill Notes that we investigated, and helped us to date the Notes. We know that the Goodwill Notes were written after 1815 because of a reference to "General" Abraham Vail. He achieved that rank in 1815, so the Notes could not have been written before that year. Johannes Miller III died in 1835 in Montgomery. His father, John, died in 1774, and his grandfather died in 1782. Johannes III was a respected leader in Montgomery, but we found no

PHOTO CREDIT: SARAH BROWNELL, 2017. FROM THE PAGES OF "THE GOODWILL NOTES," DOCUMENT IN THE BULL STONE HOUSE COLLECTION. IN THIS SECTION, GENERAL ABRAHAM VAIL IS REFERENCED.

record that he was working on a history of Orange County, as the unnamed author of the Goodwill Notes said he was writing.

Our research shows that Peter Bull, the family's first genealogist, was the author of the notes. The researchers of the Blue Book made clear in their report that they were just making an educated guess based on the connection between Samuel Eager and Miller, and didn't really spend time trying to credit the notes. They spent more time comparing the document to Eager's work, which is nearly word for word. They and other local

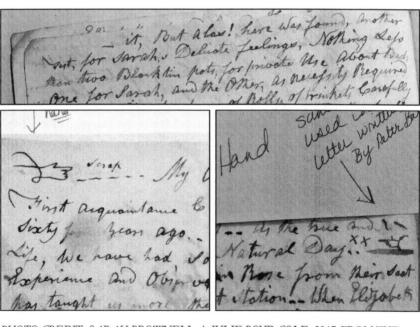

PHOTO CREDIT: SARAH BROWNELL & JULIE BOYD COLE, 2017. FROM THE THE BULL STONE HOUSE COLLECTION. TOP PHOTO IS A PAGE FROM "THE GOODWILL NOTES," BOTTOM LEFT IS A PAGE FROM A LETTER WRITTEN AND SIGNED BY PETER BULL. BOTTOM RIGHT, IS A PAGE FROM "THE GOODWILL NOTES." BOTH AUTHORS USED A MANICULE, A FORM OF PUNCTUATION USED TO HIGHLIGHT A CERTAIN PIECE OF INFORMATION.

PHOTO CREDIT: JULIE BOYD COLE, 2017. DOCUMENT IN THE COLLECTION AT THE GOSHEN PUBLIC LIBRARY LOCAL HISTORY ROOM, THAT CONNECTS GEORGE EAGER TO PETER BULL.

historians in 1965 were convinced that the Goodwill Notes were the same notes referred to by Eager.

PHOTO CREDIT: SARAH BROWNELL / JULIE BOYD COLE, 2017. DOCUMENT FROM THE BULL STONE HOUSE COLLECTION. LETTER FROM JENNIE DURYEA CRANSTON, PETER BULL'S GREAT-GRANDDAUGHTER.

We investigated thoroughly the connections between Peter Bull, Samuel Eager and Sarah Wells Bull. During our search through documents at the Stone House and the Goshen library, we realized that the handwriting on the Goodwill Notes was the same as many other documents written and signed by Peter Bull. We found identical capital letters and similar phrasing. We also found similar punctuation not found among the other family documents.

We interviewed a police officer who was a handwriting analyst in Florida and asked for her perspective. She said handwriting is very unique from person to person, and is not easily copied.

Further, Peter was born in 1753 and died in 1843. Peter was Samuel Eager's first cousin once removed, and both men were alive at the same time and traveled in the same circles. Peter's daughter married Samuel

Sheet o. N. 1

A few, Selected, Recollected
Sketches ... Relative to William Bull and Sarah
Wells ... Selected from the most Authentick Sources
And Documents, Which Can be found in the County of
Orange And State of New York. They were, two
Enterprising Young People, Unknown to Each other, Who,
Nevertheless, Sallied forth, into A Howling Wilderness
Of Aborigines — Wild Beasts And Rattle Snakes ...
into A tract of Country, However, at Situated in the Old
County of Orange — Bounded Easterly & South Easterly
By the High hills of the Highlands, South Westerly, by the
State Of New Jersey — Westerly, by the Shawangunk
Mountains — Northerly and Northeasterly, by the Old
County Line, Supposed to Divide the Counties of Ulster
And Orange, And A Line Commonly Called the
North West Line Running from the tract of Country
Now, Supposed to Comprise, Between One Hundred and
fifty thousand, to two Hundred thousand Acres of Land
And formerly, as Well as Latterly, Known by the Indian
name Of WAWAYANDA ...
The Native Original Right, Of This tract of
Country, called Wawayanda, it appears, Was
Claimed by twelve Indian Chiefs, Whose Names
Were as follows, That is —
Rapingonick — Wawassoraw — Moghopuck
Cornelawaw — Nanowitts — Arowimack
Quimbosts — Clous — Chowekhass
Chingopaw — Oshasquemonus — & Quilapaw —
These twelve Indian Chiefs, It
Seems Conveyd this tract of Country Calld Waway
-anda, as above Described, to 12 Civilized Gentlemen
At Haverstraw; John Bridges & Co on the 5th of March
1703 See Libr B in the Clerk office for the
County of Orange — It Seems also, That the
Patent Was Granted by the then Government Of
New York, to the Company of Gentlemen John Bridge
& Co On the 29th Of April 1703 Liber. B. page 1st

Eager's brother, George. Peter was the local Democratic-Republican party
chair in 1822 and oversaw the nomination of Hector Craig for Congress in.
Eager was an Orange County attorney. In 1830, he succeeded Craig in
Congress. Peter died in 1843, just three years before Eager published his
history of Orange County.

The Goshen, NY, newspaper, The Orange Patriot, printed a
submission from Peter Bull in March of 1809 that shows his longstanding
willingness to print his political opinions. It read:

> "May the spirit and energy of genuine republicanism sweep
> away all error sanctioned by authority, and the science of truth,
> virtue and happiness be its reward."

Eager's brother, George, Peter's son-in-law, was the executor of Peter's
estate, and oversaw the distribution of the estate, including his papers. We
found at the Goshen Public Library Local History Room one of Peter's
many documents that connects the two men, and shows clearly Peter's
handwriting.

Samuel also used other documents of Peter's as sources for his
published history, and printed some of Peter's letters in full in his book. It
is unclear why Samuel didn't give Peter credit for the handwritten account
when he indicates in his book that he knew who wrote them, but the
mystery might be explained by the politics of the day. During the period
between the 1820s and 1830s, Peter Bull endorsed Jacksonian politician
Hector Craig. Samuel Eager became an anti-Jacksonian politician and
replaced Craig in Congress.

It is plausible to speculate that Eager avoided giving a political foe credit for the "find" of the firsthand account of Sarah Wells Bull's story. Yet, in order to maintain the credibility of the story, he had to report that he knew the author was her ancestor with access to the account from Sarah.

We found more exciting links between Sarah Wells and Peter Bull. Peter lived on his father's farm from birth to grave, 90 years. The farm was adjacent to the Bull Stone House estate's southern side and Peter's life overlapped his grandmother's by 43 years. He had a good deal of access to his grandmother, living next door for all those years.

In studying Peter, we found he was clearly interested in the family and county history by evidence of his continued work on the family genealogy, referenced earlier. In 1820, Peter wrote a letter to his cousin on his mother's side, Margaret Welling, and asked her for their family history. He told her he was writing a history of Orange County and collecting stories from family members. Peter's mother and Margaret's mother were sisters, and the daughters of early Orange County settler Peter Mulliner. Margaret wrote back acknowledging his work. Her letter can be found in the Stone House today.

Margaret Welling wrote on Jan. 29, 1821:

> In reference to "Yours of 25 of Novem. 1820, informing me of (your) desire to write a history of Orange County and requesting of me to give you some information on our grandfather Peter Mulliner ... for my parents and I cannot see wherein that it will be any addition to the history for thou knows the individuals settlers of the country of Orange for them did all belong to the government that they did settle under ... but be it as it may, I shall comply for thou obliges a friend its will serve as amusement to look over ... our grandfather Peter Mulliner was born in the land of Great Britain in Staffordshire ... in the year 1684 and at a certain age was sent to the city of London ..."

Margaret's letter is three pages written with quill and ink on parchment, with the wax seal still affixed to the edge. It is a fascinating account of the Mulliner side of Peter's family tree and an excellent example of Peter's effort.

Peter Bull was known in the community for his written word and witty sense of humor; his nickname was "Peter the Poet." He penned a comical poem that was printed on a local Hamptonburgh tavern, called Heard's Inn back then and Bulls Head Inn in more recent days. He famously, satirically nicknamed his homestead surrounded by the hellish swamp "Paradise."

Peter worked as an attorney, surveyor, and transcriber of documents for people in his community, and there are still documents among the tice, that a meeting will be holden at the Court House in this village, on the 22d day of November next, at ten o'clock in the forenoon, for the purpose aforesaid; and to request that you will attend and become a member of said Society. We are very respectfully yours,

To Peter Bull, Esq.

JAMES W. WILKIN,
DAVID R. ARNELL.

Purgatory, March 31st, 1818.

GENTLEMEN OF THE COMMITTEE:—You will see by the enclosed note that the first motion for an Agricultural Society in the County of Orange was in Goshen, in 1808. The first and second meeting was respectable, but did not organize, and appointed another for that purpose, when a number of respectable farmers from Montgomery attended in order to become members. But alas! it had perished in embryo for want of vital energy to give it a form.

PHOTO CREDIT: JULIE BOYD COLE, 2017. PAGE FROM SAMUEL EAGER'S BOOK. SEVERAL OF PETER BULL'S LETTERS WERE USED, INCLUDING THE ONE PICTURED. PETER BULL USED THE LANGUAGE "BUT ALAS!"

historical record with his signature. Also, Eager used and credited Peter's history of the Orange County Agricultural Society for his book.

Eager printed verbatim the letters Peter Bull had written about the Agricultural Society, in which Peter's voice is clear and has phrasing similar to the Goodwill Notes. For example, Peter uses the phrase "But, alas…" to start a sentence in a signed letter in Eager's history. The phrase, though not uncommon, is used in the Goodwill Notes. Of course, this is not proof, but adds to the circumstantial evidence that shows a similar voice. Though not uncommon generally, we could not find this type of "voice" in Johannes Miller III's writing.

In 1815, Peter's son, Peter Mulliner Bull, died at a young age. In fact, the elder Peter outlived his wife and four of his seven children. This poetic obituary was published in the Orange County Patriot and rings with the tone of Peter's pen:

"On Sunday morning, the 14th instant, Mr. Peter Mulliner Bull, of this town aged 28 years.
The heart when tun'd, its tender strings
Chime with the soul, sweet music brings
To harmonized the whole;
When death cuts short the chord that ties
The link of nature, bursts and dies
With agonizing Soul.

All this must be 'tis nature's laws,
All movements in the eternal cause,
Mix'd pleasures, joy and pain;

The power that form'd us, says we must
Mix with the Earth, our kindred dust
Before we live again."

To further clarify authorship of the Goodwill Notes there are several references in them which help ascertain the date they were written; based on those references, the Notes had to have been written after 1815. Peter Bull died in February 1843. He didn't leave an official recorded will, but he left several pages of instructions for after his death. He wrote:

"A written prelude to the subsequent scrawl and written Deed of Conveyances: Whereas I, Peter Bull of Purgatory,..." He starts his written deed to give his land to his sons-in-law. " ...

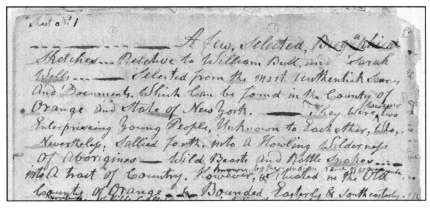

PHOTO CREDIT: SARAH BROWNELL, 2017. FROM THE DOCUMENT COLLECTION OF THE BULL STONE HOUSE. FIRST PAGE OF "THE GOODWILL NOTES" THAT SHOWS PETER BULL'S INTENTION TO WRITE THE HISTORY OF ORANGE COUNTY, NEW YORK. **BELOW,** AN 1817 DOCUMENT FROM THE BULL STONE HOUSE COLLECTION SIGNED BY JOHANNES "JOHN" MILLER, GRANDSON OF WILLIAM AND SARAH BULL. THE TWO DOCUMENTS ARE CLEARLY WRITTEN BY DIFFERENT HANDS.

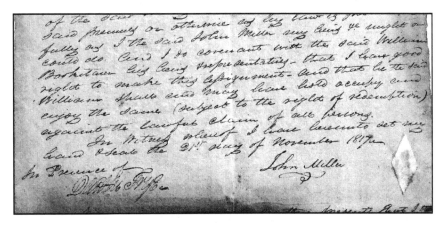

Nevertheless I seemingly wish to live a little longer .. at least while Health and what sense and memory remains yet my Crackt pate for I find the little endearments of Innocent Infancy & of Infantile Youths are the sensible Toys of Old Age for which I wish to live, being sensible that I have arrived to the that period of life commonly called a Second childhood …"

Peter left behind writings that are witty and intelligent, too numerous to print here. We found more than a dozen pieces of Peter's work in the Stone House collection, at the Goshen library, and in Eager's book.

For all these reasons, it is very clear to us that Peter Bull was the author of the Goodwill Notes and was the first to put pen to paper about Sarah's journey into Orange County as Goshen's first white woman settler.

Whatever the reason for Samuel Eager's particular way of crediting, or more mysteriously avoiding naming his source for the Goodwill Notes, after we compared the 40 pages of the Goodwill Notes with the pages of Peter's known documents and the signed document of Johannes Miller III, it is clear Peter Bull was the author of the written story.

The handwriting and voice are unequivocally the same as "Peter the Poet." In knowing who wrote the Goodwill Notes and why, we feel confident that we have an account of Sarah's expedition from someone who heard the story firsthand from her and worked hard to be as accurate as possible. In this light, the 40 pages have a whole new perspective that we found very exciting. We will address this in later chapters.

Sarah's story was re-told several times after Samuel Eager's account. E.M. Ruttenber and L.H. Clark wrote "History of Orange County, New York" in 1881. About 30 years later, historian Russell Headly wrote "The History of Orange County" in an attempt to "straighten the line" of the record of a county that he believed had been embellished.

In 1909, Outing magazine published an article by Bull descendant Frank Barkley Copley, called "The Pioneer Maid of Wawayanda," another romanticized account of Sarah Wells' first days as a frontier settler in Orange County. Copley was born in 1875, died in 1941 and was Sarah and William Bull's great-great-great-grandson in the line of Thomas. He didn't credit his source either, but it does appear that he based a lot of his version on Eager's book. Her story has shown up in a number of other publications throughout the years.

In 1974, the volunteer historians and genealogists in the family published the last known printed account of Sarah's life in the "The History and Genealogy of The William Bull and Sarah Wells Family of Orange County, New York," what we call The Blue Book. Their notes stored at the Stone House show that they worked methodically in their

1726 *(Continued)*

22 Sept.
597 JOHANNES HOOGTEELING, junior, j. m., born in Albany, and MARRETJEN
HOORNBEEK, born in Raysester [Rochester], and both resid. there. Banns registered,
28 Aug.

22 Sept.
598 JOHANNES MILLER, j. m., born in Hoogduytsland [Germany], and JACOMYNTJEN
SCHOONMAKER, j. d., born in Raysester [Rochester], and also resid. there. Banns
registered, 28 Aug.

[Date of marriage not given]
599 BURGER MEYNDERS, j. m., born in Nieuw-Jork [New York], and MARYTJEN
HOFMAN, j. d., born in Zaven-gonk [Shawangunk], and resid. there. Banns registered,
28 Aug.

22 Sept.

MARRIAGE RECORD OF JOHANNES MILLER AND JACOMYNTJEN
SCHOONMAKER. THEY HAD ONE SON, JOHN. HE EVENTUALLY MARRIED
ESTHER BULL, DAUGHTER OF SARAH AND WILLIAM BULL. BURGER
MEYNDERS, ALSO LISTED HERE, WAS A LIFELONG FRIEND OF JOHANNES I,
EVENTUALLY MOVED TO NEWBURGH AND THEN MONTGOMERY, WHERE
HE SERVED WITH JOHANNES AS A CHURCH ELDER. **BELOW,** IS A MARKER
AT THE CEMETERY OF THE LUTHERAN CHURCH ACROSS THE STREET FROM
JOHANNES MILLER'S HOME.

THE GERMANTOWN CEMETERY

THOSE WHO SETTLED THIS PORTION OF THE TOWN OF MONTGOMERY WERE PRINCIPALLY
LUTHERANS FROM GERMANY WHO HAD COME TO THIS "NEW WORLD" SEEKING OPPORTUNITY AND
RELIGIOUS FREEDOM. HERE THEY PLANNED TO FOUND A CITY. A ROAD EIGHT RODS WIDE WAS
LAID OUT, ALONG WHICH THEY MADE THEIR CLEARINGS AND ERECTED THEIR LOG CABINS ON
THIS SITE THEY ERECTED A LOG CHURCH AND THE REMAINDER OF THIS PARCEL WAS SET APART
AS A CEMETERY FOR THEIR LOVED ONES. THOUGH THE MARKERS HERE ARE PLAIN AND SIMPLE
THE PEOPLE BURIED BENEATH THEM WERE ANYTHING BUT PLAIN AND SIMPLE. THESE WERE
PEOPLE WHO CONQUERED A VIRGIN WILDERNESS AND GAVE THEIR LIVES TO ESTABLISH OUR
GREAT NATION AND THE TOWN OF MONTGOMERY.
    AMONG THOSE BURIED HERE ARE MEMBERS OF THE BOOKSTAVER, MILLER, MOULL RISELY
SHAFER, SMITH AND YOUNGBLOOD FAMILIES.
    MAY WE NEVER FORGET THEIR SACRIFICES AND EXPLOITS. MAY THIS SITE ALWAYS BE
RESPECTED AND TREATED AS HALLOWED GROUND
                                        R. L. WILLIAMS, HISTORIAN 1994
ERECTED THROUGH THE GENEROSITY OF MANY DONORS AND THE ENCOURAGEMENT OF THE
MONTGOMERY TOWN BOARD.

research. They investigated every detail of the stories of Sarah, William, and
their children, and put it down in the pages.

To the outside world, Sarah's journey into the wild might not have been
much more heroic than any other American settler, man or woman, of the
day, but her efforts bring pride to her descendants, so much so that we keep
writing about her. Her journey didn't stop on the banks of the Otter Kill in
1712. She found a way to make the best of her circumstance, against the
odds, raise a large, healthy family, and help found one of early America's
important communities.

In 1909, Headly wrote in his book: "The history of our county can not
be studied too often; for it is one of great interest, and the record reveals a

proud one. There is no section of the country processing more historic interest, nor does one exist, as closely identified with those crucial events connected with the formation period of the Republic."

During Sarah's lifetime, she saw Manhattan's population explode from 5,000 people to 60,000, and Orange County grow from 600 Europeans and Native people to nearly 30,000. It become completely settled by people from around the world. Sarah started her life in the wilderness in a tree-branch wigwam built in a few hours and ended it living in a four-story stone house that took her and her husband 13 years to build, and still stands today. She was an orphan when she came to Orange County, with no family. When she left, she had hundreds in her family.

She entered the undeveloped land as an impoverished servant with a master and when she left the earth, she was considered wealthy and by every account so far, a servant to no one with a mind of her own. She forged a path through Orange County that bears her name. It is not hyperbole to say that Sarah survived the depths of loneliness, the threat of beasts, plagues and wars, and lived to tell about it to hundreds of descendants. Those descendants have now told thousands of her descendants.

She lived in and shared a community with some of America's founding fathers: George Washington, Alexander Hamilton, Aaron Burr and John Adams, signers of the Declaration of Independence and the U.S. Constitution, and hundreds of soldiers who fought in conflicts of that century. She lived among those who wanted the freedom to build a better government and created one of the longest and strongest democracies in modern history. She began her life under the rule of English kings and queens and she left this world under the rule of law and elected representatives.

There is no need to romanticize any of Sarah's life. It is remarkable standing on its own. Her journey into the "howling wilderness," as Peter Bull describes it, is just a part of what makes her tale so fascinating and worth retelling, no matter where she began.

PHOTO CREDIT: JULIE BOYD COLE, 2017. SARAH BROWNELL SEARCHING
THROUGH RECORDS AT ST. ANDREWS EPISCOPAL CHURCH IN WALDEN.
WILLIAM BULL WAS A MEMBER AND HELPED BRING THE CHURCH TO
ORANGE COUNTY IN THE EARLY 1700S.

CHAPTER 6
THE EFFORT

One more important tradition has been carried out from the beginning:
the Bulls worked at building families, recording their history, and passing it
on. With a family this big, there were bound to be many types of
personalities and enormous differences, but hard work was a common
thread.

William Bull and Sarah Wells worked hard at building a life for their
family, and their efforts are still seen today. Each of their children raised
families, built houses and managed farms. Two of their sons served in the
French and Indian War, one of their sons fought in the American
Revolution, and all of their children contributed to their communities. The
grandchildren of the two settlers put in equal effort to keep the family ties
together despite distance, political differences, wars and every day
challenges.

Subsequent generations of descendants have spent many hours of their lives tracing distant branches of the family tree and made sure as many Bulls were told the information as often as possible. During 150 years of reunions, family members created new ways to share stories about their Bull ancestors at the annual picnic; they read lists of those who died in that year and announced the past year's marriages and births.

Over 300 years, the Bull family has had enough people among them to keep the torch burning from one generation to the next. You have highlighted some Bull family members in this publication, but there are so many more who have worked to keep this family together.

This responsibility may be the most valuable reason for the continuation of the Bull Family.

These four pillars of the Bull family – the Stone House, the annual reunion and picnic, the recorded genealogy, and the effort generations of descendants have put in to their historic family – have kept the thousands of Bull descendants together for hundreds of years and allows this legacy to continue as each new generation is born and more descendants are added to the fold.

PHOTO CREDIT: JULIE BOYD COLE, 2017. THE OTTER KILL, WHERE SARAH WELLS SPENT HER FIRST NIGHTS IN ORANGE COUNTY, NEW YORK. SHE SPENT THE FIRST NIGHT ON THE LEFT SIDE AND THE SECOND ON THE RIGHT.

PART II
CHAPTER 7
SARAH WELL'S STORY

The story of Sarah Wells, known as the "Pioneer Maid of Wawayanda," is the beginning of the history of the Bull family in Orange County. It starts when the orphaned teenage Sarah Wells, an indentured servant in Manhattan to the English couple Christopher and Elizabeth Denne, traveled by sloop to New Windsor and hiked into Orange County to the banks of the Otter Kill.

Sarah became the first white settler of Goshen in 1712, the first white woman married in the town in 1718, and the mother of 12 children. She lived beyond her 100th year. By any calculations, Sarah was remarkable. The details of just how and why she ended up in the New York frontier have been foggy for decades and have been the subject of many investigations and family debate. Her orphan status in the Bull family lore has stymied decades of family historians and amateur investigators.

Maybe her children and grandchildren knew exactly where Sarah came from or the names of her parents, or maybe she didn't share that part of her life as she worked to raise her own children and survive in the frontier.

Either way, her origin story has not come through history with much information, and we descendants have been left to wonder who she was and where she came from.

The researchers of the "Blue Book" in 1974 told us:

> "The Dennes had no children, but in their household they had a servant girl named Sarah Wells, to who they were much attached. She was eighteen and had lived with them several years since being orphaned. Denne, having full confidence in this girl, decided to send her on ahead with the settlement expedition, while he and Madam Denne would follow soon after."

Over the years, other family sleuths have offered several theories and speculations:

- Was she was born on Staten Island?
- Was she was the daughter of a minister who drowned in a ferry crossing in New York harbor?
- Was she was a child of parents lost during an Atlantic crossing?
- Was she the daughter of Philip Wells of Staten Island?
- Was she a blood relative of Christopher and Elizabeth Denne?

Samuel Eager said in his publication in 1846 that she was the "adopted" daughter of the Dennes, she had lived with them from a "tender age," and that she didn't remember her birth family. He says he collected information from his elders and never heard Sarah's story directly from her.

Our Blue Book historians investigated Eager's account of Sarah's origin and ruled out a few of Eager's details. Most importantly they found that Sarah was not adopted by the Dennes or a blood relative of the couple. They also spent enormous effort to trace all of the Wells families of the middle colonies, and ruled out all but Philip Wells of Staten Island. There, they reached a dead end. They wrote:

> "Who her parents were is a matter we shall probably never know. It is doubtful she even remembered them herself. But this has not stopped later generations from guessing." (page 56)

In their research notes, there was a letter from an historian that said she had ruled out Philip Wells as a potential father to Sarah. Our research showed the same because of the documented death date of Philip Wells.

Let's look at the facts that we do know:

1. Sarah's birth record has not been found, but family lore says she was born April 6, 1694 or 1696;
2. She was a settler in Goshen on the Otterkill in 1712, according to

several written histories of the county and family lore;

3. She married William Bull in 1718, according to several written histories and the family lore;

4. She was of child-bearing age at least between 1721 and 1745, when her 12 children were born;

5. We have no record of when she came to live with the Dennes, but we have many records of the Dennes in New York City, and in Surrey and Kent, England;

6. The Goodwill Notes reports that Sarah was "bound to the Dennes" by "public authority" as a house servant;

7. The Dennes promised Sarah, but took years to fulfill it, 100 acres for her service to settle the patent;

8. She and William built the Stone House and lived there;

9. William left a will dated 1755;

10. Neither Christopher nor Elizabeth Denne left anything to Sarah or mentioned her in their wills;

11. Sarah died in 1796.

PHOTO CREDIT: JULIE BOYD COLE, 2017. THE TUSTEN BRIDGE OVER THE OTTER KILL, WHERE SARAH WELLS FIRST SETTLED.

CHAPTER 8
THE JOURNEY TO WAWAYANDA

We are incredibly grateful to and lucky that Peter Bull, Sarah and William's grandson, wrote down the story of Sarah's expedition into the wilderness of Orange County. Not many families can say they have the written account of their progenitor in America. His work has given historians through the centuries insight into how our ancestors lived in the early colonial period and he gave our family a peek into the strength of our amazing grandmother.

The 40 handwritten pages of the Goodwill Notes tell the story of Sarah Wells' expedition with three hired hands and three Native Americans from Manhattan to what is now Orange County. Sarah was acting on behalf of Christopher Denne, who held 2,000 acres of the Wawayanda Patent in 1712. Denne was part of a group of men and women who owned the patent of more than 150,000 acres of lower New York between the Delaware and Hudson rivers.

In 1703, England's Queen Anne granted the speculators the right to develop and sell the land. As of 1712, no one had yet put shovel to earth to start a settlement. These patent holders were not settlers; they were investors.

These businessmen hoped for a financial return on their initial investment, and showed no interest in leaving Manhattan to move into huts in the wilderness among the natives of Wawayanda – until Christopher Denne.

ILLUSTRATION CREDIT: CORNELIS JANSSENS VAN CEULEN [PUBLIC
DOMAIN], VIA WIKIMEDIA COMMONS. VINCENT DENNE OF DENNE HILL,
KENT, ENGLAND, IN 1640. HE WAS THE OWNER OF DENNE HILL,
CHRISTOPHER DENNE'S COUSIN AND A MEMBER OF ENGLISH
PARLIAMENT. VINCENT DENNE DIED IN 1693 AND HIS ESTATE PASSED TO
HIS DAUGHTERS.

CHAPTER 9
THE DENNES

Christopher Denne was born in 1668 in Faversham in Kent, England. He was a descendant of a large estate owner, Robert De Dene, who was in King Edward's court in 1042. The estate in Kent, called Denne Hill, had been in the Denne family for six centuries. However, neither Christopher, nor his brother Michael, were in line to inherit the estate. They were distant cousins and had no claim to the land or its wealth.

As the boys came of age, Michael moved to London and became a baker. He married and had two children, Christopher and Mary, who also remained in England. Michael's brother, Christopher, learned the carpenter's trade, moved to Surrey and met and married Elizabeth Jones in 1690 at the Church of England's St. Mary church in Newington Parish. But Christopher had much loftier goals, more on par with his cousin's regal line.

CITY HALL AND GREAT DOCK, 1679.

ILLUSTRATION OF EAST RIVER DOCK, WHICH WAS MANHATTAN'S ONLY WHARF. CHRISTOPHER DENNE WAS ONE OF THE TWO DOCK MASTERS.

He sought to become a landowner. Elizabeth must have shared Christopher's desire to better their station, because like many lower and middle class people of the time, they decided to emigrate to the New World. They left London and embarked on the seven-week-long sail to New York.

The Middle Colonies – New York, New Jersey, Pennsylvania and Delaware – had only been settled by Europeans for about 60 years. In 1700, the population of the four colonies in total was less than 55,000 people, made up of traders, religious freedom seekers and Old World settlers looking for a better life. The native population was dramatically shrinking, as many of those who survived the diseases introduced decades earlier headed west.

The interior of New York between the Delaware and Hudson rivers was the ancestral home to an Algonquian-speaking tribe called the Munsee. Munsee Country was once home to as many as 50,000 indigenous people living in villages of longhouses and wigwams on dozens of quick streams and rivers throughout the northeast. But disease –smallpox, yellow fever, measles and malaria – brought unwittingly into the New World by the exploring Europeans, killed thousands of men, women and children who had no immunities to the plagues. By 1700, the Munsee people had lost nearly 95 percent of their numbers and were reduced to less than a 1,000 people in all of the Northeast.

Christopher and Elizabeth Denne had no children and arrived in New York City at a time when there were only about 300 homes tightly packed on the southern tip of island. They were among about 5,000 settlers of free and enslaved people from the Netherlands, France, Africa, England, Ireland, Scotland, and Germany. By contrast, London had a population of 550,000.

Almost immediately, Denne and his wife connected to many of the influential English merchants in New York. In 1702, Denne became a "Freeman," what they called a recognized citizen of the city. Less than a year later, Denne was part of a group of 12 men awarded the Wawayanda land patent, which made up about 150,000 acres in Orange County. Wawayanda was the Munsee name for the territory. A dozen sachem, (leaders each band of native people) sold the property to Dr. John Bridges and his fellow patent holders, who were all well-connected "Freemen."

In 1702, Denne had more good fortune. Denne and two business partners went before the Common Council of Aldermen of New York City and asked the local government leaders for the lease to operate the city's only wharf. If granted, they would be able to collect fees from every one of the thousands of trade ships coming in and out of the city for years. According to author Arthur Everett Peterson who wrote in 1917 in his book *New York as an Eighteenth Century Municipality Prior to 1731*:

> "Capt. Lancaster Symes, merchant, Gerrett Van Horne, bolter, and Christopher Denne, carpenter, were the trio (selected). Their term was to be twelve years," according to the the book New York in the Eighteenth Century.
> The council told the men, "For the first three years, you are to pay one peppercorn rent and for the remaining nine, 30 pounds yearly."

Since a peppercorn was their way of saying there was a grace period of no rent due, Denne and his partners stood to collect handsomely even after covering the operating expenses of running the city's only dock. But there was a catch. Peterson wrote:

> "You may receive all dock revenues, including such from as many cranes as they might erect," the alderman told them. "But you must clear away the dock mud down to the sandy foundation and raise the height of the wharf one and one half feet to its previous condition. Also, you are to construct a sewer from the fish

bridge to the other common sewer in Broad Street and it must be finished by June."

The men also received the authority to bring before the mayor anyone indebted to the men for unpaid fees. The deal could have been lucrative and should have brought the men the fortune Denne sought.

However, less than a year later and like with all other dock leases before, the joint venture began to fail. First, Dutchman Van Horne dropped out of the partnership, and then the city began what would become a decade-long investigation into the partnership for mismanagement and unpaid rent to the city.

The Dennes had arrived in New York at a time of economic downturn. The demand for beaver fur in England had weakened. Trade was changing in the province due to regulations imposed by the Old World. It was harder for the middle class, made up mostly of new English immigrants, to move up to the economic ranks, where the older, wealthier Dutch merchants still held the top rungs.

> "Aspire as they might to look and act like the great merchants of London, with their townhouses and coaches, New Yorkers, who were not already opulent in 1700 rarely rose to such heights during the early years of the eighteenth century," wrote Cathy Matson in *Merchants & Empire: Trading in Colonial New York*, published in 1998. (Page 129-130)

Instead of becoming rich, Denne was amassing debt and a negative reputation. In 1708, Denne was briefly jailed for a month for confiscating the boat of a New York assemblyman in a heated exchange about unpaid dock fees. Ironically, Denne was now an assistant alderman on the city council and apparently falling into the traps of the local politics that led to such struggles.

An assemblyman's boat is "as good as any man's boat as collateral for his debts," said the defiant Denne. It took the mediation of influential leaders to free Denne and force him to claim it had been a misunderstanding

Despite this volatile time for the Dennes in the city, they were still well-connected. Denne and his wife Elizabeth rented their home from John Hendrick and Johanna De Bruyn. They were a wealthy and connected Dutch couple and owned many properties in Manhattan. John died about 1709. At the time of Johanna's death In 1711, she had four daughters and had been widowed three times.

John De Bruyn was a prominent leader at Trinity Lutheran Church in Manhattan, where Dutch, Swedish and German immigrants congregated. The Dennes lived in Johanna's Dutch-style row house on 34 Pearl Street, just a block away from the dock where Christopher was in business with her son-in-law, Lancaster Symes, also a Wawayanda patent holder.

Denne, an Episcopalian, was also well-connected to Trinity Episcopal Church, a Church of England house of worship. Many of the prominent Englishmen and women congregated at this church. Denne was hired by the Episcopal church leaders to build pews and repair woodwork at the edifice. He had also been hired to oversee repairs at the Crown's Fort George, at the tip of Manhattan.

Despite the aid of wealthy and influential people, Denne's dream of fortune and prominence faded from reality during his decade in the city. In 1711, Johanna died and left a will that attacked two of her daughters. She left the Pearl Street home, occupied by the Dennes, to her youngest daughter, making unclear the Dennes' place of residence. Her will below is recorded in the Abstracts of Wills on file in the Surrogate's Office, City of New York (Volume II. 1708-1728), Pgs. 51-53:

JOHANNA DE BRUYN. In the name of God, Amen. I, Johana De Bruyn, widow and sole executrix of John Hendrick De Bruyn, being aged and infirm. My executors are to pay the legacies left by my husband which are not yet paid. I leave to my loving neighbor, Cornelia Low, the gold ring I have used to wear upon my first finger. I leave to the children of my eldest daughter Petronella, that is to say, Johanes Ten Eyck, Maria Ten Eyck, Hendrick and Eva Ten Eyck, all that tenement and house where I now live fronting to both streets, between the tenement of Allard Anthony on the west and Benjamin Blagge on the east. But Hendrick Ten Eyck, her husband, is to have no share thereof. I leave to Johana and Elizabeth, the two children of my second daughter Sophia [Teller] all the dwelling house and tenement in New York, wherein Richard Stillwell now lives between the tenement and house wherein the widow Van Horn lives on the west and Paul Droillet lives in on the east, reserving to my daughter Sophia if she comes back from Jamaica the rents of the same during her life; Also the interest of £50 if she takes upon herself the charge and nurture of the said two children. I leave to my third daughter, Johana Jamieson, all that tenement and dwelling house situate and lying over against the house in New York, where I now live, whereof Christopher Denne is the present tenant, and lying between the tenement of Thomas Roberts on the west and Benjamin Blagge on the east, and from the street to the water side or Dock. I also give her £100. I leave to my son-in-law, David Jamieson, £20, and make him executor. I release to my children all they are indebted to me, except the bond of my son in law, Lancaster Symes, the present husband of my daughter, Catharine Symes, and Thomas Speed, to my late husband John Hendrick De Bruyn, for £50, which Lancaster Symes did own that he received from Thomas Speed, but now detains in his hands. And also accepting the £30 which my daughter Catharine has craftily obtained from me since my husband's death. I leave to my daughter Catharine all that piece or parcel of ground which is near and adjoining unto the land of the Dutch Church. I also leave her £400. All the rest of my estate is to be divided into three parts: One part to the four children of my daughter Petronella, one to my daughter Johana Jamieson, and one to my daughter Catharine. My executor has power to sell houses in Amsterdam in Holland. I desire that my daughter Petronella be not dissatisfied, for my gift is not made through any disrespect to her but because her husband, who deserves so little at her hands, should reap no benefit. Before my daughter Catharine, or her husband, Lancaster Symes, receives any benefit from this my will, they shall convey to all my other children all claim to the estate of her uncle, Balthazar De Hart, or her father, Matthias De Hart, or anything due to her first husband, James Larkins. Dated November 30, 1709. Witnesses, Robert Livingston, Oliver Teller, Elias Boudinot, Thomas Bayeux. Codicil. August 30, 1710. Confirms the above, and gives to the two children of her daughter Sophia £200. She also states that her daughter Catharine has paid £15 of the £30 owing to her. Proved before Henry Wileman, Esq., being authorised and confirmed by Governor Hunter, January 20, 1711.

[NOTE. The house and lot left to the children of Petronella Ten Eyck is now No. 35 Pearl Street, and the lot in the rear on Bridge Street. The lot next west of this, No. 33 Pearl Street, is the lot on which the first Dutch Church stood. The old church lot was bought by Henrica Anthony, the widow of Allard Anthony, and she was living there at the time of her death. The house and lot left to Johana Jamieson is directly opposite No. 35 Pearl street, and is No. 34. The house and lot left to the two children of Sophia Teller, is now No. 63 Pearl Street. The lot next to the Dutch church, which was left to Catharine Symes, is on the northside of Exchange Place, a little east of Broad Street.]

The city Common Council's frustration over the dock management reached legal levels in 1712. The council began a lawsuit against the men for debt and mismanagement. The dock, which was located on the East River, was dirty and falling apart, and the man-made inlet was filled with garbage. By now, Denne was out of money, credit and reputation.

Adding to the sense of urgency and pressure in the Denne household, one of the other Wawayanda Patent holders, Adrian Hooglandt, was killed in April 1712 during a citywide revolt of the African slave population. On that night, a group of enslaved Africans set fire to several buildings in the hamlet and then shot at the white men who rushed to put out the blazes.

Dozens of Africans were killed on that night, and nine white men were murdered. In the weeks that followed, more slaves were convicted and executed for their involvement in the revolt.

The terror of the event so gripped the city that it wasn't easily forgotten over many years, and as a result in 1741, the city authorities went on a "witch-hunt" style round-up of blacks and whites they believed, falsely, were plotting another revolt. They publicly tortured and hanged them using medieval methods long deemed inhuman, in order to scare off any other potential rebels.

In 1712, tensions were high for other reasons as well. Denne and his fellow Wawayanda Patent holders were concerned that the Crown might remove their land rights because they had not yet developed a single acre. They knew they needed to make the patent productive for the Crown and that they were on borrowed time.

There were others in the colony creating successful settlements nearby, which were getting the attention of the Queen Anne. German Lutheran Rev. Joshua Kocherthal brought 50 refugees from the Rhine River basin to the shores of the Hudson River along Quassaick Creek. They were Lutherans and Calvinists fleeing Catholic French aggression, high taxes, poor land and unusually brutal winters. When they arrived in America, they quickly cut a grid for a village that grew into Newburgh.

Just to the south, New Windsor was home to a small development by Scotsman Patrick MacGregory and his meager group. Also at that time, another Scotsman, Robert Livingston, was moving thousands of German "Palatines," the name coined by the English for the refugees from the Rhine River valley area called the Palatinate, into New York. Livingston and New York Governor Hunter agreed to move the refugees out of London, where they had flooded and overwhelmed the city, and into camps north of Kingston to work for Queen Anne in a scheme to produce pine tar for her military ships.

The Wawayanda Patent holders' strategy of land speculation rather than land development was becoming increasingly risky in the politics of the day. English monarchs had taken away land from patent holders before and given it to others they favored. In fact, this royal practice so upset the colonists over the years that it became one of the reasons they rebelled at the end of the century.

In 1712, the Wawayanda Patent holders knew the clock was ticking on their investment and they were getting left behind in the land development race of the early colonies.

With all these pressures, Denne realized his time in Manhattan had run its course and he was out of options. If he didn't take action, his last opportunity in the New World would be wasted.

> "Let us not, however, forget the deplorable state of these, our nine year patentee speculators, who found that speculation alone would not support itself, at least, in its application toward the political civilization of Wawayanda, in Old Orange County," Peter Bull wrote in the Goodwill Notes. "This was clearly and fairly understood by Christopher Denne, one of the company & patentee, who sought his fate – that he must run aground sometime, that he might as well die in the wilderness on his own premises, as in the city of New York."

But Denne wouldn't risk his life alone in the wilderness. He would be with his wife, Elizabeth, and his indentured teenage servant, Sarah Wells. At that time, as many as 60 percent of the population of New York were either slaves or indentured servants, whose life choices were governed by others. Most teenagers, even those born into wealth, were placed into indentured service by their parents or guardians in order to learn a trade. Children, in fact all people, were expected to contribute to the small and remote colony. Even Benjamin Franklin was once an indentured, teenage apprentice as a printer. Thirty percent of boys learned their father's trade. Sixty percent learned a new trade through others.

Indentured servants, bound out by parents, became the property of the masters and had to obey. Only the court could step in when the relationship went sour. Sometimes parents sued the masters for ill treatment toward the teens, or for not fulfilling the contractual obligation. Sometimes the masters sued because the servant ran away.

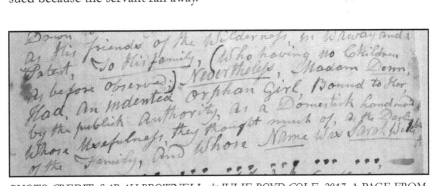

PHOTO CREDIT: SARAH BROWNELL & JULIE BOYD COLE, 2017. A PAGE FROM "THE GOODWILL NOTES" FROM THE BULL STONE HOUSE COLLECTION. IT READS: "MADAM DENN HAD AN INDENTED ORPHAN GIRL, BOUND TO HER BY THE PUBLICK AUTHORITY, AS A DOMESTICK HANDMAID ..."

The city government realized that some masters were taking advantage of the free labor pool and were not properly training their servants. These young men and women were entering the workplace without the skill the city leaders needed them to achieve, so the Common Council decided to regulate the practice. They enacted a law in 1711 outlawing handshake deals and required all apprentices to be by contract.

According to Apprenticeship & Apprenticeship Education in Colonial New England & New York, by Robert Francis Seybolt:

> "Every freeman in The Oath of a Freeman of the City of New York was required to take the following oath YE SHALL SWEAR that within the first year ye Shall Cause him the apprentice to be Enrolled or Else pay such fine as Shall be reasonably Imposed upon you for Omitting the same 3 This Act applies to poor law apprentices as well as to voluntary apprentices It will be recalled that the Duke of York's Laws strictly required that Parents and Masters do bring up their children and Apprentices in some honest and Lawful Calling Labour or Employment And the records indicate that in every case Overseers of the Poor and Churchwardens bound out poor children to some Merchant or handiCraft Tradesman Many poor girls were of course bound out to Dames but these women promised to teach their apprentices some useful occupation."

> "The usual term of apprenticeship according to English legislation was seven years and it must not be completed until the apprentice was twenty one years of age In the Province of New York however the Common Council Act of 1694 permitted four year terms which action was in effect an annulment of the law of the mother country Such a law also operated in contravention to the primary purpose of the apprenticeship system the production of skilled craftsmen But early in the next century it was recognised by the city authorities that the four year term was inadequate the average apprentice could not successfully learn a trade in so short a period Att a Common Council held at the City Hall of the said City on Tuesday the 30th day of October Anno Dom 1711 the earlier law was repealed."

The people in the young Colonies worked together in keeping tabs on the servants. and if a servant ran away, the master would often post in the newspapers asking fellow settlers for help in locating the runaway. Only the court could undo the bond before the contractual length of obligation expired. Here are a few examples of the ads that were published in the newspapers of the day:

> "Ran-away from his master Seth Sweetzer of Charlestown, in New England. August 15, 1703. A young man, named John Logen, about 19 years of age, of a middle stature, black hair, by occupation, a taylor, he's fraid to be done to Long-Island, thence to Pennsylvania. Whosoever shall take him up & convey him safe to his Master shall have 4 pounds reward," was printed in the Boston News-Letter on Thursday, June 5, 1704.

> "The above-nam'd Odell is one of a middle stature, slender & streight body, black hair, thin visage, holding his head somewhat on one side in his walk, who is known often to have changed his name," printed Thursday, August 14, 1704 in the Boston News-Letter.

Orphan children in New York were the responsibility of the authorities, and that responsibility was taken seriously. The New York Common Council appointed two men to act as "orphan wardens" every year. Churches also selected from among their congregations, elders who took care of orphans, widows, and the poor. Wardens acted as the guardians of orphans. They placed the youngest children in families for adoption and signed pre-teens and teenagers into bondage as apprentice servants.

Author Delber Wallace Clark wrote in 1916 in The World of Justus Falckner:

> "Private generosity, administered by the churches (in the early 1700s), did whatever was done for the orphans, the worthy aged poor, and such widows as had no adequate support. One of these deacons (in New York City's German Lutheran Church) was John Viets. He was a promising and active layman. His removal to new England a little later deprived (Rev. Justus) Falckner of a good helper."

Homes for orphans were not common in the early part of the 18th century. In order for orphans to become productive members of society, if they were old enough, they were quickly assigned to families as servants. The small society in New York, created by the giant and successful corporation called the West Indies Trading Company, learned early that it was in the best interest of all if everyone in the colony was thriving and contributing. They invested time and money to see that happen. Homelessness, peddling and vagrancy were illegal.

Generally, adults contracted to service signed various lengths of enslavement based on the mutual goal. Twenty-six-year-old William Bull signed himself into an indentured service contract in 1715 with Wawayanda Patent holder Daniel Crommelin. Children were generally released from their indenture when they reached the age of consent, 21 years old, and were expected to know a trade or how to keep house by the end of the term. English masters were expected to teach their foreign wards to speak English if they didn't already understand it and sometimes, they were required to teach them to read.

All this was part of an effort to create valuable citizens for the New World. People were considered a commodity, as much as beaver skins. The leaders of the hamlet could not afford to allow a single person to be unproductive. This approach, first developed by the Dutch company, continued for more than a century and helped make New York become one of the most successful cities in the world.

In Sarah's case, Peter Bull writes in the Goodwill Notes that she was an orphan, bound by contract to the Dennes. She was 16 years old and a maid, and under the authority of Christopher Dennes in 1712. We were able to determine Sarah's age by the record of her death entered into the church records of Blooming Grove Congregational Church on the day of her death, by her pastor the Rev. Benoni Bradner. We found the record in the Goshen Library Local History Room. Rev. Bradner recorded:

"Death. April 21, 1796, Sarah Bull, 100 years and 15 days old."
(Transcript of the records of the Blooming Grove Church)

This record provided new information and third-party confirmation of Sarah's age and settles this long-held confusion by the family. It also gives us a window into the last decade of Sarah's life. But we will discuss more of that later.

PHOTO CREDIT: JULIE BOYD COLE, 2017. BLOOMING GROVE CONGREGATIONAL CHURCH TRANSCRIPT IN THE COLLECTION AT THE GOSHEN PUBLIC LIBRARY LOCAL HISTORY ROOM THAT RECORDS THE DEATH OF SARAH WELLS BULL IN 1796.

In 1712, Sarah was a teenager and did what she was ordered and contracted to do: serve as a maid in the household. We read dozens of indentured documents of New York from 1690 to 1707.

Unfortunately, most of the records from 1707 until 1718, when Sarah was most likely bound to the Dennes, of indentured apprentices in New York were lost, according to the state historians. In the records we did review, we found no mention of Sarah Wells or Christopher Denne. We did, however, learn about common practices of the time. In each document we reviewed, the contract established the length of the service, the expected duties and the reward for a completed contract. Here is an example of an indentured apprentice contract:

Recorded for Anthony Farmer, the 9th, day of December 1697:

> This Indenture witnesseth that Walter Hopper aged thirteen years or thereabouts by & with the consent of John Edmiston Commander of the Priche Elizabeth of Barwick upon Tweed now riding in the harbour of New Yorke to whose charge he was by his parents committed hath for and in consideration of the sum of thirteen pounds curr. money of New York to him the said John Edmiston in hand paid at and before the ensealing and delivery of these presents by Daniell Plowman Commander of the Sloop Ann now riding in the harbour aforesaid as well as his own free and voluntary will put himselfe apprentice unto the said Daniell Plowman, etc. "the said apprentice or servant" to serve for seven years from date. Signed, May 19th, 1693. Walter Hoper, John Edmeston. In the presence of Matthew Plowman, Will. Sharpas.

And another:

Recorded for Mr. Anthony Farmer, 17th day of December, Anno. Dom. 1698:

> Indenture dated May 15, 1693, of Frances Champion, daughter of Frances Champion, with consent of mother, to Anthony Farmer and Elizabeth Farmer, his wife, as an apprentice and servant, for nine years from date. Said Master and mistress in addition to other matters "to instruct the said Frances to Read and to teach and to instruct her in spinning, sewing, knitting or any other manner of housewifery, etc." Signed in the presence of Frances Champion, Jno. Eldridge, Jn. Basford. Acknowledged, December 17th, 1698, before Jacobus V. Cortlandt, Esqu, Alderman.

We did not find a single indenture that required a teen to lead a troupe of hired hands into the wilderness to stake a land claim for the master, or an apprentice who received land as a reward. It is highly improbable that Sarah Wells was required by the contract to lead Denne's expedition. She most likely could have refused and stayed in New York, though her future would be risky and she would likely be placed with another master.

Denne did not have a position of strength in his negotiation with Sarah. He was secretly running from debt, dodging a lawsuit against him by the city, and was without money or a good name to secure credit. Peter Bull writes in the Goodwill Notes that Christopher Denne didn't demand, but asked Sarah if she would take on the task, and that Sarah thought it was a ridiculous idea.

Peter writes:

"Upon hearing this, Sarah (as she said), cast her eye around, took a glance at the Indians ... and then turned her back upon them all in a kind of dismay and with, as it were, a pouting, grumbling silence ... too plain to be concealed __ disgusted with the proposal and said to herself, 'Is this the fate of orphan children, a poor destitute girl, without a guardian or protector, who could scarcely dare think herself a woman, to be huddled and crowded on board a vessel ... and with a motley group of strange men?' "

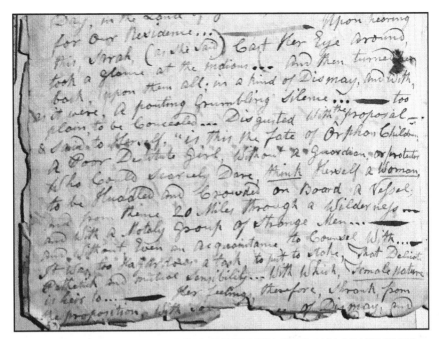

CHAPTER 10

SARAH'S CHOICE

However disgusted Sarah felt when Christopher came to her in the spring of 1712 with the frightening proposal to settle the highlands, Sarah quickly considered it. Christopher told her that he wanted her to lead the small expedition without them. He promised they would follow her sometime later, according to Peter Bull's account. Though Denne tried to make the mission seem plausible and Sarah capable, the teenager struggled with the idea.

Peter writes:

"Christopher Denne spoke kindly to her, and said, 'Sarah, we place our entire confidence in your faithfulness relative to this business … We confide to your care – we have no desire of being otherwise separated from you, than for the mere accomplishment of a settlement in the wilderness where we expect to be united in company again … perhaps forever... While life may last …"

Denne didn't back down, and instead sweetened the request. He offered Sarah an unprecedented bounty of 100 acres in the settlement at the end of her service. Denne would cut the acreage from his 2,000-acre stake. The bounty was much more than the common payment. Most teenagers left their service with a skill and clothing, not money or land.

"To secure to you a livelihood … as an independent means of living, I will give you, a hundred acres of extra bounty land, at the end of your servitude for your faithful service … and that we may live as friends and near neighbors, through life."

Peter Bull writes in the Goodwill Notes that Denne worked to convince Sarah and explained to her what might not have been apparent: the land bounty would give Sarah the means to determine her own destiny. She would no longer be a servant or dependent on strangers. After a decade-and-a-half of living at the mercy of others and the tragedies that resulted, the idea of independence gave young Sarah a powerful seed of hope, she tells Peter Bull.

"The hundred acres of bounty land sounded large and cheering to Sarah's ear … and having no desire of being separated from 'Madam Denne' the only female friend she had in the world; she therefore, the more readily assented to their proposition…"

In one conversation in May of 1712, young Sarah took stock of her prospects and chose Denne's monumental adventure. She had no one to talk to about her decision, to help her weigh the pros and cons, she tells Peter. She had no one to warn her of the dangers or encourage her to take the chance. Just the Dennes, who had a desperate and vested interest in the outcome of her decision. Yet Sarah made her decision quickly. She would go with the unknown men to the land of Wawayanda and try to survive long enough to win her freedom and a new direction for her life.

In 2017, during an Open House event at the Bull Stone House, I was extremely fortunate to meet a 90-year-old visitor. She told me that she too had once been a 15-year-old indentured servant. Aldona Jonynas, of Las Vegas, described how she was a World War II refugee in Lithuania with her family. For four years, they lived in a displaced persons? camp, poor and with no hope of a better life. An official from Canada came to their camp and offered anyone who would sign, free travel to Canada and jobs as household servants. At the end of the service, they would become citizens.

PHOTO CREDIT: SARAH BROWNELL, 2017. JULIE BOYD COLE STANDS INSIDE
THE HULL OF A DOUBLE-MAST, REPLICA SAILING SHIP UNDER
CONSTRUCTION IN ST. AUGUSTINE, FL. THIS SHIP IS ABOUT THE SAME SIZE
AS COMMON HUDSON RIVER SLOOPS OF THE EARLY 1700S AND SHOWS THE
AMOUNT OF CARGO IT COULD CARRY.

She told me how and why she took the offer, left her parents and sailed
across the Atlantic to a new land.

"It was my only hope of a real life," she said, standing in the main
hallway of the Stone House. She was scared but hopeful that it would work
out, she said. She and her friend left their family and country and sailed to
Canada alone, as teenagers. She told me her story as her daughter stood
nearby, how her decision gave her a happy, nearly century-long life. She had
just finished a tour of the Stone House when we began to talk. She glanced
around the house of Sarah and William in awe and said. "But, I didn't
create all this."

Even to another indentured servant 200 years later, Sarah and William's
accomplishments are impressive.

At the end of May in 1712, with Sarah's agreement, Denne's unlikely
plot was now set and ready to be put in motion.

Young Sarah may not have been aware of the politics of her master's
position. Nevertheless, she was aware of how much of her fate was outside
of her control. Born at the turn of the 17th century meant that she was
born into a world where liberty was a not a right for most.

Denne kept his expedition secret from most people and shared it only
with his closest friends. He was leaving behind debt to more than one
creditor and he may have been been in a land race with the other patent-

PHOTO CREDIT: *DXEDE5X (OWN WORK) [CC BY 3.0 (HTTP://
CREATIVECOMMONS.ORG/LICENSES/BY/3.0)], VIA WIKIMEDIA COMMONS. THE
REPLICA SLOOP "CLEARWATER" SAILS NORTH ON THE HUDSON RIVER IN JUNE 2007.
THIS SHIP IS SIMILAR TO THE SHIP THAT CARRIED SARAH WELLS OUT OF
MANHATTAN TO ORANGE COUNTY.*

holders. The group had agreed years earlier to award extra acreage to the first of them to settle the land. Daniel Crommelin and Benjamin Aske, two other men still on the patent at that time, soon followed Denne's tiny expedition in 1712. Aske and his representatives Christian Sneaker, Jo Wesner and Lawrence Decker, claimed and settled the town of Warwick. Daniel and his son, Charles Crommelin, claimed what is now Chester.

According to the Goodwill Notes, the Dennes, Sarah, and Christopher's associates, some of whom were his fellow patentees, spent the day getting ready for the evening sail up the Hudson River. Christopher and his friends worked to find willing tradesmen and collect supplies. Elizabeth helped Sarah pack.

How strange, rushed, and uncertain it must have felt for the young woman and Madame Denne to pack, when they really had no idea what to expect. Sarah was leaving a small but developed city and the comforts of the Pearl Street townhouse. She was headed to undeveloped land neighboring a small village of indigenous people. Nevertheless, Sarah tied up her linen and woolen clothes. Inside the bundle, young Sarah stashed a few trinkets and toys she could play with on her journey, according to Peter Bull. Maybe she tucked inside her tight package tops, playing cards or jump ropes, common toys of the day. Peter didn't tell us specifically. Regardless, she might not have realized then that in the days, weeks and maybe even years ahead, she would have little time for leisurely amusement.

Peter Bull does tell us that the Dennes packed up the household items they were putting in Sarah's care: a coffee pot, wooden trenchers, bowls, two pails, two kitchen kettles, and bedding tied in bundle. After the women

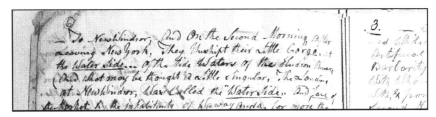

PHOTO CREDIT: SARAH BROWNELL, & JULIE BOYD COLE, 2017. A PAGE FROM
"THE GOODWILL NOTES" IN THE BULL STONE HOUSE COLLECTION.

had everything ready, and Christopher returned, they were able to share one last meal together before they hurried to the boat.

Everything was loaded on the sloop, including the three Native American men and the three tradesmen. The young servant girl was the last to board. With little fanfare, Sarah stepped on board and looked back to the Dennes standing on the dock. As the captain began to cast off the ropes, the Dennes quickly said farewell, according to the Goodwill Notes.

As the sun set, the sloop sailed with a stiff wind into the north. Sarah watched as New York City quickly faded out of sight. Would she ever see Madame Denne again? Would she ever see Manhattan again? What would become of her? The boat was crowded with supplies, two cows, two bulls, two horses, two dogs, and men she did not know. The rush of fear, she told Peter Bull, was only controlled by her overwhelming sense of hope. Sarah hoped that she would survive. She hoped that Madame Denne, her only friend in the world, would soon follow her into the wilderness. She hoped that this was the beginning of a new life; one that would be filled with security and happiness.

After a while, sailing along the deep waters of the Hudson River, the pace of the sloop slowed. The breeze that had taken them so quickly out of New York harbor had slowed as well. The current of the Hudson River flows with the tides for miles north. The Munsee people named the river "Muhheakantuck" for its north and south current , which translates in English to "the river that flows two ways."

The captain, with the help of all the men on board, put out the oars and began to row to keep the boat moving north to Plum Point, New Windsor. By late afternoon of the next day, the sloop arrived and anchored offshore. The tiny outpost had been home to Patrick MacGregor's Scottish settlement for nearly 30 years and the waystation where traders put in during their travels between Albany and New York City.

To the south of the outpost was the point where Murderer's Creek, now called Moodna Creek, empties into the Hudson. Legend says that the creek was named because a family of settlers were killed by local Indians at the creek, but historians today say it's more likely a tall tale than fact. The creek winds eastward around the hills of the Highlands into the interior of the country, eventually meeting the Otter Kill near Goshen.

After spending the night on the sloop, Sarah's expedition unshipped in

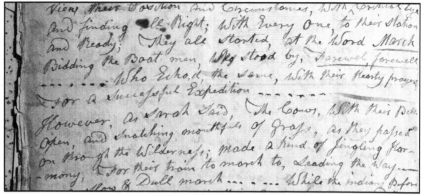

the early morning at Plum Point while the ship was aground in the low tide, she told Peter Bull. He writes that the small troupe unpacked their supplies and animals, and walked to shore on the exposed sand flats of the riverbed.

> The Goodwill Notes read: "The cows were first unshipped and their bells unstopped, with the most youthful Indian to take charge of those. While they browsed and grazed along shore. The horses next, with their bells stopped, and with their straw, or Irish saddles, to lade the provisions and other baggage on … The first horse was loaded with the heaviest provisions, tools and kitchen furniture, and the oldest Indian, to lead and take charge … the other horse was loaded chiefly with bedding baggage upon which Sarah's budget was fastened, and the charge of the horse given to her, with a place fixed for her to ride occasionally as she felt disposed …"

Peter did our family and historians a wonderful service when he recorded the tales of his grandmother and documented what it was like to face the frontier in the 18th century. Thankfully, Sarah was willing to tell him her story of the expedition.

She told Peter that along with the workmen's tools and kitchen items, they carried into the wild leather bags that contained bread, flour, ham, cheese and bacon. On Sarah's horse, they made a "pillow saddle" for her comfort when she would occasionally ride.

Horses were a common form of travel in 1712, but the animals could not go too far at one stretch, were high-strung, easily spooked and unpredictable. Humans could walk almost twice as long as a horse at any given stretch, so most people walked more than they rode a horse.

Once the horses were packed, the small band of men and Sarah stuffed their pockets with bread, biscuits, ham and cheese so they could quickly carve off a snack with their pocket knives as they traveled.

They planned to take an old Indian trail that had become known to the European settlers as The King's Highway, today about the same as Route 94, that linked New Windsor to New Jersey and followed Murderer's Creek into what is now Washingtonville. The highway was more of a foot path through the wilderness, and reportedly first used by the indigenous people.

Another road, also called "The King's Highway," followed a path from Virginia, through New York City and onto Boston. This roadway may have been considered part of that important thoroughfare In 1712; the Dennes planned to go further west to what is now the east side of Goshen, to the site along the Otter Kill that Christopher Denne selected as their new settlement.

Peter Bull writes:

"The whole train, being thus arranged in single file, with Sarah in the middle, the third Indian, who was to assist Sarah with her horse, was confided the care of the whole train, and walked round them all on both sides, to view their position and circumstances, with a critical eye, and finding all right, with everyone to their stations and ready. They all started, at the word, 'March.' Bidding the Boatman, who stood by, 'Farewell, farewell.' _ Who echoed the same, with their hearty prayers for a successful expedition __"

It took all day for Sarah's expedition to walk from the banks of the Hudson River to the east bank of the Otter Kill. The march through the narrow pass was strangely uneventful, quiet and rhythmically calm. The single-file hike by people of different ages, ethnicities, familiarity, and languages didn't lend itself to much easy conversation, Sarah told Peter. She kept quiet during the long hike. Sarah said she watched the cows occasionally grab mouthfuls of the long grass and listened to their bells as they walked along the trail.

Sarah told Peter Bull:

"The cows with their bells open … made a kind of jingling harmony, for their train to march to, leading the way _ on a slow and dull march __ while the Indians before could talk to each other, in their own language, and the men, in the rear could talk as they pleased __ while she in the middle might talk to herself."

During the slow, day-long march to her new home in the wilderness, the weight of Sarah's decision to take Denne's offer must have been crushing. Her grandson wrote:

> "But for all this, in her waking and sleeping dreams __ a melancholy hovered over her senses __ almost impossible for her to conceal __ As life loses its charms, so in proportion, death loses its terrors."

Sarah was just a teenager. She had lost her parents. She had moved to Manhattan from New Jersey. Yet, in 1712, she was hiking through wilderness filled with rattlesnakes, wolves and other beasts, leaving the last people she knew and traveling with unknown men to a place she had never been and with certain, life-threatening dangers.

Many others before her had succumbed to the fear and hopelessness in facing the prospects of a new start in the undeveloped New World. Decades earlier, Pilgrim leader William Bradford's young wife died when she fell off the Mayflower that had been anchored off the Massachusetts coast for months. According to the historians in the PBS documentary "Pilgrims," she had been suffering deep depression and it is believed she jumped off the ship to end her own life.

Peter Bull writes in the Goodwill Notes about Sarah Wells:

> "A forlorn hope. Her fate was sealed. How could she survive it? Could say but little. A mere spectator. A mute."

Peter was clearly amazed, like Samuel Eager, at Sarah's ability to physically and emotionally handle the expedition. He wrote about his grandmother that she was "somewhat small for her age and naturally smart," and "was light, sprightly and smart."

Intelligence might have been a disadvantage as she spent the quiet hours hiking through the wilderness on that day in May, calculating her odds of a pleasant future. In May of 1712, Sarah's fate was a complete unknown, except that she knew how common settlers were killed by accidents, Indian attacks or nature's harsh hand. Did she worry that she might starve? How long would the provisions they packed last? Would the Dennes come to Wawayanda soon or leave her there to die?

According to Peter Bull's Goodwill Notes, Denne only told Sarah that they would "follow at some later date." What did that mean to young Sarah? Was the plan that Sarah would be left alone to live in the wild until they came, or would the hired workmen and indigenous people stay with her?

EXAMPLE OF A MUNSEE PEOPLE CAMP IN THE NORTHEAST WOODLAND OF THE 18TH CENTURY.

"Could Sarah, as she said herself, dared to have given vent to her sentimental feelings," Peter Bull wrote in the Goodwill Notes, "... would have preferred weeping to smiling."

Thankfully for Sarah, her traveling companions seemed to sense her mood, or maybe they understood her task ahead, and treated her with the care and reverence of a daughter, even the youngest of the native men.

"To relieve her melancholy dreams," Peter wrote, "she would often stop her horse, cling to his mane, and descend from her pillow saddle, to the ground, with ease. And when she chose to lead her horse, this third Indian, would pass round their whole train with a critical eye, to see if all was right and nothing lost. This was a faithful trust and a satisfactory service throughout their journey and when he returned to the the horse again to lead, would often present to her a nosegay of blossoms, snatched from the bushes, as he passed along, such as the huckleberry, hillberry and honeysuckle and showed to me that they were harmless, be eating some of the blooms..."

"And when she wished to ride again, she had but to stop, The men would lay down their tools and the dogs would set by

70

them as sentinels, while the men stepped forward to help Sarah again, on her pillow saddle. They would place her again, on her saddle, like a child with all ease. All, she said, appeared pleasant, friendly and kindly attached to her. As if she was the very darling of their tender and most affectionate concern. All their friendship, seemly was concentrated around her. Nor could it have appeared more so, to her, if she had been the sole cause of the expedition."

Throughout the day-long, 20-mile hike to the site of the new settlement, the team stopped to rest and milk the cows, graze the livestock and unload the horses. After each break, they would load the horses again and carry on, Sarah told Peter.

Toward the end of their journey, they came into the Munsee village, where the three men lived with their sachem, the name used to describe the leader of the family, their wives and children, less than two miles from Denne's site.

"Passing the Indian Village, where all seemed still and quiet, when the old Indian, who had been left to take care of the home (when the three Native American men went to Manhattan with Christopher Denne just a few days before), slipped out with his hatchet, joined the young Indian, his son, with the cows and leading the way, to the east bank of the Otter Creek, nearly opposite, to where Christopher Denne had fixed upon a sequestered spot for a resident. As the sun set, the night overtook them."

Sarah and the small band of men and farm animals had arrived at her new home less than five days after Sarah was first proposed the idea in Manhattan of relocating to undeveloped wilderness.

The hike was without incident; all were well, and that was remarkable. New York's frontier was not a harmless place in the early 1700s. Wolves roamed the land in packs. Rattlesnakes were common. Weather could suddenly turn without warning. Native people and Europeans lived within dramatically different cultures that could at times lead to violent misunderstandings. Strangers, both natives and immigrants, were not easily trusted. Life in the frontier was not ever easy or without an element of anxiety.

In the dying light, the group took care of the necessities. The men unloaded the horses. Sarah milked the cows. The oldest Indian, the sachem, quickly built a fire using only his hatchet. The horses were turned loose to graze. The cows soon followed and the jingling song of the bells continued. There by the shore of the Otter Kill, the men went to work quickly in the night to build a few raised sleeping platforms under the boughs of Beech trees, to protect them from rattlesnakes on the forest floor and dew from the night sky, Peter Bull wrote in the Goodwill Notes.

Sarah put together a small buffett supper of wheat bread, milk, biscuits, cheese, ham and bacon. When all work was done, they each took from the spread what they wanted and fell upon their makeshift bedsteads in the wild, exhausted. Two of the native men went back to their village, to their wives and children. The Munsee sachem and his son took their blankets and laid them by the fire, where they slept.

It is hard to imagine what Sarah must have been thinking as she looked out over the scene lit only by the glow of the campfire and the white light of the Milky Way above. Did time stand still for her at that moment, or speed up? What was beyond the light in that vast darkness?

In the summer of 2017, Sarah Brownell, my son Campbell and I stood at the site where Sarah Wells first made camp and tried to imagine what must have gone through her mind.

Today, there is a busy road and bridge. Large 21st century houses dot the landscape. A stone wall and the slow-moving Otter Kill are the only things from Sarah's time there today. Standing there, though, it is possible to get a sense that settling the land with only what a few pack horses and cows could carry, miles and miles away from anything remotely civilized, seems as unthinkable today as it seemed to Sarah then. And yet, she did it.

Sarah awoke the next morning on that late spring day in 1712, to see the men, including the younger Munsee men who had slept at their village the night before, cutting wood at the camp. The Munsee sachem had rekindled the fire. Sarah told Peter:

> "'They made a temporary raft, in the most expeditious manner and slid over (the Otter Kill) with their tools' and went to work on the spot where Christopher Denne had fixed his site. And under the direction of these friendly and kind Natives of the Wilderness who had long wished to see the white people settle among them as neighbors, and for which purpose, their lands were sold to the white people, and which they were now about to realize."

We turned to the history to better understand why the native people of Orange County in this small village would be so helpful to Sarah's troupe. Of course, they could not have had the forethought of what European settlements were doing to the native populations' culture and way of life. Even still, the native people tried to protect themselves. Unlike some of the other native tribes, the Munsee people had survived the devastation of the 17th century. They sometimes fought the Europeans but often laid low, and

tried to get along with these outsiders. They often helped the Europeans to settle their newly purchased lands.

The Munsee were also in the minority and less powerful than other tribes in the Five Nations of the Northeast. They had for centuries learned that small family villages were more environmentally sustainable and caused fewer relationship conflicts. The Munsee preferred camps by rivers and creeks among the woodlands, where there was plenty of clean water, food and fuel. They often traveled between seasonal camps through the year and would reconnect with their larger family during annual reunions, where marriages were formed. That lifestyle was working for them in the 18th century.

The Munsee culture was matriarchal, which meant that women stayed with their small family villages and men left to marry within other villages. The dramatic reduction of the population meant there were fewer opportunities to mingle with outside families to find mates.

American Indians did not have written language. Their culture stayed alive only through verbal communication and passing down their collective wisdom from elder to child. As the populations diminished, so too did their hope for life beyond the present generation. The elders were literally watching their society die. We spoke with a Stockbridge-Munsee Community historian during our research. She told us that it was common for the Munsee people to help settlers, especially women, at the time.

Maybe this small village helped the Dennes and Sarah in the hope they would integrate into their culture, rather than the other way around. If they had the benefit of hindsight, maybe their helpful behavior might have been different; maybe not.

The Munsee people of the Wawayanda Patent met with Christopher Denne many times over the years, according to Peter Bull. Each time he visited their lands, they offered friendship and aid. They showed him how to select the best homesite and taught him about life in their country. They wanted the Englishman and his family to live among them. Their numbers were so dramatically reduced that they needed the white settlers to become a part of their community.

They were glad that Denne was finally going to populate the land, Peter Bull writes in the Goodwill Notes. But the historical account says the same. In April of 1712, before Sarah's expedition began, Denne stood with his new Munsee neighbors on the spot of his future home, on the west bank of the Otter Kill, near what would become Goshen. The eldest Indian told Denne they would do anything to help. Even for Denne, who had known this man for years, it was hard to believe, Peter Bull describes. Why would they want to help him?

Denne knew that with their help, he wouldn't be at the mercy of all other native tribes, as Elizabeth feared. They would be with friends, and not alone. On that May morning in 1712, with Sarah and her band of workmen, the Munsee people kept their promise and worked tirelessly to help get the settlement started.

On the first morning in the new settlement, the Munsee taught the workmen how to construct a wigwam common among the Northeastern people. Peter Bull's description in the Goodwill Notes of the effort matches with other histories of how the Munsee people built their homes.

> "(The men) dug holes in the ground with the spade, at the distance of about fifteen feet apart, with crotches, cut and set in the holes for posts, about six or seven feet high, all leaning inward, with poles around in the crotches and pinned together at each corner with wooden pins, and a gutter dug around, corresponding with the posts, serving to keep out the wet, and to set the lower end of the slabs or palisades in, and had begun to set some up, jointing them as close as possible with the ax. And two crotches outside of all, rising still higher to hold a ridge-pole for the roof."

Native American homes differed depending on the region of the country and tribes. Tipis dotted the west. Pueblos were built in the southwest. The wigwam was unique to the Algonquian-speaking people of the northern region of America. According to author Bobbie Kalman's account in Native Homes, published by Crabtree Publishing Company in 2001:

"To build a wigwam, the builder's first job was to trace an outline on the ground and then dig holes along it. The poles that made up the frame would be set into these holes, making the wigwam sturdier. The poles were the stripped trunks of flexible young trees. Each pole had a partner directly across from it and the pairs were curved to meet at the top in an arch. Each pair was tied together with basswood strips. The builder reinforced it with two or three rows of poles. Once the frame was secure, the cover was put on."

Peter Bull described in the Goodwill Notes how the Native American men and the three carpenters worked together on their first full day on the Otter Kill building the wigwam. He wrote:

"The carpenters were gouging and boring holes, with a five quarter auger on the outside through the palisades in every corner of the wigwam for the purpose of, first, to lay two slabs of about 12 or 15 inches broad & five feet long and jack-planed off smooth, on one side, with the ends sawed & square, to be placed at the remotest end of the hut and on sticks, crowded into these holes, on the inside of the hut and resting upon studded crotches driven in the ground, on corners fixed for their beds and bedding, with poles and light brush to be laid out on slab of five feet long, as a seat for Sarah."

He continued:
"Brought in, the east-bench and placed it at the remote end of the hut from the door, then the table plank placed there in due order, in one corner, near Sarah's seat, and with poles in the these holes studded with crotches to bear them up, as was also the other three corners for their bedding."

The Munsee family living near Sarah's settlement would live in these wigwams in all seasons. In the winter, more layers were added to the outside walls. "The roof was made of overlapping sheets of bark, which were lightweight and water-resistant. An opening in the roof allowed smoke from the campfire (inside) to escape. The hole was covered by a flap of bark that could be opened and closed with a long pole," according to Kalman.

The wigwam was also portable. The tribe would move it from one seasonal location to another, though they left the frame of poles in place for when they returned. Within this home, all family members lived; they

EARLY ETCHING OF PEARL STREET IN MANHATTAN IN 1679.

cooked, ate and slept there. "Life in the wigwam was busy and cozy," Kalman wrote.

Sarah didn't see it that way. Peter Bull tells us in the Goodwill Notes that Sarah was shocked a tree hut with a dirt floor, built in less than a day, would be her home. In fact, the home was not much different than homes built thousands of years earlier, but very different than the homes in Manhattan. There, Sarah lived in a rowhouse with the Dennes. Some homes built in New York City in 1712 still stand today. They had solid construction of stone, brick or wood with floors, windows and doors. Homes had interior kitchens and fireplaces for cooking and warmth. Though not nearly as private as homes are today, the rowhouse in Manhattan offered much more privacy than a wigwam.

> Sarah "said to herself, 'what a hole it was, to huddle in, and in the night, or bad weather.' It was all ominous against her. She turned from the door with disgust," Peter Bull wrote in the Goodwill Notes.

The Munsee people worked hard, according to Peter, to give Sarah the best that they knew to make a successful settlement. They didn't just help the workmen build Sarah's new home; they provided information about the best way to farm, live among the natives, how to boil water over the campfire, use the dogs for security, and all aspects of life there.

And of course, the small band of Munsee sent three of their four men to Manhattan to help bring the expedition up to the Wawayanda. Sarah told Peter that they also offered to camp among them indefinitely in order to serve as a liaison with other Indigenous people who might come through their camp.

Peter Bull wrote in the Goodwill Notes that the Munsee sachem said to the settlers:

> "(The younger men), if you wish it, may perhaps stay with you through the warm season and all they may require or hope from you, is to make them comfortable while they stay. As you

will doubtless, if life and health be with you all, you must have a busy summer, to prepare for the winter in your way, of what you call civilized life."

Peter Bull continued:

"The Young men assist you as a runner, and in many respects as a messenger and also in looking up and bringing the cows and horses up occasionally, for there is no fear of his getting lost in the woods. Further, should he find any of them astray or in the custody of any other Indians, he could talk to them in their own language and so adjust your claim with them and have no further trouble. While the old man (his father) is now past the meridian of active life, yet he may be of service to you, as a sentinel guardian to you and your property. Suppose for instance, this very night, a large party of our Indians were travelling through the woods upon some extraordinary occasion as sometimes happen with us, and should come to this wigwam, of this day's work, having no previous knowledge therefore __ Although your dogs might give the alarm __ which, however, they could easily quiet, they would not pass you, without making a thorough examination into the cause. Suppose they could speak only the Indian language, what could you do?"

It is clear in the Goodwill Notes that the Munsee family, now Sarah's most immediate neighbors, wanted her to succeed and would help her to do so, even if Sarah had her doubts.

Peter Bull tells us in the Goodwill Notes that during the entire expedition, Sarah was battling depression. Who could blame her, a 16-year-old girl in a dirt-floor wigwam, alone?

In 2017, I read Peter's words from Sarah Wells to a psychotherapist in Gainesville, FL. "She was depressed," the expert told me. No surprise there. I asked the Bull Stone House visitor, the Lithuanian indentured servant, about her emotions when she left her family and country and sailed to Canada. "I was very scared, but hopeful," she said. The trauma of her teenage years stayed with her for the rest of her life.

In 1712, the Munsee worried about Sarah's mood, according to Peter Bull. On the second day on the Otter Kill, the oldest Indian worried about Sarah's visible melancholy.

"She set a-musing on the log and cast a mental eye, as it were over her fate. At least, say for weeks, or for months or perhaps forever. Her spirits sunk again, below par, and she was lost in the profundity of the muse," Peter Bull wrote what came from his grandmother's own description. "Until the horses and cows with their bells, came jingling up to her, which aroused her from her waking pensive, and melancholy dream, when she slid from the log, took her pail and went to milking."

"The men observed her setting on a log, with her serious movements," Peter Bull wrote. "Was fearful Sarah was too much worried, in ferrying over so much baggage and would have her set down and take some breakfast with them, as she must feel fatigued and faint. She shook her head, but said nothing."

Since Sarah was the source of Peter's notes, she clearly remembered that trip all through her life too, just like the Stone House visitor in 2017. Ninety-year-old Aldona Jonynas had no trouble telling me in details of her emotional state of her 15-year-old self, even though 75 years had passed since she made the voyage across the Atlantic. The two women shared a common beginning and both stood in the Stone House, though more than 200 years of time passed between them. They both lived long lives with family they loved and are testaments to what human beings are capable of.

Back in May of 1712, Peter wrote that Sarah was shocked by the realizations of her dramatically changed lifestyle. Over the course of those early days, Sarah told Peter she thought about the rustic campsite, her fears, her loneliness, the tragedy of being an orphan and servant, and the unfolding realizations of every inconvenience of daily life. But in order to tell the details of her story to her grandson decades later, Sarah must have believed those details mattered to complete the story of the journey. Maybe she too saw the contrast between the beginning of her life in Orange County and the end of her life, the contrast of living in a dirt-floor wigwam and a four-story stone house.

On Sarah's first full day on the Otter Kill, the men worked hard to finish the wigwam and a few pieces of rudimentary furniture. They also built a kennel for the dogs just outside the door, where they would serve as nighttime sentries.

Peter took down several accounts from Sarah of the work:

"While two men came to the log (where Sarah was seated near the fire pit), as some of the Indians kindled up the fire, the carpenters flattened the top of the log with their axes, to serve as a table to spread our provisions on, for all was now about to be examined ..." Peter wrote. Sarah "having thus taken a glance at the business of the day, returned again to the log where the men were about finishing breakfast, late in the morning, and as they had much to accomplish in order to get all their provisions, household goods and kitchen furniture under cover by night __ They would leave her to pack all up, as she thought proper, with the assistance of the Old Indian man, and they acted accordingly."

"While she was assorting things on the log, the old man with his hatchet cut crotches, drove them in the ground, laid a pole across on the them over the fire, placed on the small chair hook trammals, hung on the pot & kettle, filled with water, kindled up the fire, and then went to work with the men."

"When she took the wooden bowls & trenchers as the water boiled in the kettle & scalded them up, and cleaned them for use, and sat them on the log to dry. Then, taking her lonely seat on the log as before. The first glance & mental view was seemly. That all was increasing for the better, until she thought of her lonely and deplorable fate. How long she sat, she knew not, when the old man came and told her, the workmen might wish to have something to eat before night & he would assist her in preparing it. Observed further, that they had bread yet and good bacon; if she was willing they would get a piece and prepare it for boiling __ and also, there was a plant near the Spring & grew in abundance along the Otter Creek, when cooked with salt made excellent food, while Sarah was fixing the bacon and got it in the pot a boiling, the old man had gathered near two pails full for the plant, dipped water on them with a bowl to wash and cleanse them for cooking, then got a small potato, for everyone in company, scraped them for boiling with the herbs, as soon as the meat was done, and all was soon completed, when by pressing the bottom of a bowl on the top of the pot, as the liquid was poured off __ then dashing the greens & potatoes at once into the bowl, and set on the log, by the meat, as the trenchers, the knives & forks were placed on the log, with bread cut & in another bowl _ the old man called to the workmen to come to dinner __ though somewhat late," Peter Bull wrote in the Goodwill Notes.

Sarah was still struggling with her depressed mood through the hard work of the day. As the men came to dinner, she walked to the hut. Peter wrote:

"She walked off as before, but to her astonishment, the hut appeared to be finished, except along the ridge, as the bark was too short, from the timber that was split as all the timber seem to peel and laid by as bark for use as they cut & peeled it. Where she had as it were, the same, or similar, thoughts to ruminate over again, and said to herself, 'what a hole it was, to huddle in, and in the night, or in bad weather. It was ominous against her.

"She turned from the door with disgust. But soon met the old man with a fire-brand, nay, every Indian was bringing fire, as if they were going to burn up the hut."

But they were not going to burn down the home they had just spent the day building, no matter how uninhabitable it seemed to Sarah. Fire was part of the construction process. Peter Bull wrote:

They "were merely to build a large fire in the middle thereof, to warm & dry, the green timber of which it was made, and while this was doing, the Indians were peeling more bark & after the fire abated soon finished the roof, with a hole in the centre, to let out the smoke, and which also served as a skylight window."

Peter Bull continued:

"And so was the other three corners fixed for their beds and bedding, with poles and light brush to be laid thereon, as in the evening & night before. They even made a long bench for Sarah out of a slab of five feet long, as a seat for her. All of which was preparing & prepared on the outside, while a large fire was blazing in the wigwam."

"When the fire abated, brought in the seat-bench first, placed it at the remote end of the hut from the door, then the table plank placed there in due order, in one corner __ near Sarah's seat, and with poles in these holes studded with crotches to bear them up, as was also the other three corners for their bedding as before described."

"When this was done, they sent off the young Indian for the horses & cows, as they were grazing, to the southward, almost out of hearing _ as the other men went to Sarah at her log table and told her they were ready to move in and wished her to bring on the coffee pot, which appeared somewhat heavy when carried in the hand, while the men brought on her budget, with a small bed, well secured and bound up with packthread, as was also her budget, the small bed was called 'Sarah's' and if possible, not to be unbound until she arrived at her place of destination, which together with two large beds, with a pair of sheets & a pair of blankets and a pair of pillows for each _ two of which had made Sarah's saddle."

The Munsee men told Sarah that it was the custom that Sarah must take possession of her new home first, before anyone else could officially walk through the threshold of the now-finished home. Peter wrote that the men told Sarah:

"It was therefore necessary she should walk in foremost ... and they would follow with her budget and bed and she acted accordingly."

Once they were all inside Sarah's wigwam home, now fashioned with beds and linens, a bench and table, and the provisions, the men folded a blanket and put it and a pillow on the long bench and asked Sarah to sit down. Peter wrote:

"While they told the whole of their arrangements in & about the order of their new building, and if she chose anything otherwise, to say how, and they were at her service, so to do. (Sarah) nodded assent but said nothing as a mere spectator. They went on and closed their arrangements, while the Old Indian brought forward his lug-pole, the trammels and crotches fixed them over the fire. The pot & kettle cleansed & filled with pure water from the Spring and rung on to boil, as the fire was kindled up."

The day had been very active, as each day had been for the last week, and the men were not only satisfied with their work, but happy with the results. Sarah was not, her grandson Peter tells us:

"She saw nothing wrong, as she said, but her situation in life _ a mere solitary hermit, as it were in society _ again, those gloomy prestiges came hovering over her senses _ as if she must sink down."

Peter Bull wrote down what his grandmother must have told him many times:

"How could she live?"

The admiring grandson noted on many of the 40 pages of notes for what was supposed to be his history of Orange County, that his grandmother was in a very difficult situation that appeared to be hopeless. He wrote those four words on the last pages of his unpublished manuscript. What followed those desperate words were these:

"As the cows and the horses came jingling up to the door & aroused her, from her waking dream, as they did in the morning, she rose from her seat, took a pail and went to milking."

For many thousands of settlers, there was no time in the daily grind of survival for grief. It was no different for Sarah Wells. No matter how scared or lonely she felt in the first days as a settler of Goshen, Sarah opted to survive one task, one day at a time.

As the troupe prepared for their evening meal, the men were happy and pleased with what they had accomplished. Sarah did not share their joy or shake her sadness. Peter wrote:

"She had but little to hope ... The place. The wilderness _ had no appearance like home and therefore had no charms for her. Place and Young woman, she said, in her situation ... what could they think? If (the men) thought at all their thoughts would be similar to hers."

As smart, young Sarah looked over the campsite that was now her home, Peter tells us that she was overwhelmed with melancholy. The Munsee men would be returning to their village. The carpenters may have been returning to Manhattan. Sarah didn't know if the Dennes would ever move to this "hole." She had been orphaned once already and left at the mercy of the authorities. Now, she was alone again, in the frontier, with limited supplies. Peter Bull's list of items that Sarah carried into the Wawayanda land did not include a firearm, only a few small knives. What would happen when the food ran out or if there was trouble with passing strangers?

Clearly, the Munsee family nearby offered young Sarah support, based on Peter Bull's notes. But did Sarah have faith in these strangers whose primitive lifestyle looked nothing like her society, which was on the brink of the industrial revolution? Regardless of what Sarah thought, she was without any other choice now. As the men exchanged congratulations, Sarah stood inside the wigwam, surely trying to conceive how she would survive, when suddenly she heard something coming from outside that jarred her from her thoughts.

"She heard a voice," Peter Bull wrote in the Goodwill Notes. "Or thought she heard a voice __ that she knew, while she seemed as if she must sink to the ground."

Sarah thought, "It must be a waking dream __ which her serious revaries had often lead her to since leaving New York."

"The voice, which she heard, was (saying) 'Sarah, Sarah,' " her grandson wrote. "It was to her like an electric shock. But on hearing the name 'Sarah' a third time, she cast her eye to the wigwam door and behold, it was Christopher Denne and his wife on horseback."

"This was too much for Sarah to bear, She lost all the fortitude which she assumed for the several days and nights past to give vent to the feelings of the heart that sensibility, with which female nature is susceptible of."

Samuel Eager tells us in his 1846 written history that at this point, Sarah fainted. It's not clear where Eager got that information, because Peter Bull did not write that down in his notes, which were Eager's source material. If she did faint, it would make sense considering the weight that had just been lifted from her young shoulders by the appearance of the Dennes. Their arrival meant that she would not be alone.

PHOTO CREDIT: JULIE BOYD COLE, 2017. THE OTTER KILL AT THE APPROXIMATE SPOT WHERE CHRISTOPHER DENNE BUILT HIS FIRST HOME. LIVED SARAH WELLS LIVED BETWEEN 1712 AND 1718.

CHAPTER 11
THE DENNES' FIRST NIGHT

Despite Christopher Denne's historic record of dodging obligations, he fulfilled the promise he made to Sarah Wells in the spring of 1712 by following her to Orange County. The act was so unexpected that Sarah was overwhelmed with shock when they arrived.

According to Peter Bull, Christopher and his wife Elizabeth arrived by horseback to the new settlement in the wilderness just 24 hours after Sarah and the men. Peter Bull's notes show Denne regretted sending Sarah ahead with just the strangers, and he and Elizabeth left the very next day out of a sense of guilt. Maybe he was also worried that he put the care of his last investment in the hands of a child.

Peter Bull did not know Christopher or Elizabeth Denne; both died before Peter was born. Christopher died in 1725 in Orange County and Elizabeth died in 1736 in Manhattan. As a result, Peter's source for the things Christopher and Elizabeth did and said detailed in his notes were either from Sarah, others in the community, or from some unknown document written by Denne. The Goodwill Notes give a good bit of detail about that first night Christopher and Elizabeth arrived, just before the troupe was about to sit down for the evening meal. As it turned out, the meal did end up as a celebration, though it appears from Peter's notes that once the Dennes arrived, the focus was placed more on Christopher Denne than on Sarah. This may have been expected because he was in fact the leader and owner of the settlement, and Sarah's master.

According to the history, English social structures were patriarchal at this time. Still, wives often ruled at home, though they held no individual standing outside the home if they were married. Married English men were the legal and sole representatives of the family to the outside world. Servants and children were considered property those men owned. Ironically, unmarried women were able to own property solely, operate businesses, and even become "Freemen" in the cities, and they were considered the heads of their households if they had children.

Christopher was the rightful leader of the settlement on the Otter Kill in 1712. For the last three days, Sarah had been treated as the honoree by the native men and carpenters. She went back to her status as servant to her masters as soon as the Dennes arrived. Peter doesn't tell us in his notes how Sarah felt about this, but historically she would have expected this turn of events.

Peter Bull filled many pages with his quill and ink about the Dennes' first night and the celebration of their first meal together in the new land. His notes read like a journal, and he attributes sentence after sentence to Christopher Denne as if he is directly quoting the man.

Peter wrote that the dinner Sarah prepared was delayed by the Dennes' arrival as the group helped them unpack their horses and get settled. Denne began to speak to the gathering about the journey he and his wife made to Wawayanda and why they had come so soon. Sarah and Elizabeth sat down to listen and the men gathered around as Christopher began his monologue.

Peter Bull wrote:

"Character, of the learned, in their varnished, whitewash, of rhetoric, which serves, as the artificial and insidious means, to conceal the barbarity of civilized high life __ with which & with whom we had been accustomed & associated with & from habit, had become with us, a kind of second nature __ but we detested ourselves and repented of the hazardous folly of imitating the fashion of high life __ we could not stay where we was __ something must be done __ yet if possible, to live & die together and conceal our woe if Elizabeth could compose herself, a few moments I would get some female confidential friend to come & stay with her, while I might find some means to meet or pursue Sarah __ either to meet her on horseback as we had assured & flattered her, or to pursue, by water up the Hudson River, in order to find her somewhere, or learn the last of her."

It is clear from Peter's notes that Christopher Denne was critical of his own behavior as a New Yorker, a businessman, and as Sarah's master. It is also clear that Christopher enjoyed pontificating; at least that is what came down through the century between when Christopher supposedly uttered these words and Peter wrote them down.

"I then went to seek the means for our departure, as my own credit was lost. But in name, I was obliged to communicate my views & wishes to some of my Patentee friends, who as before, made my case their own. Who, in the most friendly & obliging manner, wished me to give myself no further concern how to get off: But to return to Elizabeth and make her as easy as possible, and assist her in getting ready __ and we will endeavor to get everything ready, said they, for your journey, and meet you on the ferry stair, as we did last evening, and they acted accordingly, furnished us with two saddle horses with bells, with a woman & a man's hunting saddles. Saddle-bags and portmanteaus for each horse," Christopher apparently told the gathering of new settlers, carpenters and natives along the Otter Kill.

Peter Bull didn't identify those patentees, just that they were his friends. We know from Elizabeth Denne's will, written in 1735, that Vincent Matthews, son of original patentee Peter Matthews, received half of the Dennes' Orange County property. So it is certainly plausible that the Matthews helped the Dennes raise the money for their own expedition to catch up with Sarah Wells in 1712. We also know that Christopher was business partners with Gerritt Van Horn, a brother of John Van Horn, one of the patent holders.

The Van Horns were a wealthy Dutch family that lived in New Jersey just west of Manhattan. It is possible that the Dennes stayed with them in New Jersey the night before they left for Orange County. Lancaster Symes, another patent holder mentioned earlier, was Denne's dock master partner; it is also possible that Christopher was ducking out on Symes, since it appears he was dodging the dock debt with the city. Daniel Crommelin and Benjamin Aske – two more Wawayanda patent holders – planted their stake in Orange County soon after Denne. Each of these men seemed to have money, though it is unclear if they would be willing to fund Denne's trip north. Various records also suggest that both men were also in debt.

Peter Bull wrote in the pages of the Goodwill Notes about the Denne's first night at the Otter Kill, and the notes read like a transcription of a Denne diary, though we were not able to locate one. Peter wrote this on his pages in the Goodwill Notes in the middle of Denne's account of the journey: "To return to the Journal of Our Journey." The meaning of the words is not clear. One thing is for certain: Christopher Denne died in Orange County, at his home along the Otter Kill, which he called "Denne Hill,", in 1725, so we know Peter wasn't quoting Denne directly.

Peter wrote that Denne continued to speak to the gathered settlers and described the journey he and his wife took into the wilderness:

> "One pair of saddle-bags were filled with the choicest provision for our journey. __ The other saddle-bags and portmanteaus were brought to us at our lodge-room to be filled with our clothing, and whatever we chose to place with them, and where they had rolled up several medicinal phials of cordials, such as hartshorn, peppermint, pennyroyal, & together, with a small canister of choice tea, and a due proportion of refined sugar, broke in small lumps for use, to which we added Elizabeth's small tea plate, crowded full of ribbons, small pocket knives, trinkets and toys to be distributed among the Indian woman and children occasionally, and all was in readiness for us, as we met them in the dusk of the evening on the ferry stair, together with two blankets for each horse. One to be placed under the saddle, and the other to be the covery of all, and a pillow for Elizabeth to ride on, to make her seat the easier in traveling __ all of which appears, noted in a memorandum given to us, as our bill of fare."

According to Peter Bull's account in the Goodwill Notes, Christopher continued speaking to the troop as they all gathered in the camp right after the Dennes' arrival and in interruption of the dinner Sarah had just finished preparing. Peter continued Denne's address:

> "And now our dear girl, our adopted child, as you have done our business & have been faithful to us, by sacrificing inclination to duty and after we had detested ourselves in the error and folly of imitating by insidious means, the fallacy of high life; remorse __ stimulated and prompted us to act & to do our duty and with the providential aid of our friends in New York and who also crossed the ferry & put up with us on the Jersey side of the Hudson River and assisted in fixing us off in the morning, For as they said, we 'were doing the business for them' __ when we parted with melting hearts __ and their sincere prayers, for our success __ we jogged on __ for I dare not allow my thoughts to reflect back on what had lately past; But kept conversing on what appeared new to us on our path, as we rode on."

According to Peter Bull's written account, Denne tried to keep his wife's spirits up, just as the Munsee men put effort into cheering Sarah the day before. Peter's history of the journey showed that the two women involved were battling fear, anxiety and depression after leaving Manhattan and heading into the unknown. Peter wrote in the notes that Christopher said that night:

> "And as cheering as I could, to prevent Elizabeth's spirits from sinking below par __ and thus we arrived the first day's riding, to near the cascade or falls in the Ramapo Stream in the mountains where we put up, at a hut, for the night __ and early in the morning of this day, we started again __ and grouping a winding and crooked passage __ through the mountainous Hills and valleys, until we came through into "Wawayanda" near the mountains, since called, Sugar Loaf, to an Indian Village __ where we could not learn any intelligence relative to our expedition with Sarah from them."

The route taken by the Dennes from the north shore of the Hudson River into the Wawayanda Patent followed what is now called the Ramapo River along the New York State Thruway, over the mountains and into Chester until they eventually reached the settlement from the south, unlike Sarah and her group. They came into the settlement from the east.

Peter Bull wrote that Christopher told his gathering that he and Elizabeth were searching for Sarah while they rode through the forests of north New Jersey and Southern Orange County, though it's clear the

Dennes knew and instructed Sarah and the troupe to take the Hudson River route into the settlement. Nevertheless, at each weigh station they sought news of Sarah.

According to Peter, Christopher continued:

> "We jogged on to Rumbout's (one of the Native sachems who signed the Wawayanda Patent) residence, yet no intelligence. We concluded to keep on to the Little Village and residence of these our friends and natives of the woods & soil, who live about a mile and half east from here, where we proposed to put up for the night and if no satisfactory information was to be had, tomorrow we would have endeavoured to reach the tide waters of the Hudson River."

The Dennes did not need to go that far. They found Sarah and the troop exactly where Denne had told them to set up camp. Christopher told the gathering that they were prepared to make a full circuit all the way back to Manhattan on the Hudson River if they couldn't find Sarah. Apparently, Denne feared the worst in having sent Sarah ahead, according to Peter's Goodwill Notes. Sarah was, by the standard of the day, a "city girl." The Dennes speculated on how they would feel if they never found Sarah.

> "Remorse would have stung us deeper & deeper __ and we must soon have spun but a wretched existence __ perhaps together __ and to use your own expression __ 'As life loses its sensible charms, death loses its terrors!' "

Peter Bull writes in the Goodwill Notes that on that first night at the Otter Kill, Christopher told the group they were planning to bypass the Otter Kill settlement spot, apparently assuming that Sarah never made it there, but that since they were making good time and it was still daylight, Denne decided once there to show Elizabeth the site.

> "The opportunity was favorable as the sun was yet above the horizon to ride a little out of our way, to show Elizabeth this sequestered spot, which I had selected as a resident," Christopher told the group, according to Peter's notes. "When we behold those, our Indian friends, on full speed, which we feared as runners with some disastrous news relative to our hazardous expedition.

> "But think, O think!! What our hearts felt as so sudden a transition from fear to joy __ by hearing all was well, & Sarah preparing for supper," Christopher Denne told the troop. "We

urged on as these men led the way and flew before us to the door of this spacious hut."

As Sarah listened to her master speak to the small band, did she show any sign that she didn't share his opinion about the fledgling camp and in fact thought it a "hole?" Peter Bull didn't tell us. He did describe a dramatic contrast between the expedition before and after Christopher and Elizabeth Denne arrived. In the days that Sarah was alone with the carpenters and natives, there was little conversation and a lot of hard work. The native people were concerned about Sarah's melancholy mood and Sarah was critical of the habitability of the camp.

Sarah was a lowly servant girl, but she was the center of attention of the men of the expedition. They treated her like the proprietor of the camp. After the Dennes arrived, Christopher took over and spoke more in that one evening than the six men and Sarah had spoken in the past three days together. It is fair to say that Peter Bull paints Christopher Denne as a bit full of himself, though Denne heaped praise on the men for their efforts to get Sarah safely to the settlement site and for the work they had already accomplished.

> "As appertaining to the human species _ we repeat it _ by saying perhaps there never was, nor ever will be, more fidelity, and a more Christian feeling of sympathy & charity _ in so motley a group of people __ It is a question whether there ever was, in Wawayanda, or ever will be, in the civilized Goshen of Wawayanda, a purer sentiment of Christian fidelity, sympathy & charity expressed by uniform action __ and realized with unaffected joy & sorrow, exhibited in this providential wigwam of one day's work __ this evening and where an offering of pure Christian devotion is displayed, without hypocrisy and religion without priest-craft."

Priestcraft was a derogatory description about people who put more focus on the laws of religion than on Christ's message of love for all. Denne clearly appreciated the kindness and dedication shown by these men. Denne also made note of the accomplishments of the two women in the troop:

> "Be it remembered, that Sarah Wells has obtained the laurel __ that is, the name being the first civilized white woman, who set foot on Goshen ground, and Elizabeth Denne, the next & within twenty-four hours of each other, as the first improving settling of Wawayanda __ yet it was, through the fidelity of Sarah to & for us; and the faithful concern of the company,

concentrated around her, which has accomplished this providential habitation for us, this evening."

Peter Bull tells us in the Goodwill Notes that the Dennes brought gifts for the indigenous people, like many European settlers of the frontier did. He wrote:

"And now my faithful friends, the Natives of the soil & woods: here is four blankets which we have brought here this evening on horse-back ; there is one for each of you, take them, as an acknowledgement from me, for the fidelity of your faithful services __ and after supper & when our conversation __ in this association of truly Christian sentiments, with our "neighbor as ourselves, shall seemly lag __ and we may feel inclined to repose you will, and each of you will, take a blanket, & in your own way, make your abode with us, for the night and this spacious wigwam; the work of your own hands for their appear ample room for us all, and which closes my sentimental narrative for the present ..."

By Peter Bull's count, there were four men from the nearby Native village, three carpenters from Manhattan, Elizabeth, Sarah, and himself, a total of 10 people, in the camp that night. Wigwams of Northeastern America varied in size and could be built to hold up to 60 people. Peter Bull describes a wigwam that was more rectangular than round and had "corners," and one that could sleep at least 10 adults, and house their supplies and newly made furniture. No wonder Christopher was amazed.

After Christopher spoke, the men and women of the new settlement went back to preparing for dinner. Elizabeth helped Sarah with finalizing the now-celebratory buffet. Elizabeth pulled from her saddlebags the provisions they brought with them: bread, coffee, "choice ham," cured and dried beef tongue and cheese, "choice tea, sugar and chocolate, which was used to make hot chocolate. While Sarah boiled water, Elizabeth set on the rustic table made from a log, delicate china teacups and saucers. Sarah mixed the greens pottage and potatoes in a wooden bowl and set it on one end of the table.

For the first time since she had left Manhattan, Sarah had an appetite, and the food finally smelled good. She tasted her creation and realized that it was good. She told Peter that it was the best thing she had eaten during the entire expedition and that finally, her mood improved. Sarah told her grandson that "had not this providential meal have taken place, it might perhaps been out of my power, thus to have received (the Dennes that evening.)"

Christopher was so impressed with what was to him unusually prepared food set out on the handmade table in the long wigwam, that he said, "Elizabeth, we must taste of Sarah's new invented cooking here in the woods." His wife replied, "Not only the bacon and green pottage is of Sarah's new cooking here in the woods, but all that is newly prepared on this her table this evening, as the bread, the milk, the coffee, the tea and the chocolate, which is now in readiness and steaming, before us, are of Sarah's preparation, and the table is, or was, made for her."

In the early 18th century English culture, servants and children did not sit at the dining table with the adults. Servants ate elsewhere and children, even in the frontier, would mill about the adults accepting food off the communal plates. But on this night, Christopher and Elizabeth Denne were so delighted with Sarah's ability to prepare a full meal in the middle of nowhere by campfire that they decided to make an exception to the standard dining behavior.

Peter wrote:

> "It would be necessary, at least for this evening, for (Sarah) to preside, at this serious yet festive board, and therefore, let us bring her bench alongside that she may act accordingly," Christopher said. "And the bench is long enough to hold us all three, and we will sit, one of us, on each side of her & help her to distribute the present fare among our friends around us.

> "This proposal was so unexpected to Sarah as almost to overcome her with the coy & delicacy of her feelings, but upon a little reflection, she complied & took her seat. As all was ready, Elizabeth said she would commence the course by taking a small sniff from her small phial of Hartshorn."

Hartshorn was an early form of smelling salts, or ammonium carbonate, and was made by boiling down the horn of the European red deer. People used the smelling salts to revive them and according to Peter, Elizabeth used the sniffer often during her trip north. Christopher decided to use the Hartshorn as a celebratory start to their festival.

Peter wrote:

> "I shall therefore, before offering any of these restorative cordials of mine, I shall take of them a little myself, so taking up her smelling bottle of Hartshorn, took a small snuff, and handed it to Sarah, who did the same and then to Christopher, who cautioned the men to be moderate __ then taking a small lump of refined sugar with a few drops of the essence of

peppermint to brace the stomach and so on again to the men, who received it with a sensible satisfaction.

"While this was doing, Sarah took a small slice of bacon with her new greens & a piece of a potato, and placed them on the trenchers, for Elizabeth & Christopher ... all being thus prepared, Christopher spoke to the men & said 'If there be anything on this table at present, prepared for supper which you would prefer, one and all of you, speak & we will endeavor to serve you.' Whereupon the carpenters spoke and said, 'We had it in contemplation, first, to preserve our old bread, which was yet good, and in the next place, to hansel our new building, of one day's work, with some kind of rare festivity, prepared for supper, when we made known our wishes, to Sarah, about which she was engaged, when you ... came to the door and which is now in readiness for us on the table, and we have discovered nothing as yet, to charge our opinion and first impressions, we shall therefore, prefer Sarah's new milk from the cows, her new bread baked in the pan for the first time, together with her coffee, now smoking on the board before us: Nevertheless, we are willing to taste whatever your kindness may think proper to bestow so as to complete the festival on this evening supper.' To which the Indian men all nodded assent and they were served accordingly by Sarah."

Elizabeth and Christopher did eat the food that was prepared by Sarah and said it surpassed their expectations. The greens were unusual to the Dennes' palette, and they considered the plant food on par with "pigweed," or plants that were used for hog food. Still, the method of preparation over an open campfire that Sarah had already learned from the native men tasted surprisingly good to the Londoners.

"For the bacon in cooking with the greens had seasoned them, with a proper relish, to them at present, equal to, if not superior to common pigweed. Then, they took a dish of coffee with Sarah. After which, Elizabeth served round her chocolate, old bread & cheese, when this was used, she cleansed her china cups & saucers, with the tin dishes in hot water and then served round the tea, the refined sugar together with those delicate cakes designedly prepared as it were to close the evening's festival.

"Christopher Denne arose from his seat, and stood up with the men, (who had no seats to sit at the table) and said, 'It is a singular sacred & providential circumstance realized in congregating so motley a group of people, as is in this assemblage here this evening. And yet to have no other connection, than a sudden, trifling or small acquaintance, nevertheless has fulfilled their engagements. And I say to you my friends of the woods and Natives of the soil, it is your prudential fidelity & parental providential care _ with these workmen with you, from New York, that have conducted this long wished for expedition of mine, in these woods, and to the very selected and sequestered spot, I designed for a residence. I feel at a loss for words, my friends, to express my gratitude to you all.'

"When I consider the prudential sympathetic and parental concern, which your behavior and actions expressed towards this, our adopted & orphan child, and which has brought her safe to our arms & embraces this evening __ while it was our duty, to have accompanied her, throughout the hazardous campaign ... but when remorse stung us to the heart, for the neglect of duty we repented of our weakness, folly and wickedness, for attempting to keep up & imitate the glossary of the farcical Barbarian and the pitiless sophistry of the learned in their dignitarys of high life.

"While it was remorse that stimulated & prompted us to our duty; Yet it is to you my friends whose honest minds, benevolent disposition, good hearts & willing hands, has erected this commodious building. Where in the morning of this day, was a perfect wilderness, and now a convenient habitation for us all, to assemble and congregate together this evening."

Christopher appreciated the pole and bark wigwam far more than Sarah. Of course, he was well-versed in political relationships, while Sarah was not.

Christopher thanked the band of men over and over, according to Peter Bull's Notes. But, within the pages and confirmed by other historical records, the Englishman may have aggrandized his feelings about the effort and his "love" for Sarah.

Though Peter gave us Christopher Denne's words, the historic record gave us his actions. Why did Denne send an untrained, teenage girl alone into the wilderness to stake his claim just days after he had returned from the location and just hours before he decided to make the journey himself?

In the early 1700s, adopted children were not asked to serve the family beyond what a blood relative would be required to contribute.

Within the Goodwill Notes, Sarah is clearly treated as a servant, not a child, and tasked with something few servants would have been required to do alone. We found in the records that often children were adopted and became part of the family, like any other biological child, just like modern times. They took the adoptive family's last name, and you can find their names in wills, and in family genealogies. One example is the adopted daughter of Robert Livingston, mentioned earlier. She was a Palatine refugee adopted by Livingston when she was four years old. Livingston took in six other children at the same time, but this girl became his daughter and was mentioned in his will.

Christopher and Elizabeth left nothing to Sarah Wells Bull in their wills, though Christopher wrote his will in 1706, likely before she started her service with them. Elizabeth wrote her will after Christopher's death. He died in 1725 or 26 and Elizabeth wrote her will in 1735.

Christopher Denne's will:

> 1724-25; Abstract of the Will of Christopher Denne; Liber 10, page 25; written 21 September 1706; proved 6 February 1724-25; Christopher Denne New York carpenter; to wife Elizabeth, all my property in the Parish of St Wilfred, Canterbury, Kent, England and also the land of Wawayanda Patent, Orange co, NY and other properties. Witnesses: William Bradford, William Sharpas, J Stevens. [source] Abstracts of the Wills in the Collections of the New York Historical Society.

Elizabeth Denne's will:

> In the name of God Amen I Elizabeth Denne of New York widow and executrix of my late husband Christopher Denne of Dennhill in Orange County being of advanced years but of sound mind I leave to Mary Day and Christopher Denne children of Michael Denne late of London baker who was the brother of my late husband 50 each I leave to the said Christopher Denne my silver Tankard To William Bradford Jr of New York pewterer 50 To Flora Matthews spinster 10 and my walnut Secretaire To Sarah Jones of New York spinster one of the daughters of my brother Thomas Jones late of Kent England 200 and all my household goods To Mary Parker another daughter of my brother Thomas Jones my silver mugg To Elizabeth Sharpas 30 To her father William Sharpas 50 as an acknowledgement of my affection for them I leave all the rest of my personal estate to my kinsfolk Mary Parker Thomas Jones and Jonathan Jones children of my brother

Thomas Jones deceased I leave to my said kinswoman Sarah Jones and to Vincent Matthews of Matthews field in Orange County all the lands and real estate not sold by me I make William Sharpas Gent executor Dated December 9 1735 Witnesses Isaac Van Hook Katharine Eustace John Fred Proved January 14 1736/37.

In 1712, Christopher offered Sarah a reward of 100 acres in Orange County if she accepted the mission to lead the expedition. But Christopher never fulfilled his promise. After he moved to Orange County, he lived another 13 years but never deeded Sarah the acreage from his 2,000. Years later, Elizabeth deeded the 100 acres to Sarah's husband William and their 8-year-old son John. Over the years, the family has assumed that these acres were the promised bounty – though William paid for the land.

During the decade that Christopher and Elizabeth lived in Manhattan, the record shows that Christopher owed money, was jailed for theft and was about to be sued by the City Council because he did not fulfill his obligation as the dock master. By the time he moved to Wawayanda, he was running away from his debts in Manhattan and could no longer borrow money for his ventures.

Peter Bull wrote that Denne kept Sarah's expedition secret, and only a small number of people knew about it.

Since Christopher didn't have an admirable track record and it is plausible that Sarah didn't respect her master either. Though it was common in the early 18th century for new parents to name their children after grandparents, honored family members, and friends, Sarah did not name any of her 12 children after Christopher or Elizabeth.

On the Dennes' first night on the Otter Kill in 1712, when the meal was over, Christopher dismissed his entourage but called the men together.

> "Let us sit down and compose ourselves a little __ before we repose on our beds to rest __ through the reminder of the night __ as the true and natural sabbath for each natural day," he told the men.

Sarah and Elizabeth got up from the table and began to clear the dishes. They put the table to the side of the wigwam and Elizabeth said she would clean the dishes, according to Peter Bull's account. Elizabeth told Sarah:

> "While you may proceed to unbind your bed, which Christopher show you and called it yours when shipt on board the boat, and for you not to loosen it until you came to your place of destination."

Sarah walked to the spot in the wigwam where the men had built her a bed stand and she unpacked her bundle of bed linens.

Peter Bull wrote:

> "But alas! Here was found another test for Sarah's delicate feelings. Nothing less than two black tin pots, for private use about beds, one for Sarah, and the other, as necessity required. Together with an abundance of rolls of trinkets carefully put up; as those of small jack knives and other small pocket knives, ribbons and toys for her occasionally to distribute among the Indian women & children as appeared by the bill of fare accompanying them, with garden seeds."

Though Peter does not elaborate further, apparently the pots were chamber pots for Sarah and maybe the entire troop, to use to void their bladders and bowels. When Peter wrote these notes in the 19th century, indoor plumbing had not yet been invented. People used outhouses or indoor chamber pots and disposed of the waste by dumping the pots outside their homes. One hundred years before Peter wrote the notes, when Sarah was young, privacy was less of a concern, but Peter seems to indicate that even back then, a communal, one-room wigwam had its drawbacks for young Sarah.

As Sarah made her bed, Christopher went over the list of seeds packed in her bundle.

> "The Season now required to be put in the ground ... Christopher said that if all else was well in the morning they would endeavor to attend to it."

The sky was now dark and lit only by the moon so Christopher invited the native men to sleep that night at the wigwam with them. The moonlight was enough, the native men said, to return to their village safely. They wanted to get back to the women and children and needed to plant seeds for their farm, they told Denne. The sachem and his son would stay with the Dennes and the other two men would head back to their village, they told Christopher.

As a thank you, Sarah gave each man a knife and Elizabeth gave them dedicated cakes from the table, with ribbons and toys for the women and children at the Munsee village. Elizabeth asked the men to bring their wives and children back as soon as possible so they could all meet.

> "For they were the only people in these woods, she considered as neighbors or had any actual knowledge of," Peter wrote.

The Munsee men told Christopher that the oldest man and his son would stay with Dennes through the warm season.

"You must have a busy summer, to prepare for the winter in your way, of what you call civilized life," the Munsee man said.

And with that, the first full day at the settlement along the Otter Kill came to a close. Sarah lived within a few miles of that settlement for the next 84 years.

Peter Bull did not go beyond that night in his notes found at the Goodwill Church in 1965 and used by Eager in 1846 for his book. The rest of Sarah Bull's life story came through history in bits of documents and family stories. But if not for Peter Bull's foresight in documenting Sarah's first-hand account of her journey into Wawayanda wilderness in 1712, and Samuel Eager's and his descendants' care in keeping them, Sarah's early accomplishments might never have been known. We must also thank the Goodwill Church, which still stands in Montgomery and serves a vibrant community, for their care in keeping these 200-year-old treasures and giving them back to the then-Bull Stone House caretaker and resident, Jo Brown.

.

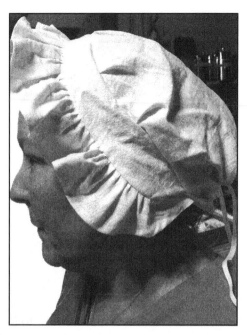

PHOTO CREDIT: JULIE BOYD COLE, 2017. SARAH BROWNELL MODELS A TYPICAL HAT WOMEN WORE WHILE WOMEN WORKED IN THE 1700S. WE FOUND THIS HAT IN AN AUTHENTIC CLOTHING STORE IN ST. AUGUSTINE, FL, THE OLDEST CITY IN THE UNITED STATES.

Chapter 12
SARAH'S LIFE BEGINS IN WAWAYANDA

Sarah Wells was just 16 years old when she traveled by sloop and horseback into the wilderness of the Wawayanda lands. She stayed for more than eight decades and she died and was buried at the top of "Burying Hill" at her farm. The story of Sarah's life in Orange County has been handed down from one grandchild to the next, from descendant to descendant with only a scattering of written records and backup, as Samuel Eager wrote in his history.

We know, for example, that in 1714, Sarah's name showed up in a survey commissioned by Christopher Denne on his tract of land. On the document, apparently as a boundary marker, is "Sarah's Hill." This, we assume, refers to a location on the property named for some unknown reason after Sarah Wells. Maybe this was a spot where Sarah went to be

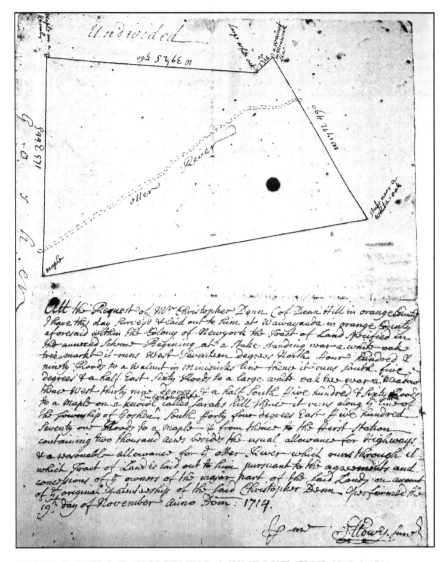

PHOTO CREDIT: SARAH BROWNELL & JULIE BOYD COLE, 2017. A 1714
SURVEY COMMISSIONED BY CHRISTOPHER DENNE AND AMONG THE BULL
STONE HOUSE COLLECTION REFERENCES "SARAH'S HILL" AS AN
APPARENT LAND MARKER.

alone and think, just as Peter Bull described in his notes she did in her first days in Wawayanda, or maybe it was where she did the wash. We don't know. But the data is just another point that connects Christopher Denne to Sarah Wells. The notation does suggest, as our family lore does as well, that Sarah was living with the Dennes in 1714.

If we were standing with Sarah, on that spring morning ,on the banks of the Otter Kill, we would see a slow-moving and winding stream about

50 feet wide. We would hear the babbling water, birds in the air, and many insects buzzing around us. Beyond the banks, we would see a meadow to the north and south and a vast forest beyond. New York, like most of the North American continent, was covered in virgin forest of hardwoods and pines. Indigenous people at one time numbered in the millions on North America, and in the tens of thousands in New York. But, in 1712, the populations of the native tribes were nearly wiped out by European diseases and war.

At least 600 native people lived in Orange County when Sarah settled at the Otter Kill. Peter Bull pointed out in the Goodwill Notes, at least 10 men, women and children lived about two miles to the east of Sarah's camp with the Dennes.

We turn to the historic record of the country to help us understand Sarah's lifestyle in the early days of Orange County. According to author David Freeman Hawke in his book Everyday Life in Early America, the first wave of settlers came to the New World aboard wooden sailing ships in groups of like-minded people numbering less than 100. Like Jamestown and Plymouth, which were developed in the early 1600s, these first settlements were small, communal villages. A generation later, in the early 18th century, people were moving out of the towns those first settlers established and into the undeveloped land of the interior. They took dangerous risks for cheap land, independence and freedom.

In the villages and hamlets, people could rent an existing house and earn a living as artisans, merchants, sailors and traders. They could hire tradesmen and housekeepers to provide the needed services. But in the frontier, settlers knew that in order to survive, they would have to build a home and do the farming by themselves. Carving a homestead out of the forested wilderness with minimum resources in the early 18th century was excruciating work, Hawke said.

> "America might be a land of promise, but 'the promise was to the diligent rather than to the adventuresome.' There was wood for fires, but he must first 'cut and fetch it home' before he could burn it. There was wood for housing, but he 'must build his house before he would have it.' In short, men had in America 'all things to do, as in the beginning of the world' and one of the first things to do was clear the land."

It took a long time to clear the forests in order to plant. We know that Christopher Denne picked a spot on the Otter Kill that was situated between two meadows. This may have given him a head start on the effort, but he still needed wood for fuel, to build their cabin, and for basically everything.

Christopher Denne was a businessman in Manhattan, and a failed one at that. He may have been a carpenter in England but he most likely did his work in existing structures there with supplies bought from a mill and used modern tools of the day. If something broke, and he didn't have the skills to fix it, he could hire someone to do it for him.

In Wawayanda, he had none of those advantages, and the stakes were much higher. Without a successful hunt or harvest, they could starve. Without a roof over their head, the winter could kill them. Without fuel, the night could kill them. Without wood, they could not produce much of anything to sustain them in their new settlement.

> "Although farms differed in detail from colony to colony, all shared four characteristics," Hawke said. "They were cut off from daily contact with the larger world; they were, up to a point, self-sustaining, they were family-run; and, by modern standards, they were small."

Christopher Denne started his settlement in Orange County with the help of one indentured servant girl, three paid Manhattan carpenters and four Munsee men. We don't know how long the carpenters stayed with the Dennes, but it is likely that they stayed long enough to help him build a log cabin.

Sarah's second full day at the Otter Kill camp was likely very similar to everyday that followed for years. According to Hawke, for more than a century, women spent every day cooking at least two meals a day for the family, preparing food for storage, making yarn, thread, clothing, candles and soap; and tending to milking cows and kitchen gardens.

We found a handwritten recipe book dated in 1854 and written by Sarah Wells Bull's great-great-granddaughter Anna Bull Weeks, daughter of Ebenezer Bull and Jane Pearsall, our great-great-great-grandparents. Anna Bull Weeks was raised in the Stone House. Anna's father was the son of Daniel Bull. It was Daniel who saved the Stone House from a foreclosure sale decades earlier, and gave the home to his son.

Anna was born in 1829 and returned as an adult to live in the Stone House with her brother, Ebenezer Bull II, after her husband died in 1874. Anna did not know Sarah Wells, but her grandparents did, so her recipe book is very interesting. She wrote it just a few months after she first left the Stone House and moved to New Jersey with her husband, and it appears it was a collection of her favorite recipes from elder family members. The book gives us a glimpse into what was passed down and our ancestors' daily activities.

Historians say that there was very little deviation from the daily schedule throughout the year for women for the rest of their lives. Sarah had her hands full with the daily efforts to survive. Christopher Denne likely worked on the construction of their log cabin and hunting. Peter Bull wrote that they had with them four horses, two cows and two dogs. Sarah was likely in charge of milking the cows, as Peter Bull wrote. Elizabeth likely ran the kitchen and sewing with Sarah's help.

Settlers in New York in the early 18th century did not grow crops for cash, so it is unlikely that Christopher Denne maintained a cash-crop farm or had reason to take produce to market. Eventually, farming in New York changed and wheat was mass produced for market sales; it became known as the "breadbasket" of England. Denne might have tried this crop but it is more likely he learned from the native people how to grow corn, beans and squash. Peter Bull describes in his notes that the neighboring Munsee family did teach the settlers how to plant. The native people taught settlers around the Middle Colonies how to plant the "three sister" crops so that each plant worked symbiotically and successfully.

Hawke writes that "Every farmer grew corn, a miraculous plant, equally nourishing to man and beast, immune to most diseases, easy to raise – it took no more than fifty days a year of a farmer's time and thrived in a field of girdled trees – and easy to harvest. The yield per acre was high, about seven times that of wheat or barley.

> "Every farmer grew corn, a miraculous plant, equally nourishing to man and beast, immune to most diseases, easy to raise - it took no more than fifty days a year of a farmer's time and thrived in a field of girdled trees - and easy to harvest. The yield per acre was high, about seven times that of wheat or barley," Hawke wrote.

> "The settlers adopted their corn culture entirely from the Indians. They planted when the Indians told them to – "when the white oak leaves reach the size of a mouse's ear" – and the way they told them, dropping several kernels in holes three or four feet apart, later 'hilling' the seedlings by scooping soil around them for support, then fertilizing them with herring, which flooded up the streams to spawn during the late spring.

> "When the stalks were two or three feet high, beans and pumpkin seeds were planted around them, Indian fashion; the stalks served as beanpoles and gave shade to the pumpkin vines. Indians taught settlers how to harvest the corn, how to grind it into meal, how to preserve it through the year. The settlers also accepted most of the Indian dishes and their Indian names - such as pone, hominy, samp, and succotash."

It is plausible that the interaction Hawke described was exactly the way Sarah and the Dennes communed with their Munsee neighbors and that friendships were created. She certainly spoke kindly about the tribe to the author of the Goodwill Notes. Peter Bull wrote that the Munsee people helped the Dennes and Sarah figure out how to survive in the wilderness.

We found another interesting document in the Virginia Bull Meath collection that hints at the interaction between Sarah and the Munsee tribe; found in Anna Weeks' recipe book:

"Aunt Martha's Indian Bread: 4 teacups of meal, 4 cups of sour milk, two hand full of wheat flour, 4 tablespoons of molasses. Saleratus (which is baking soda)."

"Indian Pudding: 3 pints of milk. 10 tablespoons of meal. 3 gills of molasses. Pat of Butter. 1 egg. Bake 2 hours."

"Indian Pudding: 1 qt of milk scalded. Stir in a pint of meal, a teacup of molasses, a teaspoon of salt, 6 sweet apples cut very small. Bake 3 hours."

"Indian Pudding Boiled: 1 qt of milk, 2 eggs, small piece of saleratus, meal to make it stiff"

"Pone Bread. 1 qt of buttermilk, 2 eggs, 1 teaspoon saleratus, a little salt. Make a batter with Indian meal."

"Indian bread. 3 qts of Indian meal. 1 qt of sour milk. Tablespoon of saleratus. 3 eggs. Salt."

"Indian Bread: 1 pt of milk, 1 teaspoon of soda, 1 egg. ½ cup of lard melted. Salt."

It is interesting to consider where Anna got all of these "Indian" recipes since by the time she wrote the cookbook, there were no more villages occupied by native people villages left in the county.

In 1712, we could find no records to show when Sarah and the Dennes moved out of the wigwam and into a log cabin. We can speculate based on general history and a few other histories that it wasn't long before they had a more permanent home. It is plausible that Sarah didn't spend many nights in the stick hut she called a "hole."

The Bull family stories handed down through the generations describe that the Dennes eventually built a small log cabin on the Otter Kill. The log cabin appears on a map of Orange County homes built before 1810,

researched and drawn by Anne Olmstead Peet for Roscoe W. Smith
(copyright 1936).

Peter Bull wrote in the Goodwill Notes that the native sachem warned
Denne on his first night in Wawayanda that he would need to get to work
and quickly plant and cultivate crops and store enough food for the winter.
The historic record of Orange County tells us that the winters were so cold
in the early 18th century that the streams would freeze solid. When the
Otter Kill froze over in the winter, it made travel easier, since settlers and

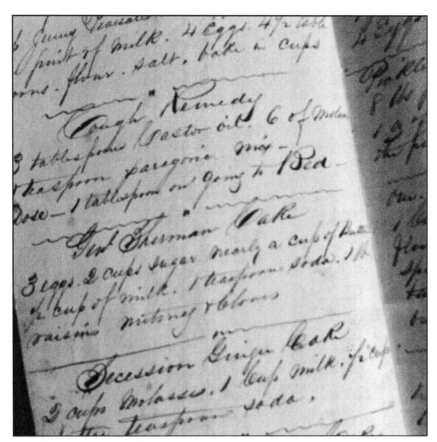

PHOTO CREDIT: JULIE BOYD COLE, 2017. FROM THE VIRGINIA BULL
COLLECTION, A PAGE FROM ANNA BULL WEEKS 1854 RECIPE BOOK.

native people could simply walk over it. However, the price they paid for the convenience was biting temperatures and dangerous snowstorms.

In that first summer by the Otter Kill, the Dennes and Sarah most likely worked hard to plant, cultivate and prepare for the winter. During the winter months, after blizzards and large snowfalls, it is unlikely that Sarah spent much time outside. Whether they lived in a log cabin or still in the wigwam, the quarters were cramped.

Though there were no other European settlements near the Dennes in the early years, there was a settlement about 20 miles away in Newburgh of the German Lutheran "Palatine" refugees. About 50 men, women and children were awarded the land patent by Queen Anne as an experiment and a way to "save" the Protestant people of the Rhine River valley from the tyrannical King of France.

Another small settlement of the time was located at Plum Point on the Hudson River. The outpost was settled by a small group of Presbyterians from Scotland. They operated the trading station and river landing that became New Windsor.

The majority of the European people of Orange County in 1712 lived in what is now Rockland County at Haverstraw. When Orange County was formed in 1686, its boundaries were different than today's. Most land north of Montgomery was part of Ulster County, and all of present-day Rockland was part of Orange County.

Of the 300 Europeans and 300 natives, few were Sarah's peers. It is no wonder that when she told the story of her first days in the county to Peter Bull decades later, that she referred to Elizabeth Denne as her "only friend in the world."

We were able to uncover that another girl named Sarah, about the same age as Sarah Wells, was living in Orange County during the same time. Sarah Plettel lived in Newburgh with her mother, stepfather and siblings. She was the eldest child of Elizabeth and John Plettel, who were part of the German Palatine refugees and were Lutherans.

Sarah Plettel had a tragic life that ended in 1741 when the city of New York unfairly prosecuted her, her husband, John Hughson, and about a dozen others for trying to incite a slave revolt. The revolt never happened, and it was soon believed that the entire proceeding was fueled by hysteria, and the false and dramatic accusations of a teenager. Sarah Plettel Hughson was eventually hanged at the public gallows, along with her husband. Elizabeth, her mother, was believed to have gone crazy after the horrific event.

In the early years in Orange County, it is plausible that the two Sarahs were acquainted and maybe even friends. We did find a church record, which will be examined in later chapters, that the families knew each other. Over the next few years, we found records of babies born in and around Sarah's Orange County home with the Dennes. Elizabeth Plettel gave birth twice. Christopher Denne's slave gave birth. It is clear that the women in the Munsee camp were of child-bearing age, which suggests that Sarah lived near at least some women about her age.

We found that two of the Wawayanda Patent holders soon followed the Dennes into Orange County. Manhattan merchant Benjamin Aske moved to Warwick with his hired hands, Lawrence Decker, Johannes Wisner and Christian Snedeker, in 1712. It is not clear how long Aske stayed in Warwick, but Decker, Wisner and Snedeker stayed in Orange County and raised families.

Daniel Crommelin, a latecomer to the Wawayanda Patent group, and his son Charles, were French immigrants and members of the New York French reformed church, also known as Huguenots. They came to New York in 1695 and soon became Freeman of the city. Daniel's wife and younger son, Isaac, followed them to America. But sadly, soon after they arrived, Anne and Isaac died during a yellow fever outbreak that gripped Manhattan.

Daniel and his son Charles were merchants and by some accounts, were also pirates and slave traders. The historical record tells us that piracy was very common along the trade routes of the Atlantic Ocean as colonists in North America and the Caribbean tried to avoid English tariffs and regulations of goods. England prevented the Colonies to produce many items, such as wool and wine, so as not to compete with the demand for English products. Piracy was a way to circumvent those regulations.

Crommelin bought thousands of acres in Wawayanda and soon after, Denne developed land that is now the town of Chester, NY.

Until 1714, when the village of Goshen was subdivided into sellable lots, Sarah and the Dennes had few neighbors beyond these groups. In the last of her teen years, Sarah most likely had very little social life beyond the gatherings, and little help in sharing the workload of developing farms. It is hard to imagine that the day-in and day-out of living in a one-room rustic house with the English gentry couple was anything but hard and stressful for Sarah.

During the snow-filled winters and rainy springs, they were confined to this one room together. During the summer days, they labored from sunrise to sunset to prepare for the year. As Hawke said, building a homestead in the interior of America was not for those seeking adventure, but for those willing to toil day after day just to survive. Since Sarah did not name a single child of her 12 after Christopher or Elizabeth, which would have been customary, it is plausible that the relationship became strained as these untrained people tried to make a life in Wawayanda.

In 1714, after the lots were cut and land was divided across the patent, people by the dozens began to move into the wilderness west of the Hudson River, and Sarah was no longer so alone. Aske created the village of Warwick, and Crommelin began to work on what would become Chester, and his tavern called Greycourt. By 1720, the population had more than doubled and by 1730, there were more than a half a dozen growing communities within the present-day boundaries of the county. Hundreds of families set up homesteads along the Wallkill River, the Otter Kill, Murderers' Creek, the Neversink, the Delaware, the Rampo and the Raritan. Orange County's population of white settlers and African slaves grew rapidly.

We found within the Lutheran church records that eventually Christopher bought a young African slave named Mercy. On September 16, 1716, Mercy's son, William, was baptized by the traveling German Lutheran minister Rev. Justus Falckner in Newburgh at the home of Jurgen Loockstead, a German immigrant whose second wife was Elizabeth Plettel, the Palatine refugee mother of Sarah Plettel, mentioned earlier. The record reads:

"At the same time and place, b. July 10 at Goshian, Orange County, Christopher, child of Samuel Seely, and wife, Charlotta. Witnesses Christopher Dean and wife Elisabeth.

"At the same time and place, William, child of Will, Mr. Aalsupp's (Alsop) negro and Mercy, Mr. Christopher Dean's baptised negress."

Denne, like many people in New York in the 18th century, owned at least one African American person as a slave. At this time, households of status in New York might own one or two people from Africa to handle household duties. They did not own large populations of enslaved people like those plantations in the South, which were managing cash crops and capitalizing on the enslaved labor.

We don't know to what extent Sarah was "friends" with the peers who lived alongside her in those early days when she was between 16 and 21 years old, but we were able to recreate the picture of those who surrounded her:

The women:
- Elizabeth Denne, her master's wife, was old enough to be Sarah's mother;
- Mercy, the Dennes' slave women, bore a son in 1716;
- Two Native women at the Munsee camp who had children and were married;
- Elizabeth Plettel Loockstead, the German Lutheran immigrant married to George and living in Newburgh;
- Sarah Plettel, daughter of Elizabeth, and about the same age as Sarah Wells;
- At least one woman living at the Plum Point trading post.

The men:
- Christopher Denne, her master, 30 years older than Sarah;
- Four Munsee men of two generations;
- George Loockstead, Elizabeth's husband;
- At least two men who managed Plum Point in New Windsor;
- Benjamin Aske of Warwick, a generation older than Sarah;
- Daniel Crommelin, a generation older than Sarah;
- Charles Crommelin, the same generation as Sarah.

HOLLAND SOCIETY OF NEW YORK CITY LUTHERAN, VOL I, BOOK 85,
RECORD OF BAPTISMS IN NEWBURGH BY THE GERMAN LUTHERAN
CHURCH MINISTER JUSTUS FALCKNER, INCLUDING THE CHILD OF
CHRISTOPHER DENNE'S SLAVE AND THE SON OF SAMUEL SEELY.

According to authors Martha and Bill Reamy, who wrote Pioneer
Families of Orange County, New York in 1993, there were 115 male heads
of households in present-day Orange County by 1714. By 1716, there were
hundreds of settlers who began to develop all the land that surrounded
Sarah's home with the Dennes on the Otter Kill. As we stated earlier, by the
end of her life, the county was populated by thousands of settlers and
Orange County was no longer considered "the wilderness."

PHOTO CREDIT: JULIE BOYD COLE, 2017. MARGARET BULL'S WEDDING DRESS IS PART OF THE BULL STONE HOUSE COLLECTION. IT IS BELIEVED THAT SARAH WELLS MADE IT.

CHAPTER 13
SARAH AND WILLIAM BULL MEET

In 1718, Sarah Wells married William Bull, an Englishman and trained stonemason. He emigrated to the New World by way of Ireland in 1715. They eventually raised a family of seven daughters and five sons on hundreds of acres in Hamptonburgh, not far from where Sarah first settled with the Dennes.

William Bull was brought to Orange County as an indentured servant of the aforementioned Daniel Crommelin. The Bull family Blue Book goes

PHOTO CREDIT: CROMMELIN.COM PHOTO OF A PAINTING OF DANIEL
CROMMELIN HELD IN HOLLAND. CROMMELIN, WAS BORN IN 1647 IN
FRANCE. HE WAS WILLIAM BULL'S MASTER IN 1715.

into great detail of William's heritage and life story before he came to
America aboard a sailing ship at the age of 26, and it is a must-read to learn
more about William and his heritage.

Daniel Crommelin came to New York in 1695. He was born in France
in 1647 and died in New York in 1725, and was buried in the famous
Trinity Episcopal Church cemetery in Manhattan.

In 1715, Crommelin went aboard a ship docked in the East River in
Manhattan, looking for laborers, and found William Bull being held aboard
for unpaid passage. The family lore found in the Blue Book states that the
vessel captain cheated William on the fee. Crommelin was a connected and
wealthy merchant in Manhattan. He paid for the balance on William's
passage and brought him back to Wawayanda to help build his home.

Crommelin's reputation was sketchy, according to the accounts
maintained by his descendents. There is record that Crommelin funded his
expedition into the Orange County wilderness with ill-gotten gains which
included piracy, slave trading and pilfering his young orphan cousins'
inheritance. In contrast, Crommelin was also active in the French Reformed
Church on Long Island and signed an agreement supporting the local
pastor in trouble with the church.

Whatever the makeup of Crommelin's character, he did provide
William with a way out of his "imprisonment" at the Manhattan dock.

We don't know very much about William's service with Crommelin,
except that he built at least two structures on King's Highway: a small stone
house which is still used as a residence today, and a tavern called Greycourt.

We could not find the document indenting him to Crommelin. We do know that New York State lost all of the indenture contracts made from 1708 to 1718, the time when William Bull was bound to Crommelin. It is plausible that the length of service was completed when the work on the estate was finished. According to the Crommelin family historians at crommelin.org, William finished the tavern in 1716. It was the main gathering spot for all travelers through the interior of the Hudson River valley. The tavern was eventually razed, but a cornerstone was saved and placed in the exterior northwall of the Bull Stone House.

According to crommelin.org, William Bull, with the help of Richard Gerrard, completed the Stone House in 1718. We could not find corroborating records of this partnership, though William and Gerrard appear together on a deed as recipients of 2,600 acres in 1723 during a time when the entire county's northern boundary was in dispute, and the authorities re-issued deeds and set new boundaries. Without the actual indenture between William and Crommelin, we do not know when the contract ended.

Using the trail of records in New York City, it does not appear that Crommelin ever actually called Orange County his primary home. It is more likely that he occasionally visited to check on his investment. He died in 1725 in Manhattan and his son, Charles, took over ownership of Greycourt. By 1740, Charles was deep in debt and lost the estate as a result.

The family lore tells us that William came to Orange County soon after he set foot in the New World. Imagine what the young man must have been thinking as he traveled into the vast, forested mountains of the interior lands. Whether he traveled by sloop on the currents of the Hudson or through the forest by horseback, it must have been overwhelming and exciting. In Europe, a tradesman had no hope of owning any of the lands which had already been developed for hundreds of years. Here, there were miles and miles of virgin, undeveloped land for as far as he could see. Despite the chaos in his arrival, before him was the opportunity that drove so many other immigrants to face the potentially deadly sea crossing.

By some historical accounts, as many as 60 percent of the population of New York in the early 18th century were indentured servants, apprentices or slaves. The colonies needed labor in order to cultivate resources. The English Crown did what it could to get people there working, including the support of bondage.

As an indentured servant, William was bound by a legal contract to Crommelin, in all likelihood for three or more years. To further understand the life of an adult contracted for service, we turn to historian Hawke in his book, Everyday Life in Early America. He wrote:

> "The master's power was all but absolute. He could rent out the servant, buy and sell him like any other commodities. He

could bequeath him as private property. During his years of bondage the servant was in effect a slave with no real rights. If he survived bondage he often had to hire himself out to another master."

It was illegal and socially unacceptable to mistreat a servant in the early 18th century in the Middle Colonies, though it was often hard to prevent a master from abuse. We don't know how William or Sarah were treated day to day by their masters. Historians tell us that masters were expected to take care of indentured people as one of their own, provide food and board. Masters were expected to teach servants – both men and women – how to speak, read and write English.

"Treat them as you would your children," Hawke quoted John Cotton in 1655. "Give them both the liberty and authority you would have them use, and beyond that stretch not the tether; it will not tend to their good nor yours."

Servitude fell into three categories in the Colonies: slavery, indentured apprentices and indentured servants. Slavery, as we know, was most often permanent bondage and affected most Africans and some Native Americans. Sometimes masters would grant slaves their freedom through their last will and testament, but often they were included in the list of property doled out in bequests.

Indentured apprentices were teenagers bound by a guardian through a legal contract to someone who would teach them a trade or housework. These contracts usually expired when the apprentice reached 21 years old, the age of consent. The servant was then free to leave and go about his or her life as desired.

Lastly, adults were bound as indentured servants by a legal contract. An adult would put themselves in service usually in exchange for money, goods or land. The length of the service varied from contract to contract. Very often, when an indenture reached the end of the term, the servant would sign up again with the master or with another because they had no other option.

Though marketing campaigns throughout Europe painted a picture of the "land of milk and honey" and free land, indentured servants rarely were given land as reward for their service. Many a master did not want servants to compete with their own efforts in the New World and avoided such deals. Money was problematic in the colonies as well. Each country in the Old World had their own form of currency, which resulted in each colony using different forms of money. The indigenous people used wampum (strings of seashells) for trading. The quid pro quo for a term of hard work was most often a barrel of corn, a bushel of wheat, or some other goods.

According to Hawke:

> "If thrifty, diligent, and not cheated by the new master, he might accumulate enough money to buy land. It comes as no surprise that few indentured servants later became prominent leaders. The system worked well in that it provided a labor force in a land short of manpower. That is the most that can be said for it."

Remarkably, both William Bull and Sarah Wells ended their bondage with land. William Bull bought a tract of 100 acres in 1718. They went on to create a legacy of thousands of descendents and a homestead that lasted much longer than most settlers', including both of their masters.

The Dennes died with no other legacy but Sarah Wells' remarkable life. Elizabeth sold their house and about 1,100 acres of the estate on the Otter Kill in 1729 to William Mapes, according to the Sackett family record published in 1897. At some point, the house was razed. Elizabeth moved back to Manhattan, where she died in 1735. There is no sign of the Dennes in Orange County or Manhattan today, and we could not find where either are buried.

Crommelin died penniless and with the words of his cousin, the guardian of the two young orphans Crommelin supposedly left destitute: "What consoles me is that if we are not punished for our crimes, at least there is a God who knows how to avenge us of such perfidy." On the crommelin.org website is this: "Therefore, in losing all of his hard-won assets at the end of his life, Daniel may have 'reaped what he sowed.' "

Once free of indenture, Hawke said it was rare that the experience, and the trauma of it, was forgotten. According to Hawke

> "When he acquired land, he carried indelible scars that would shape his own conduct as a master. Former servants who became small planters, it has been said, were persons who learned about proper forms of behavior, about acceptable patterns of human relations, about exploitation and competition, about careless resolute blows and embittering frustrations, while they were servants."

Many bound servants fled their masters. Some filed suit before the court asking to be released. But that was difficult. When a servant or slave ran away from their master, a classified ad was often published in the newspaper. Some examples:

As published Oct. 31, 1726 in the New York *Gazette* by William Bradford:

"Waters, William (b. In Hartforshire), age c. 35 – runaway from Stephen Beaks of Chester Co., PA."

Printed Sunday, November 17, 1720 in American Weekly Mercury, Philadelphia, Pennsylvania:

"Runaway from his master John Brome of Calvert County, in the Province of Maryland a servant named John Pike age about 22 years, he is a west country-man of a middle stature fresh colored black hair, a little beard, a husbandman by calling. Whoever shall take up the said servant and bring or secure him so that his said master may have him again shall have ten pounds as a reward paid by John Brome."

As far as we know, William Bull did not run away, and did help to complete the Crommelin estate.

As one of the first three settlers of the Wawayanda interior, Crommelin selected the site for building his compound on what became King's Highway in Chester. According to crommelin.org:

"In Daniel's time, the area in which he chose to settle was a principal route to Trenton, New Jersey from Newburgh, NY. Along the King's Highway (now Route 94) Daniel operated the Gray Court Inn and a residence - stone buildings constructed by Irish mason, William Bull, and Richard Gerard."

Crommelin picked a spot just six miles south of Denne's property on the Otter Kill, where Sarah was living with her masters. We don't know how often Sarah and William saw each other during those first three years of William's life in Orange County, but the historic records tell us that there would have been a good deal of interaction between the two small settlements. Life in the frontier required cooperation and trade among the farmers, Hawke writes.

"Everyday life was from the beginning tied to the world beyond the farm. Paths led settlers to other farms, to and from social events, but equally to spots where they exchanged goods. … From the beginning trade permeated the everyday life of every farmer."

With just six miles between them, William and Sarah were close neighbors even as the population exploded. According to the Documented History of the State of New York by Christopher Morgan, published in

1849, there were about 1,200 people living in Orange County in 1723. Ulster County, which included Montgomery and Newburgh, had a population of 3,000 people.

We know today that whatever their interactions, they led to marriage and a life raising a dozen children within only a few miles of where they met. Whether they carried scars of their servitude, as Hawke said was common, we don't know. But our investigation found that both were fiercely independent and did not seek leadership or the limelight. As Hawke's research suggests, the two formerly bound servants did not become prominent leaders of their community.

In August 1718, family lore and local history says that William Bull and Sarah married. The story handed down through the generations and documented by Samuel Eager in 1846-47, and the Blue Book historians in 1974, is that William Bull insisted that they marry following the Church of England, or Episcopalian, rituals. The family historians write that a magistrate, John Merritt, read alone the "banns of marriage" three times from three different doors of the log cabin on the Dennes' homestead, and after there being no objection, the two were wed. We could find no church or government document of this event, though the crommelin.org historians suggest that the wedding was actually held at Greycourt, not the Dennes' log cabin.

Again, we turn to history to help us understand the story and fill in the blanks.

Our romantic and sentimental cousin, Samuel Eager, tells the story of love that brought the two settlers together. But that is most likely a construct from Eager's 19h century mind than the actual sentiment of the two people of the 18th century.

During the early 1700s, marriage was more commonly formed as a commitment to make a life together with a suitable mate rather than a union of love-struck partners. Marriage for love only became the norm 100 years after William and Sarah met. The historic record does not rule out love as part of a marriage, and in fact, the partnership often created a loving relationship, but it was not Cupid's arrow that started them.

In 1718, William was 29 years old, about the average age men married for the first time in the colony. Sarah was 22 years old, also about the average age women married for the first time. William had just purchased 100 acres of land, and Crommelin's Stone House was completed. Sarah's indenture would have been finished with the Dennes when she turned 21. Bonded servants were not allowed to get married, according to Hawke.

Though marriage was more of a business arrangement than a romantic one, it was still the expected lifestyle choice, even in the wilderness. Unlike patriarchal marriages in England or New England hamlets, women's roles in marriage in New York were different. First, men outnumbered women as much as seven to one, according to Hawke:

"Comely or homely, strong or weak, any young woman was too valuable to be overlooked, and most could find a man with prospects," he wrote. "Women could not be treated brutally or tyrannically. If intelligent, thrifty, and hardy, she became more than a helpmate, as were English wives. She became a partner, sharing in her husband's efforts to scrabble a living from the wilderness."

Sarah Wells was capable, thrifty, hardy and intelligent, as we know from Peter Bull's account. The stories handed down about her all point to an independent woman who faced many challenges, including raising her last five children alone after William died. William was very lucky that she agreed to become a settler of Wawayanda. Hawke wrote:

"As inevitable as the once-indentured woman married when free, she remarried when her husband died, especially if she had no son old enough to manage the farm. But now she could be choosy and more demanding. Into the marriage she brought property and possible children who could work the land. She also brought the experience of a previous partnership and an authority that her English counterparts had never shared She was not someone who could be pushed around easily. Legally, she remained inferior to her husband, and she could not participate openly in public affairs, but within the family she had a very strong voice."

There is no doubt that Sarah was a strong voice in her union with William. All of our research backs up this characterization.

PHOTO CREDIT: JULIE BOYD COLE, 2017. THE BULL STONE HOUSE IN THE
BACKGROUND. IN THE FOREGROUND IS A PORTION OF A STONE WALL.

CHAPTER 14
CONSTRUCTING THE STONE HOUSE

Nestled on a rise in Hamptonburgh, NY, and surrounded by rolling
green pastures, is the Bull family Stone House. It is about 300 years old and
has, until recently, been continuously occupied, first by William and Sarah
and then their descendents.

The house has four floors with wide-plank floorboards, thick stone walls, an indoor spring and sits on a foundation of bedrock shale and slate. It is one of the few, if not only, stone houses in America still owned and used as a residence by the family of the original settlers.

William and Sarah Bull began to build their homestead a few years into their marriage while they lived in a log cabin on the site. The land they owned, like all acres throughout the once glacier-covered county, was littered with stones of all sizes. According to family lore, the couple began to collect stones and over the course of 13 years built the home.

The Blue Book historians write a beautiful account of the history of the Stone House, and it is an amazing homestead to visit. The property was believed to be used as a fort during the French and Indian War, was struck by lightning, and most dramatically, stood through a major earthquake in 1727.

After the nighttime earthquake violently shook New York, Sarah woke and told her husband, "William we have lost our new house," and in the morning, they did find a massive crack in the south wall of the massive home, according to Samuel Eager's account.

For 300 years, the home has been the site of many family reunions, family weddings, funerals, pageants, and many other social events, as well as all types of farming.

The family tradition, based on the lore handed down by Sarah and William's great-grandson, Ebenezer Bull (our great-great-great grandfather), who owned and occupied the house in the 19th century, is that the settlers began construction of the Stone House in 1722 and finished it 13 years later (Blue Book historians).

During the years of the enormous stone structure's construction, William continued his work as a hired mason and contractor to build homes throughout the county. In fact, William Bull continued this work until his last year of life (Blue Book).

Sarah gave birth to their first son, John Bull, in 1721. Seven more children came over the next 14 years: in 1723, she gave birth to William; in 1725, to Sarah; in 1727, to Thomas; in 1729, to Isaac; in 1731, to Ester; in 1733, to Mary; and in 1735, to Margaret.

While building the Stone House, the growing family farmed, most likely wheat and corn, along with food for their kitchen. According to Eager, the Bulls would travel to Fishkill, on the east shore of the Hudson River, to have their grain milled. He writes one family story handed down about Sarah that speaks to the resourcefulness of a mother in the wilderness:

"On one occasion, (William went to Fishkill) and did not return at his usual time, and Mrs. Bull fearing some accident had befallen him, tied her infant son to the bedpost and went off to meet him. She met him some halfway to New Windsor, trudging homeward, tired and weary with the

weight of his load. ... They returned ... found the child safe and still tethered to the bedpost."

According to the Blue Book historians, we are not sure of the date the couple moved into the Stone House, but they believed it was completed in 1735. William died about 1756, which means he lived just 20 years in his beautiful home, far less time than many other descendants who have occupied the house.

BY JIM.HENDERSON (OWN WORK) [CC0], VIA WIKIMEDIA COMMONS. ST. MATTHEW'S EVANGELICAL LUTHERAN CHURCH, THE OLDEST LUTHERAN CONGREGATION IN MANHATTAN AND WAS ORIGINALLY CALLED TRINITY LUTHERAN CHURCH. THE FIRST BUILDING FOR THE CONGREGATION WAS BUILT IN 1671 BUT WAS DESTROYED A FEW DECADES LATER. THE NEXT BUILDING WAS THEN DESTROYED IN THE MANHATTAN FIRE IN 1776. A SERIES OF BUILDINGS HAVE BEEN BUILT OVER THE YEARS.

CHAPTER 15
BIRTHS AND BAPTISMS

2-1 John Bull, b. 5/3/1721, bpt. Sept. 15, 1721, by German Lutheran Rev. Justus Falckner in Newburgh
2-2 William Bull, b. 3/13/1723

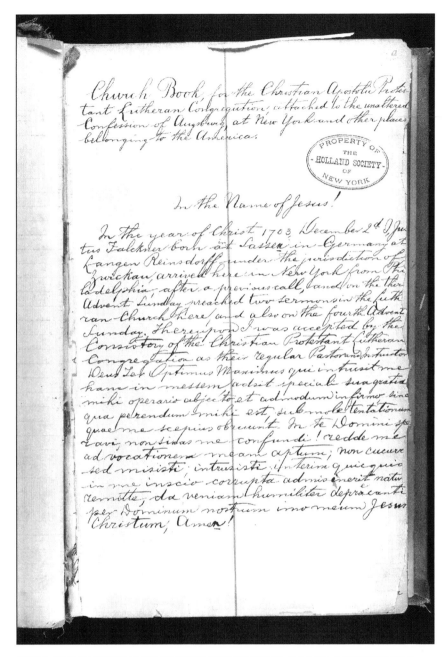

Church Book, for the Christian Apostolic Protestant Lutheran Congregation, attached to the unaltered Confession of Augsburg, at New York and other places belonging to the America.

In the Name of Jesus!

In the year of Christ 1703 December 2d I Justus Falckner born at Lasser in Germany at Langen Reinsdorff under the jurisdiction of Zwickau, arrived here in New York from Philadelphia, after a previous call, and on the third Advent Sunday preached two sermons in the Lutheran Church there, and also on the fourth Advent Sunday. Thereupon I was accepted by the Consistory of the Christian Protestant Lutheran Congregation as their regular Pastor and Instructor. Deus Ter Optimus Maximus qui in messem suam adsit speciali sua gratia mihi operario abjecto et admodum infirmo, sine qua perendum mihi est, sub mole tentationum quae me saepius obruunt. In te Domine speravi, non sinas me confundi! redde me ad vocationem meam aptum; non cucurri sed misisti; intrusisti. Interim quicquid in me inscio corrupta admiserit natura remitte, da veniam humiliter deprecanti per Dominum nostrum imo meum Jesum Christum, Amen!

HOLLAND SOCIETY OF NEW YORK CITY LUTHERAN, VOL I, BOOK 85, THE FIRST PAGE THE TRANSLATION OF THE GERMAN LUTHERAN CONGREGATIONS OF NEW YORK AND NEW JERSEY. THIS "CHURCH BOOK" WAS STARTED BY REV. JUSTUS FALCKNER AND WRITTEN IN GERMAN.

2-3 Sarah Bull Booth, b. 9/1/1725

2-4 Thomas Bull, b. 12/27/1727

2-5 Isaac Bull, b. 11/17/1729

2-6 Esther Bull Miller, b. 5/29/1731, practicing at German Lutheran church

2-7 Mary Bull Booth, b. 2/3/1733, bpt. By German Lutheran Rev. Michael Knoll

2-8 Margaret Bull Horton, b. 5/1/1736

2-9 Catherine Bull Faulkner b. 5/24/1738, sponsored baptism in German Lutheran church

2-10 Ann Bull Eager, b. 11/3/1740

2-11 Richard Bull, b. 5/29/1743, practicing at German Lutheran church

2-12 Eleanor Bull Weller, b. 3/4/1745, worshipped in the German Reformed congregation in Montgomery

In the eight years since Sarah Wells Bull first settled along the Otter Kill, the population in Orange County had exploded, and with that growth came more and more signs of the civilized world. More farms, roads, taverns and churches became part of the fabric of the county's landscape. Goshen was now laid out as a village, and a team began construction of the towering First Presbyterian Church in the center of town.

Traveling pastors from many denominations, including Episcopalian, Presbyterian and Lutheran, began to circulate among their brethren scattered around the county as early as 1708. A Presbyterian minister named "Treat" was believed to be traveling through the county in 1715 and then in 1719; Rev. John Bradner was appointed to the new Presbyterian church in Goshen. An Episcopalian minister was believed to have helped congregants in the county start three log cabin churches about 1730. The Dutch Reformed Church was flourishing in Ulster County and Albany.

We found this record about the Dutch Reformed Church in Montgomery, also known as the "Brick Church," in the Goshen Public Library Local History Room:

When the fertile Wallkill Valley came to be settled its population represented different nationalities. The Dutch established trading posts at the mouth of the river on the site of the village of Rondout (now Kingston), as early as 1614, six years before the Pilgrims landed on Plymouth Rock. The first settlement was broken up by Indian hostilities and the second one, begun between 1630 and 1640, shared the same fate.

Tradition tells us of a raid of Indians upon Esopus in which many white settlers were killed or captured, and that a band of courageous pioneers followed the Rondout creek and Wallkill river till they came upon the Indian camp at the junction of the Shawangunk and Wallkill. These persons seeking to release the captives were well pleased with the view of the plains of New Paltz, and a migration began shortly after -- the first settlers being Hollanders, Hugenots and Germans.

Meanwhile from New Windsor and Goshen came English, Scotch and Protestant Irish, who made their homes in Hamptonbergh, Wallkill, and the hills of Crawford. The exact date of arrival of the settlers who founded this Church cannot be determined. Dr. Van Zandt in his historical Sketch says :"We shall not be far from the mark if we date the beginnings of the settlement - as early as 1725".

Thus there were settlers here prior to 1732, and it is probable that they had a religious organization and meetings for worship. It was in 1732 that this Church was organized by Domine Geogius Wilhemlus Mancius, Pastor at Kingston, with an election of the first Elder, Johannes Jong Bloet, and the first Deacon, Jacob Boochstaber.

"On confession were received to the fellowship of this Church,1732"- Michael Krans, Margriet Maul, Cathrina Maul, Johannes Krans, Jacob Sinsebach Magdalena Sinsebach, Benira Newkerk, Aitje Menges, wife of Stephanus Christ, Elizabeth Menges, wife of Lawrens Christ, Gertrout Jong Bloet, Frederick Weller, Anna Margretta Kochin, Maria Gertrout Stemer, wife of Philip Melsbach, Maria Cathrina Stemer, Elizabeth Stemer, Geertje Klearwater, wife of Johannes Newkerk.

The first Baptisms as of April 17, 1734 were Stephanus son of Stephanus Christ and Annatje Menges, Jacob son of Phillipus Melsbach and Maria Gertrout Stemer, Johannes son of Chrsitian Eboltz and Maria Eliz. Christ, Annaatje daughter of Christoffel Maul and Anna Juliana Searing.

The first marriage record is dated October 23rd,1734, and that of Johannes Krans and Elizabeth Klearwater.

It is said that the earliest settlers had no time ever to build themselves log cabins for shelter, and actually burrowed in the earth during the first long winter, at which time Elizabeth, daughter of Jacob Boochstaber and Anna Maria Menges was born.

In Manhattan, Trinity Lutheran Church, the Dutch Reformed Church, the French Reformed Church, Trinity Episcopal Church, and a synagogue were all serving their congregants. In the small village of Newburgh where the aforementioned Palatine refugees settled in 1708, a small wooden church was built for their exclusive population of German Lutherans. Some of these congregations, including the Presbyterian church in Goshen, St. Andrew's Episcopal Church in Walden, and Trinity Episcopal Church in Manhattan, are still active today.

During the early 18th century, baptisms, marriages and deaths were recorded by pastors and in most cases, the church records were the only official documents of the milestones in a person's life. Marriage licenses,

PHOTO CREDIT: SARAH BROWNELL, 2017. ST. ANDREW'S CHURCH IN WALDEN, NEW YORK. WILLIAM BULL HELPED GET THIS CONGREGATION STARTED IN THE EARLY 1700S. HE HELPED WITH THE BUILDING OF A LOG CABIN CHURCH. THIS BUILDING WAS BUILT DECADES LATER.

though available, were not required. No government agency kept birth or death certificates, though both were very important in a community.

Because age was the basis of many laws and social norms, it were important but often estimated. In order to know when someone was old enough to consent to be married (21 years of age), they had to know when they were born. Even slaves' birth dates were collected because among other reasons, New York slavery laws applied differently to different generations of those in bondage as slavery was phased out.

In England, under the rule of the Church of England (also known as Episcopalians in America), baptism was required, and it was one way for the Crown to keep track of their subjects. Most Protestant denominations required infant baptism. People could not become a member of a church without first proving they had been baptized, whether done during infancy or adulthood. Quakers, an exception, did not believe in any form of baptism and did not practice the ritual; they did keep records of births within the congregation. Mennonites also did not practice infant baptism and believed that only adults could choose to be baptized.

It is family lore, and recorded in Eager's book, that Sarah and William did not get married in a church or by a minister, because there was no Episcopal Church or minister available at the time of their 1718 wedding. We did find a record in the Episcopal historical documents to support this.

According to the written history of the St. George Episcopal Church in Newburgh, which was one of the original churches in Orange County, Rev. Richard Charlton was in the county in 1728 serving the "congregations of people of the plantations."

We also found that William was considered a devoted Episcopalian and helped build the log cabin church circa 1732 in St. Andrews Parish near Walden, where he worshipped. In 2017, we visited the church, which has since been relocated, but did not find any records of the wedding, the couple or their children, though the church had only a small number of historic records to study.

Sarah and William's first child, John, was born on May 22, 1721, and was baptized in Newburgh, four months after his birth, on Sept. 17, 1721, by German Lutheran pastor Justus Falckner. The witnesses, or sponsors, at his baptism were Elizabeth and George Loocksteed, the couple mentioned earlier. They were part of the Palatine refugee community in Newburgh, NY. We found a handwritten transcription of Falckner's records and the story behind it. His original records, written in German, are stored today at the Evangelical Lutheran Church of St. Matthew in Manhattan, the modern name and new location of Falckner's church.

HOLLAND SOCIETY OF NEW YORK CITY LUTHERAN, VOL I, BOOK 85, RECORD OF BAPTISMS IN NEWBURGH BY THE GERMAN LUTHERAN CHURCH MINISTER JUSTUS FALCKNER, INCLUDING JOHN BULL (INCORRECTLY SPELLED "PULL" IN THIS TRANSLATED TRANSCRIPTION.), SON OF WILLIAM AND SARAH BULL. THE WITNESSES WERE PALATINE REFUGEES LIVING IN NEWBURGH.

Falckner was a celebrated Lutheran minister and became known for keeping together the Lutherans who were scattered from Philadelphia to Albany through the early 18th century. He and his brother, Daniel, were immigrants from Germany and the sons of a Lutheran minister. They were kind, and worked selflessly to serve all the Lutherans in the Middle Colonies.

Justus Falckner was appointed to Trinity Lutheran Church on Broad Street in Manhattan in 1704, and the church in Albany. Justus was the first Lutheran minister ordained in the colonies. He took his responsibility to the people in his flock seriously. He traveled by sloop and horse on a 1,000-plus-mile circuit that stretched from New Jersey to Albany every year for 20 years. The weary minister reached the dozen far-flung, tiny congregations about twice a year, at the same time leading the churches in Manhattan and Albany. Today, the Lutheran history credits Justus Falckner with establishing the Lutheran denomination in the Colonies.

After his death, the Lutheran Church sank into disorganization and dramatic infighting that led to the brief imprisonment of several non-ordained, seminary-trained Lutherans, including Justus' brother Daniel, by the elders in New Jersey. A decade later, the German Lutheran congregation of the Middle Colonies settled down, and the infighting stopped. Daniel Falckner took over after his brother's death, and until 1732, led the Hudson River and Raritan River congregations. He and Justus Falckner both became celebrated for their efforts. Many books have been written about both men.

Rev. Justus Falckner baptized John Bull on one of his two scheduled trips to George and Elizabeth Locksteed's house in Newburgh. The Locksteeds lived on Lot 1 of the little village, then called Quassaick, and

HOLLAND SOCIETY OF NEW YORK CITY LUTHERAN, VOL I, BOOK 85, IN 1732, NEW MINISTER MICHAEL CHRISTIAN KNOLL TOOK OVER THE GERMAN LUTHERAN CONGREGATION AND THE CHURCH BOOK FIRST STARTED BY REV. JUSTUS FALCKNER.

HOLLAND SOCIETY OF NEW YORK CITY LUTHERAN, VOL I, BOOK 85, IN 1734, NEW MINISTER MICHAEL CHRISTIAN KNOLL BAPTIZED MERRIE BULL, CHILD OF WILLIAM BULL AND WIFE SARA AT "BIRGERT MYNDER'S" IN NEWBURGH.

opened their home every year to the pastor for baptisms, as the records show, until George's death in 1727. Elizabeth and at least one of her daughters, Sarah, moved to Yonkers at some point after. The record also suggests Sarah Plettel, Elizabeth's daughter from her previous marriage, was unmarried when she gave birth to a child, who was baptized on the same day as John Bull.

Rev. Justus Falckner never stayed long when he landed the sloop at Quassaick Creek. During his short time there, he handled all the marriages, comfort visits and baptisms that had stacked up over the many months since his last visit. In order for Sarah and William to have John baptized by Justus, they had to wait for his twice-a-year visit to Newburgh. Because Falckner served so many Lutheran congregations beyond his primary appointment in Manhattan, the individual churches managed their regular Sunday services on their own, but baptisms, marriages and funerals had to be handled by the ordained minister. When Falckner arrived at a congregation, he often baptized several children and married more than one couple.

John's baptism was one of eight Rev. Falckner conducted that day in September of 1721. Until we began this research, the family did not know that John was baptized in the German Lutheran church, though it has been handed down that Sarah would bring her children to Manhattan on horseback to get them baptized at Trinity Episcopal Church. We discovered through this research that John's baptism was actually performed by the Trinity Lutheran Church minister. The lore is just a little bit different from the actual fact, and a simple and understandable mistake as anyone who has played telephone can understand.

We then discovered the baptism record of Mary Bull, William and Sarah's seventh child, in the same German Lutheran journal that had John's record. She was baptized by one of Rev. Justus Falckner's successors in Newburgh among the German Lutheran congregation in 1734 when she was nine-months old.

Rev. Michael Knoll took over Trinity Lutheran Church in Manhattan and the Hudson River congregations after the years of unrest, and was generally believed to be a stabilizing influence of the congregations, though

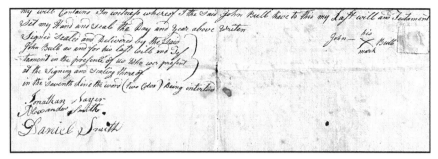

PHOTO CREDIT: JULIE BOYD COLE, 2017. THE WILL OF JOHN BULL, SON OF WILLIAM AND SARAH. THE TEXT OF THE FULL DOCUMENT CAN BE FOUND IN "THE BLUE BOOK."

no one since Falckner traveled as much as he did to so many congregations year after year.

An interesting aside: we found that Sarah's son John Bull's last will and testament, dated 1795, was witnessed by Alexander Smith. Alexander's wife, Ellen, who was also witness to Mary's baptism decades earlier. Alexander lived close to the Stone House, according to the 1790 U.S. Census.

We have not yet found the rest of the children's baptisms, but we believe that they were also baptized Lutheran. Like Trinity Episcopal Church, Trinity Lutheran Church was destroyed in Manhattan in a famous citywide fire during the Revolutionary War. The journal and several others were saved from the fire by a fast-acting and devoted pastor, which is why we have what records we do.

Justus Falckner died the same year Sarah's second child, William, was born. After Justus' death and the general neglect of the Hudson River Lutherans, Daniel Falckner served more than 20 congregations, including the Lutherans of the Wallkill River. In 1725, the Lutherans in Europe sent a minister to take over Trinity Lutheran church in Manhattan and to serve the congregations along the Hudson River, but Daniel continued to serve the neglected group for another decade.

Tensions arose among the Lutherans of the Middle Colonies; there was criticism of the appointed minister by the congregations and power plays among the ministers, both those ordained and not. Daniel was still baptizing children until he retired. He died sometime after 1745. We are still searching for his records.

We did find church records of some of Sarah's children acting as sponsors in baptisms, something that only those who were baptized were allowed to do. We also know that both Sarah and William were documented members of congregations. It is unlikely that only two of Sarah's 12 children would be baptized and also unlikely that the German Lutheran baptisms were conducted simply out of convenience, especially since William was a documented Episcopalian. It is much more likely that John and Mary's Lutheran baptisms were deliberate.

130

[new page, 4b]

The call to the altar of the Hebron Church, June 1762: the following infants came to be baptized on the 12th into the congregation, Pastor Wm Groat

David Trevers	Abraham		
wife Catharina	born September 27	1761	Joseph Trevers
	baptized June 12	1762	wife Rebecca
John Miller	William		
Esther	born June 8	} [17]62	William Gr[oat?, *ink blot*]
	baptized June 12	}	Cathar. Bull

A PAGE FROM THE TRANSLATED RECORD OF THE HEBRON (LUTHERAN) CHURCH/HARRISON MEETING OF MONTGOMERY, NEW YORK.

We found that Esther, Richard and Catherine all served as sponsors at some of the baptisms of their siblings' children, Sarah and William's grandchildren, in the German Lutheran congregation in Montgomery. Eleanor served as a sponsor in both the Lutheran church and the Montgomery German Reformed Church, called Brick Church.

We discovered that the Lutheran congregation in Newburgh was under a good deal of pressure from the growing congregation of Episcopalians. The Episcopalians wanted to use the church building in Newburgh, since the Lutherans used it just a couple of times a year, to hold services in the sanctuary when the traveling minister came. In the later 1740s, a fight broke out on the steps of the church between Lutherans and Episcopalians as they battled over control of the building. Eventually, each side wrote to the governor for arbitration.

The Episcopalians won and subsequently took over the building. The Lutherans had already been moving west in trickles, and eventually moved their congregation to Montgomery. They called themselves the Hebron Church and the Harrison Meeting. A graveyard is still there today.

We found some of the records of the Montgomery church and discovered that this was the church where Esther Bull Miller and her husband, John, as well as Richard Bull and his wife Jemima, all worshipped. John Miller's parents, Johannes and Jacomytie Miller, also worshipped there. We assume that Sarah, who would later marry Johannes after Jacomytie's death, worshipped there as well. We found records showing that there was a group of Lutherans worshipping together there, and was visited occasionally by the traveling Lutheran ministers as early as the 1720s.

We have not yet found other baptism records for the rest of Sarah and William's children, but we did find in the documents at the Stone House, the Bible of Isaac Bull, Sarah's fifth child, kept by he and his wife and

| Richard Bull Jacomime | Humphrey born February 5 baptized May 1 | } | [17]68 | Parents |

[new page, 8b]

List of adult members of the Christ Evangelical Heaven [Church] at Hebron on the Wahlkill

Wardens and Deacons

Johannes Miller and Burgher Mynders } Wardens, appointed at Newborough

Johann Georg Schmidt and David Treber } Deacons, appointed at Hebron 30 January 1757

Hanns Georg Schmidt Nicolaus Holtzländer } As wardens, elected 9 August 176[1], 12th Sunday past Trinity

John Miller, Jun., Deacon, [elected 9 August 1761]

The callings of those who served on occasion are written below

Year 1792, therefore I, Johann Friedrich Ernst, minister at Loonenburg and Claverack called the following congregants to serve: as deacons with seniority, Jacob Pitts and Daniel Schaffer—to these were added on 16 June [1792] Jacob Weldy and Hannes Schmidt

A PAGE FROM THE TRANSLATED RECORD OF THE HEBRON LUTHERAN CHURCH/HARRISON MEETING OF MONTGOMERY, NEW YORK.

documenting his family. Though this is not a baptism record, it suggests that he was a practicing Christian and supports that he too was baptized.

DATE	PARENTS	CHILD	SPONSORS
1766	Wilhelmus Weller Peternella Boll	Hendrick	Hendrick Weller Elsjen Muller, his wife
	Jacob Dekker Eva Buckstaber	Conrad	Christian Christ Elisabeth Weller
		Elsias	Hendrick Schmidt

A PAGE FROM THE TRANSLATED RECORD OF THE BRICK CHURCH GERMAN AND DUTCH REFORMED CONGREGATION IN MONTGOMERY, NEW YORK. "PETERNELLA" IS ELEANOR BULL, DAUGHTER OF WILLIAM AND SARAH BULL. ELEANOR USED THIS NAME OFTEN, ACCORDING TO "THE BLUE BOOK "HISTORIANS.

CHAPTER 16
THE CHILDREN LEAVE THE NEST

Sarah and William's 12 children were born between 1721 and 1745, which means that Sarah was pregnant or nursing an infant on and off for 24 years, at the same time that she was helping her husband build the Stone House, hold down the homestead while William went to work building other houses around the Orange County, and they managed a farm.

The oldest of her children began to leave home about the the same time that Sarah was having her youngest. It is possible, but improbable due to the dates, that all 12 children lived in the Stone House at one time with their parents. There is no denying that the house was packed like a boarding house from time to time.

The first of Sarah's herd to venture out was her eldest daughter, Sarah. According to the Blue Book, Sarah married George Booth, a neighbor and son of Charles and Mary Booth, of Neelytown, sometime before 1745, when she had her first child. Sarah Bull Booth moved with George to what was then part of Ulster County in the town of Wallkill, and was counted in the 1790 census.

Sarah gave birth to her first child, Sarah and William's first grandchild, a girl they named Sarah Bull Booth, in 1745. It was the same year that her mother, Sarah Wells Bull, gave birth to her last child, Eleanor. Sarah and George Booth had seven more children, including Sarah and William's first grandson, William Booth, and their third grandchild, Rhoda Booth, born in 1748.

The next child to leave was most likely John, when he married Hannah Holly in 1746. They had 12 children, including their first child, a son named Ebenezer, born in 1749. He became the fourth grandchild of William and Sarah. John and Holly gave the progenitors their fifth grandchild, another Sarah, born in 1750. John and Hannah lived on a farm next door to the

Danl Bull	Thomas			
Catharina	born October 22	1780	Parents	
	baptized September 30	[17]81		

[new page, 24a]

*A PAGE FROM THE TRANSLATED RECORD OF THE HEBRON CHURCH/
HARRISON MEETING OF MONTGOMERY, NEW YORK. DANIEL BULL WAS THE
SON OF THOMAS BULL, AND GRANDSON OF WILLIAM AND SARAH BULL.
HIS WIFE, CATHARINE MILLER, WAS THE DAUGHTER OF GERMAN
PALATINES.*

Stone House on the 100 acres that he received from Elizabeth Denne when he was 8 years old, according to the Blue Book.

By 1751, at a time when Sarah and William still had five children under the age of 18, the family tree began to rapidly spread its branches over Orange County. William Bull II married Anne Booth, George's sister, and they had William III in 1751. Son Isaac Bull married Sarah Mulliner of Little Britain, daughter of Peter Mulliner, and they brought Rachel Bull into the world in 1751. Daughter Esther joined in the baby boom in 1751, when she and her husband John Miller, a German Lutheran and son of Montgomery's earliest settler, gave birth to Margaret.

Between 1745 and 1784, 39 years, the children of Sarah and William produced 83 grandchildren, who were counted by the Blue Book historians. This number doesn't include the nearly dozen children who died either during childbirth or shortly after. Sarah Wells Bull welcomed at least one new grandchild into the Bull family nearly every year until 1784. In 21 of those years, she welcomed more than one grandchild.

William was alive only to meet about 20 of his second-generation offspring. After his death, Sarah saw 62 more grandchildren come into this world. William died while they had five children living with them at the Stone House and the youngest, Eleanor, was only about 10 years old. According to the 1790 U.S. Census, John, Isaac and Richard lived on farms adjacent to the Stone House property. John had a dozen children. Isaac had six. Thomas, William and Mary settled on farms nearby in what is now the town of Wallkill. Sarah, Esther, Ann, and Eleanor lived in what is now Montgomery. Catherine settled in New Windsor, and Margaret settled in Blooming Grove.

Sarah Wells Bull spent most of her adult life surrounded by children.

In researching some of the 83 grandchildren, particularly searching for baptism and church records, we found that Sarah and William's children raised their families as Christians from several denominations. We found in the church records that several of the 12 children were connected in some way to the German Lutheran and German Reformed churches in Orange County.

Baptisms

DATE	PARENTS	#	CHILD/BIRTHDATE	REMARKS
11.20.1803	Geo. & Eliz. Currin Jas. Weller	221	Amelia Currin b 12.10.1802	
11.23.1803	William Smith Rachel	222	Hannah Ann Smith b 4.21	
11.27.1803	John F. Kain Helena	223	Eliz'th Green Kain b 5.25	
11.27.1803	William Welling Elizabeth	224	William Welling b 10.5	
11.29.1803	Frederick Welling Elizabeth	225	(___)aria Welling b 12.29.1791	
	Same as #225	226	(___)ho Welling b 11.23.1793	
	Same as #225	227	(___)bert Welling b 2.16.1796	
	Same as #225	228	(___)nna Welling b 1.27.1798	
	Same as #225	229	(___)ane Welling b 11.30.1800	
	Same as #225	230	(___)harles Welling b 12.25.1802	
11.30.1803	James Galat(ian) Philander	231	(W)illilam Galatian b 11.17	
1. 5.1804	Benj'n Smith Sarah	232	(J)as. Kain Smith b 7.21.1803	
2.12.1804	Morris & Amelia Thompson May(___)	233	Frances Amelia Hurtin b 8.21.1803	
2.13.1804	Thos & Jane Geraughty & (___)(___)	234	John Wilkes b 10.12.1803	
3.12.1804	Richard W(ellingn) Mary	235	(Sa)rah Welling b 9.20.1799	
	Same as #235	236	Mary Welling b (9).17.1802	
3.13.1804	Cadwallader (Bull) Subm(___)	237	(F)rancis Crawford Bull b 3.26.1798	
	Same as #237	238	(Mit)te Maria Bull b 12.23.1802	
3.19.1804	Ambrose & Mary Crane James Curran	239	(___) Burns Crane b 8.29.1794	
	Same as #239	240	(___) Whiter Crane b (8).19.1799	
	Same as #239	241	(___) Curren Crane b 10.28.1801	
	Jno. & Emilia Curran Jno. Curran jr	242	(___)n Burns Curren b 10.10.1802	

PHOTO CREDIT: SARAH BROWNELL, 2017. PAGE FROM THE ST. ANDREW'S HISTORIC RECORDS OF BAPTISMS. CADWALLADER BULL IS LISTED AS A FATHER OF TWO CHILDREN WHO WERE BAPTIZED HERE. BULL WAS THE SON OF THOMAS AND THE GRANDSON OF WILLIAM AND SARAH BULL.

Beyond the records of John and Mary Bull's baptisms discovered in the German Lutheran records, we found records that Esther, Catherine, and Richard were connected to the German Lutheran church called the Hebron Church/Harrison Meeting in Montgomery. We discovered that Eleanor sometimes called herself Peternella, and her husband, Wilhelmus Weller, a German Lutheran and Palatine, worshipped at the German Reformed Church in Montgomery.

Ann Bull also sometimes used another name. We have records that she sometimes called herself Nancy. She married William Eager, an Irish immigrant child of William and Elsa. They worshipped at the Associate Reformed Church of Neelytown, according to the Blue Book.

Margaret Bull married Silas Horton, who was first cousins with the three Booth siblings who married William, Sarah and Mary Bull. The Booth and the Horton families came to Orange County, with several other clans, from an early Puritan and Quaker settlement at Southhold, Long Island. Many of the Southhold group started a church in 1758 near the Stone House called the Blooming Grove Church. It began as a Presbyterian Church but soon moved toward the independent Congregational model and broke its connection with the Presbytery.

We did find some records of Bulls, including Thomas' second wife, Sarah Gale, connected to the First Presbyterian Church of Goshen. But the majority of Bulls who became practicing Presbyterians were in the third, fourth and later generations.

We did not find records of any of the 12 children worshipping in the Episcopal denomination, though William Bull clearly did. We did find records of William's grandson in the records of St. Andrews Episcopal Church in Walden. We found Cadwallader Bull, son of Thomas Bull, and his wife, Submit, in the record at St. Andrews as the parents of Maria Bull, born in 1802. She was not recorded in the Blue Book. Since the Episcopal Church was the American branch of the Church of England, many of that denomination hid their connection during the Revolutionary War. In fact, the American patriots closed many of the churches during the war years. The Episcopal church only began to make its comeback years after the war.

By the time the third generation began to get married and have children, we find their records scattered across many villages, towns and denominations. The record above is from the German Hebron Lutheran Church/Harrison Meeting in Montgomery and shows the record of the baptism of Thomas Bull, great-grandson of Sarah Wells Bull, grandson of Thomas Bull and child of Daniel and Catherina "Kitty" Bull, our great-great-great-great-grandparents. Daniel was a soldier in the American Revolution, while his father was jailed for being a Tory. Catherina Miller, Daniel's wife, was the child of German Lutherans and Palatine refugees.

PHOTO CREDIT: JULIE BOYD COLE, 2017. THE ELLISON HOUSE, ALSO CALLED "KNOX HEADQUARTERS" IN VAILS GATE, WAS THE LAST HOUSE WILLIAM BULL BUILT. TODAY, IT IS A MUSEUM.

CHAPTER 17
WILLIAM BULL'S BUSINESS, DEATH AND THE FRENCH AND INDIAN WAR

About two years before William died and while he and Sarah had at least five of their youngest children living at home in the Stone House, the French and Indian War began. The primary battle ground was the Providence of New York near Albany and points north, but the settlers of Orange and Ulster counties were in near-constant terror. Some of the native people who fought for the French would go on murderous raids of homesteads, wiping out entire families as they went. Blockhouses, or lookouts, were built along the front lines to serve the frontier families during the bloody, seven-year conflict.

The Stone House, though never the site of any battle, was already built like the blockhouses of the day. According to the Blue Book historians, Sarah and William's son, John Bull, was a captain in the Orange County Militia, and son Thomas Bull was an ensign, both serving under Col. Vincent Matthews. Col. Matthews was the son of Wawayanda Patent holder Peter Matthews, and a dear friend of Christopher and Elizabeth Denne. According to the Blue Book:

PHOTO CREDIT: JULIE BOYD COLE, 2017. A SMALL STONE BRIDGE AS PART OF KINGS HIGHWAY ON THE ELLISON HOUSE PROPERTY. THIS BRIDGE WAS LIKELY BUILT BY THE PROLIFIC STONE MASON WILLIAM BULL.

> "In Jan. 1757, Capt. John Bull with others was employed building a line of block houses to help secure the western part of the county against further Indian encroachments. Although the attacks were confined to the frontier areas west of the Wallkill, the whole county lived in continual terror that hostile war parties might at any time penetrate into the more highly populated easterly areas. During this period, the Stone House was used as a fort and place of refuge for inhabitants of the neighborhood for miles around, especially at night."

Two of Sarah and William's son-in-laws also fought in the war. James Faulkner, Catherine's husband, served in the Ulster County Militia, and Benjamin Booth, Mary's husband, served in the Orange County Militia.

Sarah had already lived through the earlier years of the county, when all strangers were potentially dangerous adversaries. Now and for the next seven years, she again had to live life on high alert, with children to protect.

Despite the war, her husband took a job to build the Ellison House in Vails Gate, about 10 miles to the east on what was then King's Highway and still stands today. It is unclear how long it took to build or whether William Bull stayed overnight at the construction site during periods, but the time and distance of the job site suggests that Sarah and the children would have extended hours at the Stone House alone during wartime.

From 1715 to 1755, William Bull built many stone houses around the greater Orange County area. Besides the Bull Stone House, the Ellison House, Greycourt and Crommelin residences, he may have helped four of

138

his sons build their homes, and may have been hired to build a handful of others. Each must have taken months, if not years, to complete. Sarah was certainly left home alone with the children while he was working.

William died soon after completing the construction on the Ellison house, sometime in the winter of 1755 and 1756, according to the Blue Book historians. They used dated documents related to the construction project found centuries later to bracket William's death date. No other record of his death has been found. We don't know the cause of his death, only that he was between 66 and 67 years old.

Peter Bull and Jesse Booth, the original Bull genealogist, wrote in 1796 that William was 66 when he died. The historians of the Blue Book disputed and explained that the men likely assumed William died in 1755 because that is the year he wrote his will. Peter was only a toddler when William died and Jesse had not yet been born, so they didn't have any personal knowledge of the date.

Sarah was left to raise alone five young children during wartime. Thankfully, the families of her sons, John and Isaac, lived adjacent to her farm, and her other older children all lived close by.

PHOTO CREDIT: JULIE BOYD COLE, 2017. THE VIEW OF THE WALLKILL RIVER VALLEY FROM LAKE MINNEWASKA IN THE SHAWANGUNK MOUNTAINS. THE LORE IS THAT JOHANNES MILLER, A GERMAN IMMIGRANT LIVING IN KINGSTON, NEW YORK, RODE OVER THE MOUNTAIN RANGE, SAW THE BEAUTIFUL VALLEY, AND DECIDED HE WOULD BE BACK TO SETTLE IT.

CHAPTER 18
JOHANNES MILLER AND THE GERMAN LUTHERANS OF MONTGOMERY

Our Blue Book historians and Samuel Eager all wrote that sometime after William Bull died about 1756, Sarah Wells Bull was married a second time, to Johannes Miller. But no one had any record of the marriage, and some doubted the marriage took place. We wanted to solve this puzzle, so we too tried to find a record of the marriage.

Johannes Miller was the father of one of Sarah's son-in-laws. John Miller married Esther Bull, sixth child and second daughter of Sarah. Johannes Miller Sr. was a German immigrant and a Lutheran. He married his first wife, Jacomytie Schoonmaker, in the Kingston Dutch Reformed Church. Her father was also a German immigrant, and they lived among a community of weavers.

According to Eager, Miller and his new bride picked up and moved to the frontier of what is now Montgomery. The story handed down is that Miller was out in the frontier with a posse after some indigenous people had kidnapped members of their settlement. He rode into an open valley

WALKILL LUTHERAN/HARRISON MEETING HOUSE, MONTGOMERY, ORANGE COUNTY

CONTRIBUTED BY BART J. KOWALLIS, PH.D.[*]

AMONG THE FIRST SETTLERS in the towns of Montgomery and Crawford, now in Orange County, were a group of German settlers. They organized a Lutheran church and built a log building in which this congregation met. The building burned down in the late 1700s, and the members of the congregation migrated to other nearby churches. It was placed on the National Register of Historic Places in 1998, and a historical marker placed at the location of the old church. A few headstones, mostly unmarked, can still be found at the site, which is south of the Village of Montgomery near the junction of New York Highway 211 and Orange County Road 416. The text of the church book is in German, interspersed with Latin.[1]

CHURCH BOOK

List of those who have been sanctified in word by baptism and who have joined the Christian Church: Started the 31st day of January of the 1757th year since the blessed birth of Jesus Christ the supreme Lord of the Christian Church. By the current acting minister and erectors of the Christ-Evangelical congregation at Camp Scheinbad and etc. Hebron.

Johannes Christophorus Hartwig, with the assistance of

Johannes Millers and } Church superintendants
Burghard Meynders

Johann Georg Schmidt and } Deacons
David Trebers

[new page, 2a]
1750. Jemima born 18 June, father Johannes Miller, mother Esther, sponsors Johannes Miller sen. and Jacobina

1753. Margaretha born 24 March, baptized Jun, parents same as above, sponsors [blank] Rapp and wife Maria

---

[*] Department of Geology, Brigham Young University, Provo, UT 84602. His article, "Finding the Parents of John Moore of Orange County," RECORD 138(2007):273–83, used records from Harrison Meeting House. He thanks Roger P. Minert, Ph.D., who consulted on especially difficult German text and handwriting.
[1] A bound, negative photocopy of the church book is at the Family History Library in Salt Lake City, from which this translation was made by the contributor. Parentheses are in the original text. Ditto'd text is shown in square brackets.

THE FIRST PAGE FROM THE TRANSLATED RECORD OF THE HEBRON CHURCH/HARRISON MEETING OF MONTGOMERY, NEW YORK. JOHANNES MILLER, SARAH WELLS BULL'S SECOND HUSBAND, IS THE "CHURCH SUPERINTENDENT."

along the Wallkill River and found it so beautiful that he wanted to make it

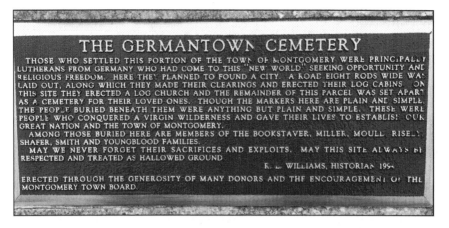

PHOTO CREDIT: JULIE BOYD COLE, 2017. THE CEMETERY AND ONE OF THE HEADSTONES IN THE HEBRON LUTHERAN CHURCH CEMETERY IN MONTGOMERY, N.Y. THERE IS NO NAME ON THE HEADSTONE, JUST THE DATE.

his home. He convinced his wife to leave against her father's wishes and carve out a homestead along the river.

In about 1727, they settled on the east side of the river, where the Orange County Airport now stands. He built a small, square stone house on a slight rise along the winding river. Unlike most of the early settlers of the Middle Colonies, they had only one child, Johannes "John" Miller. Soon, many more German immigrants moved to the area. This first settlement in Montgomery was populated by dozens of families who fled the harsh winters, political unrest and poor land of the Rhine River.

The Millers, like many of the German populations in the Middle Colonies, were Lutherans and they helped form and build the small Lutheran Church called the Hebron Lutheran Church/Harrison Meetinghouse. The church blew down in the late 1700s or early 1800s, and was never rebuilt, but the cemetery remains today at the intersection of Rt. 416 and Rt. 211.

We were able to find a English transcription of the church records of baptism and communion. A copy of the original church records, which are written in German and Latin, are housed in Salt Lake City, Utah, where the Church of Jesus Christ and Latter Day Saints has been gathering thousands of church records for decades.

Thankfully, someone already translated the records, and in that copy we find the Miller family, including Esther. Johannes Miller Sr. was one of two "church superintendents," and John and Esther's child was the first baptism in this record.

However, we have yet to find record of any marriage records there. We did find that Johannes Miller Sr. and Burghard Meynders were both involved in the Lutheran Church in Newburgh before they were involved in Montgomery. Both of their marriages are recorded at the same church in Kingston years earlier. It appears by the timing that the Hebron Church was created after the upheaval and chaos at the Newburgh Church that led to the fist fight on the church steps. Both men can be found in the German Lutheran journal of church records referenced earlier. And Meynders' house in Newburgh was used as a meeting place for the congregation before he moved to Montgomery.

Our search for a record of Sarah Wells Bull and Johannes Miller's marriage led us to the other German congregation in Montgomery, the Dutch Reformed Church called the Brick Church. We contacted Frank Gillespie, the Brick Church Historian, for help. He searched their records for Sarah and Johannes' marriage, but found nothing. He did find something else, and wrote to us in August of 2017:

> "I did find one interesting item in a book titled Genealogical Data from Colonial New York Newspapers, compiled by Kenneth Scott, page 149. Genealogical Data from NY Gazette-Mercury, 1770: 'Miller, Sarah, wife of Johannes Miller of Wallkill, Ulster Co., NY – has eloped from her husband (11/12).' What do you make of this?"

We were floored to read this, and even more so when we dug in and found the actual copy of another classified ad regarding Sarah and Johannes. This was new information to the family and it proved, of course, that Sarah and Johannes did indeed get married. We are hoping to find the exact date of the union, but we can say that their marriage must have happened sometime after 1756, when William died and when we have the last record of Jacomytie Schoonmaker Miller, Johannes' first wife.

We have read various accounts by the Schoonmaker family that Jacomytie lived into the 1760s, but have not found any actual record to corroborate the lore. We did see the gravestone pictured in the Lutheran church graveyard in Montgomery, which was interesting, but not revealing.

ABSCONDED from her Husband and Son-in-Law, about 6 Month ago, Sarah Miller, the Wife of Johannes Miller; whereas the Subscribers are apprehensive that she will run them in Debt; Therefore this is to forewarn all Persons from crediting her on either of their Accounts, as they will pay no Debts of her contracting from the Date hereof. Johannes Miller, John Miller.
Ulster County, Nov. 7, 1770.   53 6

A NOV. 29, 1770 CLASSIFIED AD PLACED IN THE NEW YORK JOURNAL MANHATTAN NEWSPAPER.

CHAPTER 19
THE END OF MRS. MILLER

On Nov. 29, 1770, printed in the New York Journal in Manhattan:

> "Absconded from her husband and son-in-law, about 6 months ago, Sarah Miller, the wife of Johannes Miller; whereas the subscribers are apprehensive that she will run them in debt; therefore this is to forewarn all perfont from crediting her on either of their accounts as they will pay no debts of her controlling from the date hereof. Ulster County, Nov. 1, 1770 Johannes Miller, John Miller"

We were shocked to find this record. Until August of 2017, we had never heard that Sarah might have left her second husband, Johannes. We dug into the history to understand this type of classified ad. As it turned out, it was very common for ads like these to appear in the newspapers of the day. Often, it was the only way that couples "divorced" in the Middle Colonies in the 18th century. English law prevented legal court divorces. Placing an ad in the newspaper let everyone know that the union was dissolved, much like we would have legal separation today. It was the reverse reason for the "banns of marriage," which was the public declaration of the union. The definition at the time of the word "elope" had to do with the preposition that followed the word. If the word "from" followed elope – rather than "with" – the couple was separating.

Sarah was one of four New York "separations" we found in the newspaper record aggregate in the Genealogical Data from Colonial New

York Newspapers by Kenneth Scott. Printed in the *New York Gazette* and *The Weekly Mercury* in 1770:

> "Dunn, Hannah, wife of Thomas Dunn, of NYC, comb maker _ has eloped from her husband (7/23)"

> "Dudley, William _ will not in future pay debts contracted by wife Mary (9/3)"

In 1769, the paper published seven ads of divorce:

> "Denniston, Elizabeth, wife of William Denniston, of Raway _ has eloped from her husband, (6/4/)"

> "Smith, Mary, wife of Hugh Smith, of Precinct of New Windsor, Ulster Col, NY - has eloped from her husband (2/26)"

We also learned that it is a myth that people did not end their unions 300 years ago, especially in the Colonies. In fact, the divorce rate in America runs in cycles and is driven by a number of economic and sociological variables. In the Colonies, for example, men still outnumbered women and that meant that women could be picky when selecting a mate. Men could obtain land much easier than in Europe, and land meant means. We found that the most common reasons for the end of a marriage differed from decade to decade and was dependent on who was leaving whom. In 18th century America, men who left the union did so most often due to infidelity, while women most often left due to "cruelty."

Marriage was still more or less considered a business arrangement, so "falling out of love" was not a reason they would even consider to leave the union. Mates were judged based on how they contributed to the family or added status, not how lovable they were.

One historian reported the winds of independence that blew through the Colonies in the 1760s and 1770s, and led to our nation's revolution, also led to women leaving oppressive husbands. Thomas Jefferson even wrote a legal brief in 1772 asking for a legal divorce in the Virginia Supreme Court, which had never been done before. That brief is widely thought to be the precursor to the Declaration of Independence, according to the Journal of the American Revolution.

Colonists had been restricted by years of the self-centered and exploitive Old World monarchies, and were all developing a taste for liberty and self-rule. It appears that Sarah Wells Bull Miller was no different. We now know that she was married to Johannes from one to 14 years. And then in 1770, at the age of about 73 years old, she left him and his name behind.

Maybe after her decades of tackling so many challenges, many inflicted on her by others, she had had enough and decided to head back to her Stone House on the Hamptonburgh hill. We can't help but be impressed all over again about the resolve of this incredible woman.

An Incident of Sarah Wells.

The following incident shows the remarkable vigor of our ancestress in her old age. who when a girl of eifteen made a first settlement in a wilderness and before that was in the habit of rowing a small boat with produce to sell across New York Bay from Staten Island.

At the bend of the Wallkill where a cross road connects the Goshen-Montgomery State Road with the old turnpike at Bodines Bridge, stands a home that was once the home of Aunt Jinnie Miller. She and Sarah Wells Bull were close friends. and when Sarah was in her hundredth year she journeyed there on horseback to visit her old friend. A storm came up and although urged to stay over night, Sarah would not consent to remain. Then the friends tried to arrange for her safety saying for her to ride the older horse, leaving the colt for the younger guest. To this Sarah did not agree, saying she "would ride the young horse as he would be more sure-footed." And ride him she did. Think of that you young people! How many of you could do it! And she was then one hundred years old.

PHOTO CREDIT: JULIE BOYD COLE, 2017. A BULL STONE HOUSE DOCUMENT ABOUT SARAH WELLS BULL'S 100TH YEAR. THE TRANSCRIPTION, PG. 150.

CHAPTER 20
A STORMY RIDE FROM MONTGOMERY

Only a handful of stories about Sarah Wells Bull have passed through the generations to reach the 21st century. One story we found in the documents at the Bull Stone House at first seemed unlikely, but after completing the research on Sarah, now seems completely plausible. We are not sure who wrote this or when it was written, but we were able to dig into the tale. Here is what we found:

We have no evidence that Sarah ever rowed a boat the nine miles of the open waters of New York Harbor between Staten Island and Manhattan. In fact, the evidence we did find makes this seem very unlikely. We were able to put a general date range on this found document by the references to Bodine Bridge and the old Turnpike. Both were constructed about 1809, according to the National Parks Service. Aunt Jennie Miller, mentioned in the tale, was born in 1767 and lived until 1850. The story was likely shared by Aunt Jennie with the younger generations. She had 15 nieces and nephews, and at least 26 grand-nieces and -nephews, who lived well into the 1800s.

We believe that by process of elimination, Aunt Jennie is Jane Bull Miller. She was Sarah's granddaughter and the daughter of Thomas. At the time, "Jennie" was a common nickname for Jane. She married her first cousin, William Miller, son of Esther Bull Miller, and lived on Johannes Miller's farm in Montgomery. She was born in 1767 and died in 1850.

We also found a baptism record for one of Jane and William's children, Carr, that lists Jane's first name as Jean.

By layering the dates, we can calculate that the document of the 1796 story was written sometime after 1809, and likely later, since Jane Bull Miller's nieces and nephews would need to be old enough to share the story. Of course, it could also be a document written much later, relaying a story handed down verbally through the generations. If it is, we know that Jane Bull Miller lived in the house of Sarah's former, second husband in Montgomery, in the spot described in the document. It also appears that the paper used was more modern than the older documents found in the house. In the early 19th century, paper was made with recycled material or

Carr Miller		**New York Births and Christenings, 1640-1962**	
New York Births and Christenings		Indexing Project (Batch) Number	C50654-1
Name	**Carr Miller**		
Gender	Male	System Origin	New_York-ODM
Birth Date	30 Sep 1801	GS Film number	823668
Birthplace	PRESBYTERIAN CHURCH,HAMPTONBURGH TWP,ORANGE,NEW YORK		
Father's Name	William Miller		
Mother's Name	Jean Bull		

Citing this Record

"New York Births and Christenings, 1640-1962," database, *FamilySearch*
(https://familysearch.org/ark:/61903/1:1:FDRT-X7X : 12 December 2014), Carr Miller, 30 Sep 1801;
citing PRESBYTERIAN CHURCH,HAMPTONBURGH TWP,ORANGE,NEW YORK, reference ; FHL microfilm
823,668.

cotton, hemp or linen. After 1843, wood pulp was added to the paper-making process and mass production began.

We also know that Jane Bull Miller was one of Sarah's 83 grandchildren. We found a few more interesting connections between Jane and Sarah Wells Bull. They both worshipped at the same church, the Blooming Grove Congregational Church. In 2017, we found in the basement of the church a record referencing Jane Miller during the time of Jane's life. Jane and William Miller also named one of their children after the beloved pastor of the Blooming Grove church, Rev. Benoni Bradner, who was Sarah Wells Bull's pastor at the end of her life. Bradner Miller was born in 1799, according to the Blue Book.

All of these pieces of information, coupled with what we know of Sarah Wells Bull, certainly give credibility to the tale of the 100-year-old woman riding horseback through a storm to get home. Nothing seemed to get in Sarah's way once she had a mind to do something. She also didn't seem to fear much, the result of having successfully faced so many dangers.

The letter pictured reads:

"An Incident of Sarah Wells

The following incident shows the remarkable vigor of our ancestress in her old age, who when a girl of sixteen made a first settlement in a wilderness and before that was in the habit of rowing a small boat with produce to sell across New York Bay from Staten Island.

At the bend of the Wallkill where a cross road connects the Goshen-Montgomery State Road with the old turnpike at Bodines Bridge, stands a house that was once the home of Aunt Jennie Miller. She and Sarah Wells Bull were close friends and when Sarah was in her hundredth year she journeyed there on horseback to visit her old friend.

A storm came up and although urged to stay over night, Sarah would not consent to remain.

Then the friends tried to arrange for her safety saying for her to ride the older horse, leaving the colt for the younger guest. To this Sarah did not agree saying she "would ride the young horse as he would be more sure-footed." And ride him she did. Think of that you young people! How many of you could do it! And she was then one hundred years old."

PHOTO CREDIT: JULIE BOYD COLE, 2017. REV. BENONI BRADNER'S
GRAVESITE UNDER THE BLOOMING GROVE CHURCH IN ORANGE COUNTY.

CHAPTER 21
SARAH'S LAST MINISTER

Rev. Benoni Bradner served the congregation of Blooming Grove
Church from 1786 to 1802, and was buried in ground which is now under
the current church structure. He died in 1804 at age 71. Rev. Bradner was
the son of the first minister of Goshen, Rev. John Bradner, of the First
Presbyterian Church. Rev. Benoni Bradner's amazing life story is chronicled
in a small book titled The History of the Blooming Grove Church by A.
Elwood Corning, published in 1929:

"As a minister of the Gospel, Mr. Bradner possessed considerable eminence. He appeared to have an extensive and thorough knowledge of the doctrines of the Bible. Subjects in divinity were, in general, family to his mind. And his acquaintance with experimental religion was evidently genuine. A becoming gravity marked his conduct in the pulpit. He seemed to possess an unusual affection for the welfare of souls, which, operating on his enfeebled frame, would sometimes, almost overcome him. His zeal, though fervid, was accompanied with a correspondent and useful degree of knowledge. He was blessed with the talents of an easy and entertaining speaker. His pubic discourses, for the most part, were, unusually, interesting and instructive … as a neighbor and friend, he was benevolent, obliging and faithful … He possessed a truly philanthropic spirit. In friendship, he was sincere, warm and engaging … As a parent, his tenderness and vigilant care were, perhaps, without a parallel. In council, in example, and in affection to his children, he could scarcely be equalled."

The beloved minister was raised by his widowed mother, and never knew his father. John Bradner died the same year Benoni was born. His mother urged Benoni to attend Princeton seminary school, and he graduated in 1755. He then traveled around the colonies as an appointed minister in the Presbyterian system; he married and had three daughters.

Bradner fought on the side of the patriots of the American Revolution. Bradner lost his wife in 1777 and was suffering from various ailments that caused him enormous pain, so he decided to go home to Goshen. After he had officially retired, then a widow and grandfather, he began to serve the congregation at Blooming Grove. Blooming Grove was loosely part of the Presbytery, but was leaning toward Congregationalism, according to historical records found at the church. By the 1800s, it had pulled its membership with the Presbyterian church and officially became a Congregational Church.

Despite the many reasons Bradner could have used to retire to a quiet life, he instead threw all his efforts into increasing the small congregation and serving others. According to Corning's account:

"His pain at times were so distressing that his cries were said to have been heard from quite a distance. When he came out of these attacks, he would sometimes say, 'if it be possible let this cup pass, but not my will, but Thine be done.' "

This is the man who was Sarah Wells Bull's last minister. However she came into the world, she left it comforted by a selfless, compassionate man. She certainly deserved it, and as her ancestors who have come to admire her so much, it brings us peace knowing that Sarah left this Earth in the hands of those who were loving.

1796

Apr 21,   Sarah Bull of Hamptonburgh 100y 15d

June 10,   Absalom Sackett   teacher at Blooming Grove

1797

May 13,   Mrs Henry Brewster Sr

Oct 10,   John Chatfield

1798

May 11,   Mrs Edward McLaughlin of North Stamford
                    New england

Mar 16,   Benjamin Youngs

June 25,   Phinehas Helm 73y

1802

Jan.8,   Capt Jonathan Tuthill 83y

1803

Jan 13,   Nathaniel Woodhull Jr

Aug 17,   Elihu Marvin 84y

Dec 7,   Susannah Tuthill 79y

1804

Jan 21,   Rev Benoni Bradner 71y

Apr. 1,   Issac Horton

PHOTO CREDIT: JULIE BOYD COLE, 2017. A PAGE FROM THE BLOOMING GROVE CHURCH DOCUMENTS SHOWS THAT SARAH BULL'S DEATH ON APRIL 21, 1796 WAS RECORDED. REV. BENONI BRADNER WAS THE MINISTER OF THE CHURCH AT THE TIME OF SARAH'S DEATH. THE CHURCH WAS FORMED IN THE MID 1700S AND WAS FIRST ALIGNED WITH THE PRESBYTERIAN CONGREGATIONS BUT LEFT THE DENOMINATION AFTER A DIFFERENCE DEVELOPED BETWEEN THE CONGREGANTS AND THE LEADERSHIP.

CHAPTER 22
SARAH'S DEATH RECORD

In 2017, a bit of a miracle happened while researching Sarah Wells Bull's life. Searching through Bull family records at the Goshen Public Library Local History Room, a very important piece of information turned up unexpectedly.

While waiting for the librarian to look up something now insignificant on the computer, a bookshelf filled with old binders of worn-out and faded labels caught my attention. ne binder's label had the dates 1734-1831. I took it down from the shelf and started to page through it. Suddenly, a page flopped open.

It took a few minutes for the words on the page to sink in.

"Apr 21, 1796, Sarah Bull of Hamptonburgh 100y 15d"

I turned to the librarian and asked her to look at it.

"Does this mean what I think it means?" I asked her. "It's her death record," Anne Roche, the librarian, told me. Someone had transcribed the church records of Blooming Grove Church and gave a copy to the library decades ago. Within those notes, Sarah Bull's death was recorded by her minister. This was new information about our ancestor. No one had known in modern day that Sarah had once belonged to the church.

Ironically, two of her ancestors still attend the church. We were able to attend the small Sunday service and wander around the building. Though it was not the sanctuary of Sarah's day, there were remnants of the old church. In the crawl space under the church, we visited the gravesite of Rev. Benoni Bradner; and we saw the original pulpit, the one Sarah saw each Sunday at church.

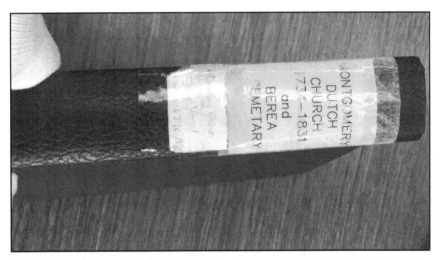

PHOTO CREDIT: JULIE BOYD COLE, 2017. A TRANSCRIPTION OF THE EARLY RECORDS OF THE BLOOMING GROVE CONGREGATIONAL CHURCH IS PART OF THE LOCAL HISTORY ROOM COLLECTION OF CHURCH DOCUMENTS AT GOSHEN PUBLIC LIBRARY.

Blooming Grove Congregational Church Record
from 1790-1830.

The Church Records from 1774-1786 have disappeared
and no accurate record can be given.

"Blooming Grove Congregational Church, Blooming Grove
is situated in the Town of Blooming Grove, Orange County
New York twelve miles west of the Hudson River and two
miles west of the Village of Washingtonville on the main
road running from the City of Newburgh to the Villages
of Chester, Warwick and Goshen.

The first Congregation was formed in 1759 by early pioneers
settling in this section, who came chiefly from Suffolk
County, Long Island, many of whom were descendants of the
Pilgrims.   It was a small wooden structure painted yellow
and stood on the spot of the present edifice, facing the
road.   It was demolished in 1823, and the present building erected in the same year, which covers not only the
space occupied by the first church, but the cemetery in
which are interred the remains of three of the former
pastors of the Congregation viz: Revs.Enos Ayres, Benoi
Bradner, Samuel Parkhurst. "   Copied from "Old Churches
of Orange County,N.Y. by Almit S Moffat, Washingtonville,
N.Y. 1927."

PHOTO CREDIT: JULIE BOYD COLE, 2017. THE FIRST PAGE OF THE
TRANSCRIPTION OF THE EARLY RECORDS OF THE BLOOMING GROVE
CONGREGATIONAL CHURCH. IT IS PART OF THE LOCAL HISTORY ROOM
COLLECTION OF CHURCH DOCUMENTS AT GOSHEN PUBLIC LIBRARY.
BELOW IS THE PULPIT IN THE BLOOMING GROVE CHURCH USED IN THE
1700S AT THE CHURCH.

PART III
SARAH'S BEGINNING

CHAPTER 23
A BRIEF REVIEW OF 1700S NEW YORK

Before we continue, let's take a brief look back at the history of New York as a pre-colonial settlement. As stated already, New York was sparsely populated in the late 1600s. The Dutch had first settled the New York harbor area in the early 1600s after Henry Hudson discovered the area in 1609. Rich Dutchmen set up the West Indies Trading Company and sent trappers and traders to New York to gather beaver fur from the vast forests that blanketed the landscape. Indigenous people sold furs to the traders, and a new economy was created.

The Dutch famously purchased the island of Manhattan from the Algonquin Indians for $24. In 1664, New York became an English colony held by the English Crown until the American Revolution. New Amsterdam, as New York City was once called, encompassed Lower Manhattan, Brooklyn, Long Island, Staten Island and several of the smaller islands. Albany and Kingston, once called Esopus, were growing settlements, too.

The 150 miles of the Hudson River were mostly wilderness used collectively by Native Americans in the area and by traveling trappers. A few small trading posts opened on the river banks. New York was managed by a governor appointed by the monarch of England. A city mayor and "common council" handled the day-to-day operations of the small town of Manhattan.

English leadership of New York changed often as monarchs changed in London. The first governors were: The Earl of Bellomont, 1698-1701; Lord Cornbury, 1702-1708; Lord Lovelace, 1708-1710; Gov. Robert Hunter, 1710-1719; William Burnet, 1720-1728; John Montgomerie, 1728-1732; William Cosby, 1732-1736; and George Clinton, 1739-1753.

In Manhattan, there was one wharf, or dock, on the East River and a wall (on what is now called Wall Street) that separated the island from the rest of the island's dense forest for protection from native people and the French.

There are thousands of records and historical accounts preserved about life in early New York, including decades of meeting minutes of the New York Common Council. There are recorded wills filed as early as 1694, baptisms and other church records, census records, deeds, voting records, and many other documents preserved in various archives and now available online.

Staten Island was first settled in 1661 by the Dutch and the French Huguenots. By 1698, it was cut into about 100 homesteads and had a population of about 727 people; many were Dutch Reformers, a Christian Protestant denomination. There was a documented census in 1706 www.nygenweb.net/richmond/1706.txt). The first city-run ferry on Staten Island was established in 1713. Long Island was equally developed, although the city operated a ferry there as early as 1700.

As stated earlier, New Jersey and Staten Island were separated by a narrow band of water. We found New Jersey and Staten Island had European settlers as early as the mid-17th century and no more than a few thousand people at the time of Sarah's infancy. When she was with her parents, there was a settlement in New Jersey called Piscataway, just over the Raritan River and Arthur Kill, from the southern end of Staten Island.

The area was settled by a group of Lutherans, Quakers and other dissenters of the Church of England. By the end of the 17th century, William Penn was granted one of the largest land patents in the colonies that included Pennsylvania, Delaware and parts New Jersey. Penn was a wealthy Quaker and might be considered one of our country's most successful land developers; he immediately began to look for settlers to help develop his land in America.

Since most wealthy Europeans and land owners would not risk their lives traveling across the Atlantic Ocean to the undeveloped New World, Penn sought out people who would. In England, Wales, Ireland, and Germany, he found land-poor farmers, religious dissenters and people who wanted to rise above their station, willing to make the dangerous journey. The early settlers calculated their chances to improve their lives and determined that they were better across the vast ocean than in the established cities and countries of Europe.

Penn filled dozens of ships in the late 1600s with settlers to populate his fledgling developments that eventually became New Jersey, Pennsylvania and Delaware.

Germantown was just north of Philadelphia and settled by Quaker, Mennonite and Lutheran refugees from along the war-ravaged Rhine River valley in the Palatinate in what is now Germany. As stated earlier, New Jersey and Staten Island were separated by a narrow band of water. We found prominent, early families from Staten island buried on the northwest side of the river in the historic Edison, New Jersey, cemetery and the history shows there was a lot of travel back and forth.

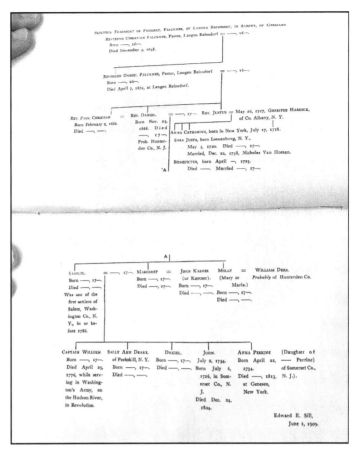

SKELETON FRAGMENT OF PEDIGREE, FALCKNER, OF LANGEN REINSDORF, IN SAXONY, BY GERMANY

REVEREND CHRISTIAN FALCKNER, Pastor, Langen Reinsdorf ═══ ——, 16—.
Born ——, 16—.
Died November 5, 1658.

REVEREND DANIEL FALCKNER, Pastor, Langen Reinsdorf ═ ——, 16—.
Born ——, 16—.
Died April 7, 1674, at Langen Reinsdorf.

REV. PAUL CHRISTIAN ═══ REV. DANIEL. ——, 17—. REV. JUSTUS ═ May 26, 1717, GERRITGE HARDICK,
Born February 2, 1662. Born Nov. 25, of Co. Albany, N. Y.
Died ——, ——. 1666. Died ANNA CATHARINA, born in New York, July 17, 1718.
——, 17—. SARA JUSTA, born Loonenburg, N. Y.,
Prob. Hunter- May 5, 1720. Died ——, 17—.
don Co., N. J. Married, Dec. 22, 1738, Nicholas Van Hoesan.
BENEDICTUS, born April ——, 1723.
'A Died ——. Married ——, 17—.

A

SAMUEL. ═══ ——, 17—. MARGARET ═══ JOHN KABNER MOLLY ═ WILLIAM DERR.
Born ——, 17—. Born ——, 17—. (or Kastner). (Mary or Probably of Hunterden Co.
Died ——, ——. Died ——, 17—. Born ——, 17—. Maria.)
Was one of the Died ——, ——. Born ——, 17—.
first settlers of Died ——, ——.
Salem, Wash-
ington Co., N.
Y., in or be-
fore 1786.

CAPTAIN WILLIAM SALLY ANN DRAKE. DANIEL. JOHN. ANNA PERRINE (Daughter of
Born ——, 17—. of Peekskill, N. Y. Born ——, 17—. July 2, 1754. Born April 22, —— Perrine)
Died April 25, Born ——, 17—. Died ——, ——. Born July 6, 1734. of Somerset Co.,
1776, while serv- Died ——, ——. 1726, in Som- Died ——, 1813, N. J.).
ing in Washing- erset Co., N. at Geneseo,
ton's Army, on J. New York.
the Hudson River, Died Dec. 24,
in Revolution. 1804.

Edward E. Sill,
June 1, 1909.

PHOTO CREDIT: SARAH BROWNELL, 2017. FROM THE COLLECTION AT THE HISTORICAL SOCIETY OF PENNSYLVANIA. A PAGE FROM "A CONTRIBUTION TO PENNSYLVANIA HISTORY MISSIVES ..." LANCASTER, PA 1909. SHOWS THE ESTIMATED FAMILY TREE OF THE FALCKNER FAMILY OF GERMANY.

CHAPTER 24
THE FALCKNER BROTHERS

In 1700, two immigrant brothers, Daniel and Justus Falckner, sons of a Lutheran minister from Germany, sailed together to the New World. The older brother, Daniel, had already seen the new continent once years earlier as part of William Penn's expeditions. He had returned to his homeland to, among other reasons, convince his younger brother, Justus, to come back with him. After arriving, the two brothers made such a mark on the Middle

Colonies that authors have written about them ever since. Delber Wallace Clark wrote in The World of Justus Falckner in 1916:

> "Justus Falckner was discovering America. From the deck of the ship which was bringing him up the Delaware River, he was sizing up the New World. He was not alone, as he compared his native Germany with the vista which unrolled before him. He was able to turn to his brother, Daniel, and point out to him how very little man seemed to have done to the vast expanse of woodland, which crowned the low bluffs on the right, and then swelled into forested hills above the marshland along the river on the left. His brother was there to hear his remarks about the fields of golden stubbled, from which the grain had lately been harvested. These tiny patches of yellow seemed insignificant in the endless throngs of trees."

Justus and Daniel landed in Philadelphia and settled in one of the communities to the north, called Germantown. Among their fellow German immigrants, they began remarkable lives. They showed incredible faith and dedication to mankind, and took great pains to reach all the scattered Lutheran flocks in the Colonies. Some even compared them to Jesus Christ.

The young standouts also became targets of scrutiny and ridicule from the establishment that had already taken hold in the young colony. Justus was able to shed the cloud of criticism more quickly than Daniel. Justus became the first Lutheran minister ordained in America in 1703, and took over New York City's Trinity Lutheran Church and the congregation in Albany. Daniel, aligned with a new religious movement led by Philipp Jakob Spener, commonly known as Pietism, had a longer battle. Clark wrote:

> "The backbone of Spener's Pietism was the meeting of small, intimate groups. Usually these are called in English, 'house meetings.' As they multiplied in Germany they became a strong of power houses which electrified German Christianity. All over the country little groups go together. Sometimes the local pastor himself favored them, and sometimes he opposed them. Though they generated a great new surge of devotion, they also created friction by magnifying the contrast between the 'converted' and the 'unconverted.' "

Germantown was founded about 20 years earlier by German Quakers and Mennonites. The Lutherans were welcomed there at first, accepted into William Penn's vision for his development based on tolerance and "Brotherly Love." But, in terms of practice, there was friction. The original settlers did not believe in the sacraments followed by the Lutherans, such as infant baptism or relationships with God through a priest. Daniel Falckner aligned with their attitudes of judgment-free love, but was still looking to bring Quakers into the beliefs of the Lutheran denomination, including baptism.

From 1700 to 1703, the brothers tried to find their place among the Quakers and Mennonites in Germantown, PA, with little success. Justus eventually moved to New York City. A yellow fever epidemic had sickened the pastor and his family, and they were in desperate need of a new leader. The Swedish Lutheran leadership managed the New York City Lutheran congregation and convinced a reluctant Justus to answer the call, leading to his becoming ordained.

In order to serve the congregations in New York City and Albany, Justus Falckner taught himself how to speak Dutch, as the services were conducted in the language. In December of 1703, he preached his first service in the small, wooden church in Manhattan. Clark wrote:

> "It was December 12, the third Sunday in Advent, eighteen days after his ordination, that Justus Falckner first mounted the pulpit under one of the two windows which the little church could boast, and looked down on his congregation. As the late arrivals walked to their places, the loose board of the floor cried out like creatures in pain. The gusts of wind which whipped up from the North River set the roof timbers creaking and groaning. The members of the congregation shivered beneath their heavy clothing."

Justus was accepted by the small congregation and led the church until his death in 1723 at age 51. He became an incredible and remarkable leader, but he did not do it alone. As he increased the number of small congregations in his fold, he leaned heavily on the Manhattan and Albany church elders, as well as the leaders of the home churches scattered around the colonies.

In Manhattan, senior Lutheran elder Major Jan Hendrick de Bruyn, the husband of Johanna de Bruyn – Christopher Dennes' landlord – mentioned earlier, was a well-connected politician in New York and Albany. He was in his 70s and Falckner's closest ally. Falckner lived with another congregant, Pieter Pietersen van Woglom van Utrecht, who was nicknamed "So Easy." Pieter owned an open boat sloop called the "Unity" that sailed the Hudson River between Albany and Manhattan. Pieter allowed Justus liberal use of the vessel to carry him between the river's Lutheran congregations.

Over the course of Justus Falckner's ministry, the congregation began to repopulate with the increase of German immigrants. Services, previously preached in Dutch, were now being presented in German. Further, the younger leaders were men more commonly of German descent, on whom Justus Falckner relied. Several young men held the position of deacon and their jobs varied between managing operations of the service and the church, and acting as wards of the orphans and poor. In the early 18th century, churches regularly collected money to support the poor, sick, widowed, and orphaned. John Viets, or de Viets, was one of the deacons of the Lutheran church. He was a medical doctor and immigrated from Germany a few years earlier. Though a dedicated servant of Justus congregation, he eventually moved to Connecticut in 1710 in search of a community more accepting of Germans.

New Yorkers at that time were increasingly worried about the thousands of Palatine German refugees who arrived in Manhattan in 10 ships sent by Queen Anne. The city was in turmoil, believing they would double the population of the small island settlement and severely tax their limited resources. The were so nervous about this population boom of "diseased" people that they forced them to live for months on Nutter's Island until the city could plan for their disbursement throughout the colony. This practice became the precursor for Ellis Island a generation later. Before Viets left, he did what he could to help Justus expand the church and manage its people.

Rev. Justus Falckner and his council of church leaders had three pressing problems, according to Clark: not enough money to effectively operate; too many Lutherans leaving to join the English or the Reformed churches; and a "shabby, run-down little chapel that could attract only the incurably loyal." The problems of the little church didn't stop Justus from working hard to reach out to all the Lutherans between the Raritan River of New Jersey, up to Albany along the Hudson. By the time Justus died, he had thousands of congregants named in the journal of his New Jersey and New York flock, and was canonized by the historians who studied him. Clark wrote:

"No one but a saint or a fool would have tried to save the New York Lutheran church in the winter of 1703-04. History has demonstrated that if Justus Falckner was a fool, he was a fool in Christ, which is another way of saying, he was a saint."

Justus documented his ministry actions until the day he died. The original "Kercken Boeck," or church book of records, was published by the New York Holland Society in 1903, according to Clark, and is one of the most detailed journals of its time.

Within its pages are some interesting bits of information about the Lutherans of the Hudson River and Raritan River valleys, including this one highlighted by Clark:

"Early in the fall after his first trip up the Hudson, Justus performed a marriage which set up a family whose homestead was to be famous in American history. On the thirteenth of September 1704, he went out to Bloemendaal and married Meyndert Berger, grandson of Meyndert Fredericksen, the old blacksmith of Albany, and Sara Uytse, of the family of Long Geysbert uyt de Bogaert. For some years the young people lived at Bloemendaal and brought their children to Falckner to baptize. Later they moved to the new settlement at Newburgh, while Justus was making pastoral visits, and he baptized other children there. At Newburgh, Meyndert built a small stone house. This house, much enlarged by later owners, was the headquarters of George Washington during the critical months at the end of the Revolution, when the American Army was quartered at Newburgh."

In 1709, Justus took over the Lutheran congregation that had settled Newburgh and were the first of the German Palatine refugees Queen Anne and Rev. Kocherthal set up in the New World. Kocherthal left his group of about 50 people in Newburgh and sailed back to England to oversee the 10-ship boat lift in 1710. Justus vowed to serve this group as well as the other Lutherans scattered along the Hudson. He visited Newburgh twice a year to perform baptisms and marriages, and to minister to the dying until his own death in 1723. Sometime during his tenure, Justus asked his brother, Daniel, to help him cover the congregations. Daniel agreed and served at least two New Jersey congregations on the Raritan River.

Rev. Justus Falckner served more than 20 congregations along the rivers of New Jersey and New York, and is credited with establishing the Lutheran church in the New World. He is still known in church history of truly living a life of Christ and love. When he died suddenly at the age of 51, all of the Lutherans would have been without a minister until another could be sent from Europe. But Daniel stepped in and picked up his brother's travel schedule.

According to author Dr. John C. Honeyman, who wrote History of the Zion Lutheran Church at New Germantown, New Jersey, in 2012:

> "... We do not again meet with (Daniel Falckner) until September 1724, when we find him recording in classical Latin, in the church book of West Camp, N.Y., the following: 'Having been called to the place of the sainted Kocherthal, and of my sainted brother, I, Daniel Falckner, Pastor at Millstone and in the Mountains near the River Raritan, have, on the last day of the month of September, 1724, baptized the following persons.

"Although calling himself pastor of the Lutheran along the Raritan, it is evident that he spent a part of his time in 1724 and 1725 with the Palatine Lutherans at East and West Camp and other places on the Hudson, where until the arrival of (Rev. William Christopher) Berkenmeyer, he probably did good service in holding the congregations together, in marrying their young people and in baptizing the children."

According to Honeyman's account, Berkenmeyer was a 38-year-old pastor from Hanover, Germany, ordained in Holland and sent to America in September of 1725 to fill the vacancy left by Justus' death.

"The pastoral labors of Rev. W.C. Berkenmeyer extended over the whole region embraced in the Valley of the Hudson, and included also the Ramapo and Hackensack (and perhaps Wallkill in New York) congregations in New Jersey. An occasional visit was also paid to the Schoharie settlement of Germans 30 miles west of Albany. In New York City, at Hackensack, Loonenburg, and Albany, the preaching was in Dutch; at Ramapo, Newburgh and West Camp, in German. Berkenmeyer was master of both languages, and also of the English."

But Berkenmeyer did not have the same commitment to the scattered Lutherans as Justus or even Daniel. Honeyman wrote:

"After six years of arduous travel, by land and water, in the discharge of his difficult office, this servant of God desired to relinquish the southern half of his spiritual charge and to fix himself permanently in the more agreeable district north of the Highlands."

With that, the New York congregations of Lutherans agreed to hire a new minister to serve the people from Manhattan to Newburgh. They set up a payment schedule of what they would pay the new minister for various services. They offered a handsome salary and fees for services. Honeyman listed:

"The united congregations of New York and Hackensack promised to the new Pastor the expenses of his journey hither, a yearly salary of 60 pounds, free residence, wood and light, and the following prerequisites:

1. 20 shillings for a funeral sermon,

2.   6 shillings for a prayer at the grave,
3.   3 shillings for a marriage notice,
4.   6 shillings for marrying at the pastor's house,
5.   12 shillings for marrying elsewhere,
6.   1 shilling for christening,
7.   3 shillings for baptismal certificate,
8.   1 shilling for churching a recent mother,
9.   60 shillings for service in a congregation outside of our corporation (20 shillings are to fall to the church.

In return for this liberal maintenance, the pastor was to live and labor in the summertime in New York and in the winter at Hackensack, and pay two visits yearly to the Palatine Lutherans at Newburgh."

After the call for a new pastor was made by the southern New York Lutherans, Rev. Berkenmeyer happily moved his family to Looneburg, which is now Athens, where he lived until his death in 1751. Though he was involved in the newly formed Synod, or assembly of Lutheran clergy in the Middle Colonies, he no longer ministered to the circuit of congregations formed by Justus Falckner.

Although Berkenmeyer was the official pastor of the New York and New Jersey Lutherans, Daniel Falckner continued to serve, apparently to the frustration of Berkenmeyer. In an attempt to organize the Lutheran ministry and remove Falckner from this post, Berkenmeyer paid Daniel a visit in 1731. After some back and forth that both confused and further frustrated Berkenmeyer, the elderly Daniel "joyfully" agreed to step down and he retreated to his home in the woods of New Jersey with his daughter. A new pastor was appointed and Daniel, apparently with the same enthusiasm and commitment as he had teaching the Lutheran doctrine, began a second career in the New World as a doctor of medicinal herbs. According to Honeyman:

"A last work concerning Rev. Daniel Falckner: History does not mention him after the year 1737, but recently his name has been found as "Doct'r Daniel Falknaneer" in an old store account-book of Somerset County, running from the above-mentioned year of 1745. He probably began to practice the healing art as soon as he vacated the pastoral office."

In December of 1732, the Holland Lutheran leadership sent Rev. Michael Christian Knoll, a 36-year-old native of Holstein in northern Germany, to the New World to serve the ministries Berkenmeyer and

Falckner vacated for a 12-month term or until another minister could be called.

Another minister did come in 1735, and set in motion one of the most tumultuous and upsetting times in the history of the Lutheran church in the colonies. Rev. John Augustus Wolf, of Merseburgh, Prussia, was sent to the New World to serve the Lutherans of New York and New Jersey, and was immediately a problem.

According to Honeyman, he was demanding to the point of arguing over money and housing with this new congregations. But it only got worse when he was accused by the congregation of "being too familiar with the young women."

> "This Wolf began his operations by showing himself in New York to be a frivolous character, full of pride and self-importance. He gave evidence that he had neither gifts nor experience in theological subjects, and especially in preaching. His congregations welcomed him with sincere affection, and although he read all his sermons from a manuscript, still the congregation had patience with him, because he gave out that he had lost his memory at sea. At the very beginning the magister ran after the young women and wanted to get married, and for his bad conduct in this respect he fell into discredit.

> "So two parties were arrayed in hostile strife, which however was settled by Pastor Berknmeyer and Pastor Knoll of New York. But even after this, Mr. Wolf did not properly perform his duties, and neither could nor would preach at any time without reading off his manuscript. He had married a farmer's daughter but lived with her in miserable strife, even beating her, and finally cast her off, after two children had been borne to him, bring a scandalous and infamous charge against her. Yet he was not able to produce any proof of the charge. This miserable life of his, and his unfitness for the pastoral office, awakened dissatisfaction in the congregations, so that they refused to pay him the salary that had been promised, and wished to have nothing more to do with him."

Wolf fought the charges and demanded his salary, eventually suing the congregations. They refused to pay but offered to pay his way back to Prussia, which Wolf refused.

"Finally, the subject was brought before the Supreme Court, which involved the congregations in heavy expenses. The lawyers got the best of it," wrote Honeyman.

The destructive relationship took its toll on the Lutherans of New York and New Jersey between the years of 1735 and 1745. Honeyman quoted the documented lawsuit before the magistrate:

"In short, within the last ten years there has been so much scandal, and so much harm done to souls, that even eternity itself would seem too short to answer for it. These two congregations importuned me for two years to come and help them out of their troubles. They shed many tears on account of their children, who, they said, despised religious instruction, because everything was in such a miserable condition."

In these years, Sarah and William Bull had five of their 12 children. This fractured state of the church would certainly explain why the baptism records of the German Lutheran journal are so cryptic and the children's records can't be found. As mentioned earlier, we found that Trinity Lutheran Church was destroyed in the famous fire before the American Revolution that burned most of the city. Also noted earlier was that some of the records, including the journal began by Rev. Justus Falckner in 1703, were saved by a fast-acting Lutheran. It is certainly plausible that Wolf didn't keep complete records, or had records burned in the fire, or had not even baptized all the Lutherans in his flock.

In fact, we believe it is possible, if not probable, that Daniel Falckner continued to conduct ministry services. He was loved by his congregants and advocated for them during the Rev. Wolf years with letters to Holland. It is very plausible that he baptised Sarah and William's other children and the records were not incorporated in the church book maintained by Berkenmeyer, Knoll and Wolf.

We have not yet found a complete set of records by Daniel Falckner, nor are we optimistic that we will, for two reasons. First, if Daniel was baptising children in the years after he stepped down, he was doing it without the approval of the church leadership. They were trying to get control of the Lutherans of the Middle Colonies. No matter how much they struggled with Wolf, they wanted just one minister acting on a behalf of any congregation. Second, Daniel's last years were spent in a home that was eventually overtaken by wilderness. Whatever he stored there, including records, might have been consumed by nature as well.

However, we hope that there are records of the rest of the baptisms of Sarah and William's children, and we will continue to search.

VIRGINIA BULL MEATH COLLECTION. PHEBE AND WILLIAM BULL V. THEY
WERE MARRIED AND COUSINS. WILLIAM V WAS FROM THE LINE OF
WILLIAM. PHEBE WAS FROM THE LINE OF JOHN. PHEBE GREW UP IN THE
BULL STONE HOUSE. WILLIAM, A PRINCETON GRADUATE, AND PHEBE
LIVED IN BRICK CASTLE, WHERE WILLIAM GREW UP. IT WAS BUILT BY CAPT.
WILLIAM BULL III. (THEY ARE OUR GREAT-GREAT GRANDPARENTS.)

CHAPTER 25
THE STORY OF SARAH'S PARENTS

Who were Sarah Wells' parents? Not much about her parents came
down through the generations. As stated earlier, we have bits and pieces of
family lore which have been shared more as possibilities than known facts.
According to the Blue Book historians, Margaret Bull Horton Seaman, who
was born more than 60 years after Sarah died and was Sarah's great-great-
great-granddaughter, passed down a theory about Sarah's parents.

Margaret belonged to the same Blooming Grove Congregational
Church as Sarah did years earlier. She wrote in 1920 that a story passed
down in her line from Sarah and William's daughter Margaret Bull, that
"Sarah was born on shipboard to a young English couple coming to
America, who both died during the voyage, and upon landing she was
adopted by Madam Denne of Staten Island."

We were able to debunk much of this version of Sarah's origin. First,
there is no record of the Dennes ever living on Staten Island, though many

records of the residents, including a 1706 census, exist. Since we found records of the Dennes in England in 1691, and then in Manhattan in 1701, it is plausible that the Dennes somehow escaped the head-counters of the day and were on the island during the years of Sarah's infancy, 1696-1697, but not likely. We did discover that ocean-crossing vessels did not "land" on Staten Island. There was not even a regular ferry between Manhattan and Staten Island until 1713. So that part of the story seems inaccurate.

Further, since an ocean crossing averaged about eight weeks, in order for this story to be true, Sarah would have had to be given to the Dennes in 1696, in the first weeks of her life. The Goodwill Notes discredit this possibility when Sarah tells Peter Bull that she remembered her life with her parents before she "came to live with the Dennes."

According to the Blue Book, descendant Stevenson Walsh, one of the Bull family's genealogists mentioned earlier, speculated in 1891 that Sarah was of French descent and that her father was a sea captain lost at sea. But Walsh offered no evidence and was not alive to know Sarah to have heard that first hand. although it is certainly plausible. Thousands of ships traveled the trade routes of the Atlantic Ocean every year in the 17th and 18th centuries during the time of Sarah's youth, and many were lost at sea. In fact, according to one historical account, the New Jersey coastal waters were littered with shipwrecks and considered the most dangerous stretch of seas of the day. Many of Denne's associates were involved in the shipping industry of the small city of Manhattan and the French Huguenots were common immigrants in New York.

Daniel Crommelin, William Bull's master in 1715, was a French Huguenot. But no documents have been found to support that a family with the surname Wells came to America from France, or that a Captain Wells was lost at sea during Sarah's early life. This information, if true, would have been documented. Nor have we found any baptism record of a Sarah Wells in the historic records of the French Reformed Church on Long Island, where Daniel Crommelin worshipped.

As stated earlier, the Blue Book historians trace the lines of the Wells families in Connecticut, Long Island, Massachusetts and Rhode Island, and absolutely ruled out any connection. "Of three lines we are quite sure: that Sarah was not descended from the prominent Connecticut family of Gov. Thomas Welles, nor from the Rhode Island family of Nathaniel Wells, nor from the family of William Wells of Southold, L.I." (page 56).

All those family trees are well documented and can still be studied today. We examined some of that work by following individuals from documented births to marriages to deaths. Since the overall population of the four Middle Colonies in total was small enough to fit into a football stadium of today, it is amazing how quickly the possibilities shrink when comparing that population to the known facts about Sarah. In the end, we came to the same conclusion as the Blue Book team and found no one who lined up with Sarah's timeline.

During out our year-long research, we studied dozens of churches' baptism, marriage, death and communion records that totaled thousands of names registered during the late 17th century and early 18th century. We looked throughout the Middle Colonies and at some records from New England, England, Germany and Wales. We found many Wells families and even a few women named Sarah Wells, since both names are fairly common names, but no one matched our Sarah. Nor did we find any "Wells" that would have possibly been her parents in those records.

We did find two intriguing records which our Blue Book historians also located. One they added to their publication, and the other they left only in their notes. They wrote about surveyor Philip Wells. He lived on Staten island and worked for the city of New York in the late 1600s. We did an extensive study of Philip Wells but found it was improbable that he was Sarah's father, despite the obvious coincidence of time and location; we will discuss that further in a later chapter. We also found in the Blue Book notes, which the historians left out of the publication, that in 1703, a Suzanna Wells was counted as a "head of household" in a Manhattan census and was recorded to have two children under 10 years old, one boy and one girl. That is the extent of the record, and she doesn't show up again. It is possible that Suzanna's daughter could be our Sarah, since she would have been 7 years old in 1703, but the Goodwill Notes make this implausible.

Sarah told Peter that before she lived with the Dennes (where, we discovered, was in a home on Pearl Street in Manhattan), she lived with her parents in New Jersey or maybe Staten Island. This would mean that Suzanna, who was without a husband in 1703, would have had to reside in New Jersey or Staten Island before that census and to have had a husband, in order for Sarah's account to line up.

Further, Sarah would have had to have lived there at a point in her childhood where she was old enough to have the memory to tell Peter decades later. Sarah told Peter that she remembered learning the use of a "set pole" and "oar" while living with her "parents" in New Jersey or Staten Island, where she said she was "reared." How old did she have to be to learn this in New Jersey or Staten Island and then remember it decades later in order to tell her grandson? We don't know, but it does make the possibility of Suzanna as Sarah's mother more and more improbable, since Sarah's account seems to suggest a different timeline in New Jersey or Staten Island.

We found within the hundreds of pages of notes of the Blue Book historians a letter written to them by a New York historian they asked to review the Philip Wells connection. The historian said she was certain that Philip was not Sarah's father. So, we did not uncover a possible connection

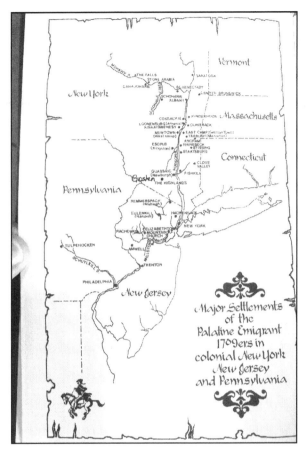

ILLUSTRATION FROM VOLUME I" BY HENRY Z. JONES, JR. PICTON PRESS
@1985 "THE PALATINE FAMILIES OF NEW YORK. A STUDY OF THE GERMAN
IMMIGRANTS WHO ARRIVED IN COLONIAL NEW YORK IN 1710.

on who Suzanna Wells' husband was, or who the father of her illegitimate
children might have been. One other piece of data doesn't line up with
Suzanna Wells as Sarah's mother: the Lutheran connection.

Since we have determined that Sarah was a practicing Lutheran by
1721, we looked for records among the early church for any mention of a
Suzanna Wells, or for that matter, any Wells family, and surprisingly, did not
find any. We didn't find Suzanna Wells in the Dutch Reformed records on
Staten Island or the French Reformed on Long Island, the closest
denominations to the Lutherans.

Additionally, neither the Dennes nor William Bull were Lutherans. They
were all documented Episcopalians. Yet we have baptism documentation
for two of Sarah's children, the first and the seventh, in the German
Lutheran church. There is strong evidence that the rest of the children were
baptized too. So how did Sarah become a Lutheran?

The most likely reason would be because she was raised Lutheran by her parents. The historians we spoke with backed up this probability. We have also learned about the minister who baptized John Bull, Sarah's first child, and know that he spent only a few days, twice a year in the Newburgh area as part of his effort to minister to Lutherans scattered up the Hudson River. In the well-recorded history of Rev. Justus Falckner, he was not scouring the countryside looking for converts. He had his hands full reaching the spread-out congregation. He would not have stumbled on the young Bull family near Goshen on his own, and somehow converted Sarah at that time to the faith.

It is much more likely that Sarah was already a Lutheran when she and William took 4-month-old John the 20 miles to Newburgh to meet up with the Lutheran pastor on his annual visit. Rev. Justus Falckner was not the only minister in Wawayanda performing baptisms, either. So, it appears that Sarah and William had a choice in who would baptize their children, and chose the Lutheran minister over William's Episcopal traveling minister, the local and nearby Presbyterian pastor, or anyone else.

Further, Sarah's second husband was Lutheran and was part of a settlement of German Lutherans in what is now Montgomery, called the Wallkill or Hanover precinct back then. In Sarah's immediate family of two

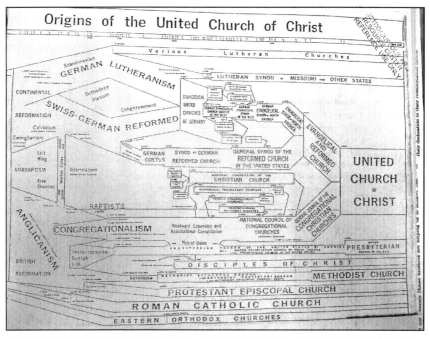

PHOTO CREDIT: EMILY BROWNELL, 2017. FROM THE COLLECTION AT THE BLOOMING GROVE CHURCH HISTORIC RECORDS. SARAH WELLS BULL WORSHIPED HERE AT THE END OF HER LIFE. THIS UNDATED DOCUMENT WAS FOUND IN THE RECORDS OF HER CHURCH THAT SHOWS THE EVOLUTION OF VARIOUS DENOMINATIONS.

PICTURE OF HISTORY MAP OF WILLIAM PENN'S DEVELOPMENTS IN PHILADELPHIA. TO THE LEFT IS THE WELSH TRACT. TO THE RIGHT IS GERMANTOWN.

husbands and 12 children, we found more records of practicing Lutherans than any other denomination.

This explanation of how Sarah became Lutheran makes Suzanna Wells even more improbable as her mother. Suzanna didn't show up in any Lutheran records. The name Wells in the early colonies of just a few thousand people was more commonly found in the Quaker records, the Puritan history, and the records of the Church of England. However, the name link is still very interesting, and one we have not ruled out.

Another speculation about Sarah's origin was offered by the aforementioned Prof. Richard Bull. We found in the notes used by the Blue Book historians, and printed in their publication, that Prof. Bull "in 1841 claimed her to be of German or Welsh descent."

We decided to dig into his assumption a bit deeper, because we couldn't understand how Richard would have narrowed to just those two, seemingly unconnected, nationalities. The people from those countries spoke different languages and were not connected by land. What did they have in common? As it turns out, the only Welsh settlement at that time in Sarah's young life was outside Philadelphia, very close to Germantown, and both communities were part of William Penn's ongoing boat lift of immigrants brought to the New World in the late 1600s. The Welsh were mostly Quakers and spoke no English. The map shows the location of the Welsh tract on the left and the Germantown settlement on the right. The German tract was populated by a people whose first language was not English.

We found Prof. Bull's notation to be the most promising of all the theories, especially since he knew ancestors who actually knew Sarah, including Peter Bull. We have one other discovery that supports Professor Bull's claim, one that never would have been available to him. DNA studies of dozens of Bull descendents have found a percentage of the French and German heritage, including my own. According to my report from 23andme, a DNA testing company, I have enough French/German DNA to support having a grandmother eight generations ago from that region. I have even more English/Irish/Welsh DNA.

CHAPTER 26
WHAT'S IN THE GOODWILL NOTES

When Peter wrote the Goodwill Notes as part of his plan to write a history of Orange County, it is clear that the 40-page document was not a biography of his grandmother, Sarah Wells Bull, but rather the beginning of the story about how Orange County was first settled by Europeans. He brought Sarah into the story because she was the first white woman to settle Goshen and the start of a flood of European developers who created his county.

We assume it brought him a sense of pride that his grandmother was part of that effort at such a young age. If Peter Bull was writing a biography of Sarah Wells Bull, then maybe he would have written on the parchment Sarah's parents' names, where she was born and the details of her orphan status. In the 18th century, the definition of orphan was any minor child without a father to care for them. It didn't always mean both parents were dead. Peter didn't explain his use of the word in the Goodwill Notes.

The Goodwill Notes also tell us that Sarah was "bound by publik authority" to the Dennes, which was a very specific designation at that time. It meant that a person with the authority of either the New York government or a church warden acting as Sarah's guardian bound her to the Dennes by legal contract, or indenture. Sarah would not have done this herself, as was the case with William Bull. Since she was a teenager and not of age, that contract was most likely as an indentured apprentice who would learn the "trade" of housemaid in the Denne household. The Dennes would have been required to teach her reading and possibly writing as well, since that was the standard of the day for young women.

It is also most likely that Sarah was in her teens when the action of placing her with the Dennes took place. Infants, toddlers and very young children were not "bound" to a family. They were adopted and raised as family members, just like today. They would not be treated as servants. Adopted infants most often were given the adoptive family surname. The Blue Book historians pointed out that Sarah and William did not name any of their 12 children after either Denne, which further suggests the type of relationship she had with the couple: one of employee-employer.

The information in the Notes strongly suggests that Sarah was under contract with Christopher Denne to learn how to be a housemaid for a specific period of time, likely until she was 21 years old. She was most likely placed with the Dennes after her father or both her parents either died or left the city and otherwise no longer spoke for Sarah, so the "publik authority" stepped in to do so.

The Goodwill Notes also tell us that Sarah knew her parents and remembered that she was "reared in New Jersey or Staten Island." Of course, this further proves by Sarah's own account that she could not have been an infant when she was orphaned and that the Dennes did not take in an infant or toddler.

Peter writes that Sarah referred to herself as an "orphan" and "barely a woman" and a "child" at the time of her Goshen expedition. Though Peter does tell us Sarah's age when she made the journey up the Hudson River, he later writes in another document, the first genealogical document he wrote when she died, that she was born April 6, 1694. Eager wrote that she was 16 years old when she led the expedition, though he didn't explain how he knew this. As of yet, no one has found a birth record of Sarah Wells. It is important to note that at that time, birth was generally recorded by the minister of the family's church. In 1694 there were several denominations of people practicing in the Middle Colonies. Everyone who was not a member of the Church of England was considered by the Crown "dissenters." Quakers and Puritans were common sects of Protestants, but

Mennonites, Lutherans and Reformers were also present in the colonies at the time.

Because so few ministers were in America in the late 1600s, parents would typically wait until a traveling minister in their denomination was near to hold the baptism and the historic records show that children might be a year or two old before a minister was available.

In the Goodwill Notes, Sarah also described to Peter that she remembered learning the use of a "set pole" and oar on the waterways of New Jersey or Staten Island. Peter was documenting why this teenage girl had the skill to ferry supplies across the Otter Kill on the second day they arrived at the campsite. This information suggests that Sarah was old enough to learn the skill with her parents. We turned to history to try to gain perspective of this and found that children were usually expected to contribute to the simplest of household tasks by the age of three, and as they got older, they were given more responsibilities.

The Goodwill Notes also show us that Sarah was more or less guessing at the location of her birth and didn't give an exact location. In 2017, Sarah Brownell and I traveled to an old cemetery in Edison, NJ, and found names of a prominent Staten Island family. Edison was then part of an Piscataway, NJ, which was one of the earliest European settlements of the 17th century. Piscataway was settled by mostly Quakers and Baptists. There are just 13 miles and the Raritan River that separate Staten Island from this part of New Jersey.

Sarah might have remembered the area of the close-knit communities, but because of her age when she left that area, couldn't pinpoint the exact location of her birth when she spoke with Peter Bull. We know by the Notes that eventually, Sarah ended up in Manhattan where she was "bound by publik authority" to the Dennes.

Another conclusion we can draw from Sarah's account in the Goodwill Notes is that she was "reared in New Jersey or Staten Island" and therefore not in Europe. It is likely that Sarah was born in America or emigrated as an infant. The journey on the ships in the 17th century were difficult and memorable. It is unlikely that a dangerous, two-month trip across of the sea would be irrelevant to Sarah or Peter's explanation of Sarah's fortitude to make a 48-hour trip from New York City to Goshen. It is much more plausible that Sarah was born to immigrant parents of the late 1600s.

The information in the Goodwill Notes given to Peter Bull by his grandmother is direct. She was raised in New Jersey or Staten Island, at a time in history when the population was very small, in the late 1600s and early 1700s. There, she lived with her parents, where she learned how to use the tools of a small boat. She eventually ended up in Manhattan, where she was contracted by a guardian to the Dennes as a housemaid. She was without a family or friends in 1712 when she had to make the decision alone to stake the land claim in Wawayanda for her master.

PHOTO CREDIT: JULIE BOYD COLE, 2017. SARAH BROWNELL DISCOVERS THE MERRELL FAMILY PLOTS IN THE HISTORIC CEMETERY IN EDISON, N.J. THE MERRELLS WERE EARLY SETTLERS OF STATEN ISLAND AND RELATED TO PHILIP WELLS, THE ONLY KNOWN PERSON ON THE ISLAND WITH THE "WELLS" SURNAME. SARAH DISCOVERED THE PLOTS WHILE WE WERE LOOKING FOR THE PETTINGER FAMILY.

She does not tell Peter Bull that her parents died, just that she was an orphan. This suggests that her father or both her parents died or left her in Manhattan. Peter also tells us that Sarah was capable of ferrying a raft across the 50-foot-wide Otter Kill because she learned to do this with her parents in New Jersey or Staten Island. This suggests that she lived there when she was old enough to learn the skill and then remember it years later.

We then turned to history to try to understand this information, which we will address in later chapters.

PHOTO CREDIT: JULIE BOYD COLE, 2017. THE WELL PUMP AT THE BULL
STONE HOUSE.

CHAPTER 27
WHAT'S IN A NAME?
PETTINGER-WELLS

In the 18th century, Europeans had all but ended the practice of last
names, or surnames, changing from generation to generation based on the
first name of the father. For example, in prior centuries John Williamson
was named for his father "William" and his son would have the last name
"Johnson." This was confusing, and record searches are still complicated
because of the remnants of this naming system. Still common throughout
Europe and the Colonies was the naming system used for first names, or
given names. It varied by nationality, but basically followed this pattern:

> First born son named for paternal grandfather;
> Second born son named for maternal grandfather;
> Third born son named for father;
> First born daughter named for maternal grandmother;
> Second born daughter named for paternal grandmother;

Third born daughter name for mother.

If there were more children, then names were selected to honor favorite siblings, aunts and uncles, or friends, especially godparents. If there there was a bad or broken relationship between the grandparents and the parents, then those names might be skipped. Sometimes parents would use a name twice in order to honor grandparents with the same name.

This naming convention led to many of Sarah and William's grandchildren being named after them, and the Bull family genealogy has dozens of Williams and Sarahs throughout the family tree. Sarah Brownell is one of those named for Sarah Wells.

If Sarah and William Bull followed the common naming pattern, then their first-born son, John, was named after William's father, but may have also been named after Sarah's father. Or William, their second son could have been named after Sarah's father. Or they could have decided not to name a child after Sarah's father. Since the next boy in their family was named Thomas, it appears that after John and William, the couple met their obligatory naming construct.

Their first-born girl was Sarah, and the next girl was named Esther, which suggests that either the grandmothers were both named Sarah or they skipped their names and went straight to naming their first daughter after her mother. We know that William's mother was Joanne, but died when William was a baby and he never knew her. At least, this is our best record according to the Blue Book historians and the records found overseas. Sarah and William eventually named a daughter Ann, which may have been a tribute to William's late mother.

Though name selection is in no way proof of motive, it does help many genealogists look for corroborating evidence. We did the same, which we will discuss in later chapters.

We found another interesting bit of information in the recorded history. According to a 19th century study of an early settler family, the name Pettinger means, in Old English, "living by a well." "Pett" or "pytt" means well in Old English, according to author F. Hinder Dale, who wrote The History of the Pittenger Family in America. We studied this and found that the word stems from the Latin word puteus, which means well or pit, according to The Development of Old English by Don Ringe and Ann Taylor.

The Pittenger/Pettinger names were introduced to the Colonies by two progenitors, one named Richard and other named Johannes or John. Richard was either from Amsterdam or Germany, and Johannes was from Germany. Richard settled in Piscataway, NJ, on the Raritan River, and Johannes settled in Germantown, PA, just north of Philadelphia and part of William Penn's settlement. It is possible the two Pettingers were related, according to the historians who have studied the families. We do know that

Johannes knew the Falckner brothers and lived near them in Germantown before he moved to Piscataway in 1700.

We found early records at the Germantown Historical Society in Philadelphia that showed the men were living and interacting in the small settlement at the same time.

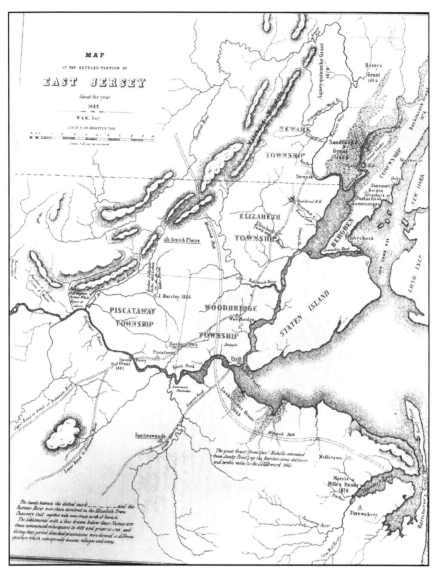

A 1682 MAP OF NEW JERSEY. PHILADELPHIA IS JUST TO THE SOUTH. ORANGE COUNTY, NEW YORK IS JUST TO THE NORTH. MANHATTAN IS TOP RIGHT.

CHAPTER 28
OUR HYPOTHESIS OF SARAH'S ORIGIN

Like many descendants of Sarah Wells Bull, we have wanted to know the answers to the mysterious questions, "Who where her parents?" "Where did she come from?" Though we have both been students of the Bull family history our entire lives, we really began to study in earnest in 2016. As an investigative journalist and non-fiction author, I thought it was high time to put my training to use and try to uncover this mystery and make my grandfather and late mother, Virginia Bull, proud.

For more than a year, we visited dozens of cemeteries, libraries, history rooms, museums and historical societies in New York, New Jersey, Pennsylvania and Washington, D.C. We spoke with dozens of people and experts in history, genealogy, psychology and handwriting analysis. We spoke with our own family historians and genealogists in order to collect as much information as we could to try and understand the data we were finding. Of course, we search the internet like crazy and spent hundreds, if not thousands, of hours studying records from the 17th, 18th and 19th centuries. We spent hours in the Bull Stone House examining records, books, photos and artifacts. And we just wandered the grounds absorbing Sarah's energy from last place she was alive on this Earth. We have had a blast, and it has been such an honor to be able to do this work. We have felt our ancestors' presences, if not their downright help in trying to unravel the mystery.

While we have not yet found the document that definitely says "Sarah Wells was from xyz and her parents were xyz," we have collected quite a lot of new information and perspectives, and when layered with what we

HOLLAND SOCIETY OF NEW YORK CITY LUTHERAN, VOL I, BOOK 85. REV. JUSTUS FALCKNER OF THE NEW YORK LUTHERAN CONGREGATION BAPTIZED FIVE CHILDREN ON APRIL 21, 1707, FROM ONE FAMILY. THE OLDEST, WAS A 10-YEAR-OLD SARAH.

already know, has helped us develop this work of documented and circumstantial information. We have also been completely amazed by the work of the volunteer and amateur sleuths who researched the Blue Book, or The History and Genealogy of the William Bull and Sarah Wells Family of Orange County, New York. We cannot say enough of how impressed we are with what those cousins accomplished in uncovering almost seven generations of descendants. The pages and pages of county and family history they gleaned without the use of the internet or cheap long-distance telephone service is incredible.

Please read this wonderful book if you haven't already. If you don't own a copy, buy one from the William Bull and Sarah Wells Stone House Association for you and your descendants. The proceeds help to fund the upkeep of the Stone House.

Upon completion of our work thus far, we do believe we know the most likely possibility of Sarah's true origin and who her parents were. We think the circumstantial evidence we have collected points to the most probable identification of Sarah Wells and pushes out other theories into more improbable possibilities. By unpacking the Goodwill Notes, who wrote them and why, we have new understanding of the story. After that undertaking, we can say that the lore passed around that Sarah was an infant orphan given to the Dennes is highly unlikely. The historical details do not support this idea either.

We have also been able to determine that it is completely improbable, as the Blue Book historians did, that Sarah was adopted by the Dennes or was anything more than a favored servant. We have also been able to debunk the story that Sarah took her children to Trinity Episcopal Church in New York City for baptism. Instead, the records show that during the years of her children's birth, she was a practicing Lutheran and at the end of her life, worshipping with the Congregationalist/Presbyterians of the Blooming Grove church. Lastly, we were able to prove that Sarah did marry Johannes Miller, her second husband, but that she also "divorced" him in 1770. This means that she most likely lived out her last 26 years at the Stone House, as family lore suggests.

We found that the German Lutheran connection was too strong to be a coincidence. We are able to prove without any doubt that at least two of her children were baptized in the German Lutheran congregation, a relatively closed congregation, and both were located in the same church record book, which had been initiated by Rev. Justus Falckner. Sarah's second husband was a German Lutheran and was the elder of the small Lutheran church in Montgomery, appearing many times in Falckner's church book. In addition to John and Mary's baptisms, Sarah's children Esther, Richard, Catherine, and Eleanor acted as sponsors to children in the Montgomery German Lutheran church, and both Esther and Richard had their children baptized there.

We dug into Falckner's church book and found many interesting entries, some which shed more light on Johannes Miller and his first wife, and in the understanding of the people of Newburgh and the pastors. Then we stumbled on one 1707 entry made by Rev. Justus Falckner that really got our attention.

Five children were baptized by Justus in New York City on April 21, 1707. They were the children of Elizabeth and John Pittenger. John, the entry stated, was not present at the mass baptism because he was out to sea and a Mr. Johan Michael Schutts stood in his place. The witnesses, or godparents, were Johan Viett and his wife, Chatarina. Viett, you might remember, was the deacon at the church in charge of helping widows, orphans, and the poor at Trinity Lutheran Church in New York City. The children's birthdates, birth locations, and names were listed, as was typical for the committed Rev. Justus Falckner to record.

The birthplaces plot a course for the Pittenger parents that began in Germantown, PA, then to Piscataway, NJ, and finally ending in Manhattan by at latest Dec. 20 of 1706, and no earlier than the spring of 1705. The eldest child, Sarah, spent her first two to three years in Germantown, then by age three was in Piscataway until between the ages 8 and 10, when her family moved to New York City. This timeline is remarkably similar to Sarah Wells' own timeline in the Goodwill Notes and places the two Sarahs at about the same age.

We then began more research to learn about the Pittenger family and found quite a bit. It turns out that Johannes Pettinger was a settler in Germantown, PA, at the same time that the Falckner brothers were there. He was a German immigrant who got into some trouble in Germantown. He was fined for fighting and for violating fence laws. We found another family of Pittengers in Piscataway, NJ, and though we could not definitively connect them to Johannes, it appears there might be a blood connection, according to the Pittenger family historians.

At the Edison cemetery mentioned earlier, we did find the graves of Elizabeth Pettinger (spelled differently than the baptism record) and her two sons, John and Philip. Both boys died young, in 1719. Elizabeth died soon after. We could not find the record of Elizabeth's husband, John, who was out to sea during the baptisms, or any further records of the girls. We did find some records in Piscataway of a John and Maria Pittenger that may be connected to the family baptized by Rev. Justus Falckner; we just couldn't find enough pieces of their puzzle to connect them for sure. That John was recorded in Piscataway in 1715. Maria was married and went on to live her life with a family.

We found nothing on the daughters, Sarah and Elizabeth Pittenger. The silent record is very interesting. The Pittenger family historians tried to track them down without any leads. They disappeared from the record, which suggests they died, got married and changed their names, or were adopted.

And so we come to our hypothesis. We believe that our Sarah Wells Bull was Sarah Pettinger, the German Lutheran who was born in Pennsylvania, moved as a toddler to New Jersey, and eventually landed in Manhattan with her mother and four siblings. Sarah Pettinger's father was a "seafaring man," out to sea when she was baptized in April of 1707 with her sisters and brothers. This lines up with our family lore that Sarah's father was a sailor of some sort. Their documented life on the waterways of New Jersey near Staten Island also lines up with the information Sarah Wells Bull gave to her grandson for the Goodwill Notes.

The Falckner brothers, or at least Daniel, knew Elizabeth Pettinger back in Germantown. Elizabeth's mother and older siblings were all Quakers there. This explains why Elizabeth's five children had not been baptized at birth, as Quakers do not believe in baptism. It is not hard to imagine that Elizabeth, alone in Manhattan with five young children, would turn to her old friends at the Lutheran Church. The godparent of the five children was listed as Johan Vietts, the Deacon in charge of the efforts for the needy, which suggests that Elizabeth and her five children were in need.

Justus and Daniel Falckner had documented reputations of converting Quakers to Lutheran and of having kind hearts. Elizabeth was not wealthy and in Manhattan with a newborn, two toddlers and two older daughters. It's not hard to imagine that she would sign Sarah and Elizabeth into indentured service, as many parents did in Manhattan. If New York had not lost the records of indentures for that time, we feel that we would have found the documents that would show Christopher Denne's contract with Sarah. However, because we do have the records leading up to 1708, we can say that Christopher Denne did not take in an indentured servant prior to that time; this leaves open the possibility that the Sarah he did take in was Sarah Pettinger.

We do know that Johan Vietts was good friends with another Lutheran, Derrick Vandenburgh, who was also a Wawayanda patent-holder, a member of the New York Common Council, and an associate of Christopher Denne. Vandenburgh was a church leader with Denne's landlord, De Bryn. Even in this small hamlet, Denne's connection to the important people in Sarah Pettinger's life is strong.

But our Sarah's last name is not Pettinger, according to the record by her grandson Peter Bull in the Goodwill Notes; we wondered if Sarah's name had been changed. Like many before us, could not find any record of a "Sarah Wells" or her mother and father in the small colonies at a time when people were well documented. Of course, we know she existed. We know by her own words that she was reared in New Jersey or Staten Island. We found an interesting letter in the notes of the Blue Book historians from a historian that asked the same questions. We asked famed genealogist Henry Jones, who has written many books on the German Palatine immigrants, if it were possible that Sarah's name could have been changed.

"Anglicization of German families did occur on occasion: 'Heisterbach' ending up as 'Oysterbanks,' 'Bergmann' into 'Hillman,' 'Bonrath' into 'Penrod,' to name a few," Jones told us. He also told us that while last names were often changed, first names were not. We found a study written by Jurgen Eichhoff of Pennsylvania State University. He wrote in 1995:

> "New names resulting from translation have only their meaning in common with the German names they replaced. Their spellings are completely different. To bring about the change, a conscious act was required, either an act of power on the part of an outside agent or agency, or an act of will on the part of the name bearer.
> "Changes imposed by outside agents seem to have taken place at the time of early German immigration. It is reported that "[w]henever William Penn could translate a German name into a corresponding English one, he did so in issuing patents for land in Pennsylvania; thus the respectable Carpenter family in Lancaster are the descendants of a Zimmermann. In many situations and at various times in American history, German immigrants or their descendants found it desirable to hide the connections to the ancestral homeland which their surnames betrayed, by having their names officially changed."

In the book Becoming German: The 1709 Palatine Migration to New York By Philip Otterness, Otterness wrote:

> "British administrators struggled to dominate a colony of diverse inhabitants from Europe and Africa while facing constant external threats to their authority from the Iroquois and the French. Entering this world in 1710, the German immigrants quickly found themselves at odds with British authorities and attempted to escape their reach by moving to the Schoharie and Mohawk river valleys of New York's backcountry. There they sought ways of living with their Indian neighbors that would ensure the viability of their new communities while feeding off further intrusion by the British."

Anglicizing Sarah's last name in order to obscure her German heritage, in a city that was completely terrified about the coming of the "thousands" of Palatine refugees, might have been done as a kindness by her godparents, the Vietts. They were experiencing discrimination because of their German heritage, according to their family history. Image-conscious Christopher

Denne might have changed her name so others would not confuse her with the dreaded refugees. Once we discovered the origin of the Pettinger name, we saw the name change as plausible. Pittenger and Pettinger were practically interchangeable. Pettinger, translated in Old English, means "a well by a meadow," and "pytt" means "well." And here we believe we have enough circumstantial information.

We will keep looking for documentation and more evidence, but at this time, we strongly believe that Sarah Wells was originally Sarah Pettinger, whose parents were Elizabeth and John Pettinger, both German immigrants. We believe that the church leaders took guardianship of Sarah and Elizabeth Pittenger and that Sarah's mother Elizabeth went back to New Jersey with her three youngest children. We believe that Sarah was bound out to Christopher and Elizabeth Denne about 1709 or 1710. We believe that Sarah's father, John, never came back into Sarah's life or died at sea. It is possible that he returned to New Jersey from his voyage, but we cannot be sure that the John Pittenger listed in the 1715 record in Piscataway is the same as Sarah's "seafaring" father. We believe that Sarah spoke English, and most likely read and wrote both German and English, based on the history of the day. We believe that young Sarah Pettinger, who was baptized at age 10 by the Rev. Justus Falckner, and sponsored by the equally kind Johan Vietts, drew some strength from her new religion and that these two men stayed with her into adulthood.

We believe that Sarah Bull did not share much about this part of her life with her grandchildren, because so little of her origin has come through the ages. Why she didn't, we can only speculate. Maybe her origin was not a big part of her life story with her offspring. By the time her great-great-grandson, Prof. Richard Bull, wrote in 1840 that Sarah was of Welsh or German descent, it appears that the family wasn't sure of her origin. We don't know if he was speaking from knowledge about a possible connection to the Pennsylvania settlement where the two nationalities converged, or was noting something he concluded on his own.

We do know that Peter Bull did not give many details in the Goodwill Notes about her origin or any explanation for why there is not. For example, Peter doesn't say that Sarah didn't know anything about her parentage; he just doesn't give many details. Is that because they didn't know or that it just wasn't important to the History of Orange County, which was the purpose of the work?

Like our intrepid ancestors, the historians of the Blue Book, we took our current investigation as far as we could, for now. We believe we have added to the history of Sarah Wells Bull, but we also hope we have inspired others to continue the search.

PHOTO CREDIT: SARAH BROWNELL, 2017. HISTORIC GERMANTOWN, IN PHILADELPHIA. THIS TOWN WAS SETTLED IN THE LATE 1600S BY MOSTLY GERMAN SETTLERS BROUGHT TO AMERICA BY WILLIAM PENN.

CHAPTER 29
SARAH SHOEMAKER &
ELIZABETH PETTINGER

In 1685, two decades before young Sarah Wells found herself on the bank of the Otter Kill, Sarah Shoemaker, a German Mennonite from the Rhine River Valley, held fast to the railing of the massive sailing ship called The Jeffries and watched as the body of her beloved husband slipped into the frigid waters of the Atlantic.

Her youngest daughter, Elizabeth, was just 11 years old. Sarah's children did not contract the dysentery that ultimately killed her husband, George.

Sarah and George had hoped to create a better and free life for their large family in the New World settlement of Quaker William Penn. They most likely had heard him speak of his vision and promise their fellow Palatinate citizens of a place where they would be left to worship in the manner they believed, and would receive land they of their own. Though they were both raised as Mennonites, they aligned easily with those of the Quaker faith. Both faiths held similar beliefs of pacifism and freedom.

The Rhine River wound through the Palatinate and separated the cities and states of present day Germany and the kingdom of France. It flowed from the Swiss Alps through Rhineland to the North Sea in the Netherlands. The once-fertile land was sought by kings and queens for centuries, but in the 17th century, it had been stripped of its timber, carved up by warring factions and laid bare by freezing winters. George, and his extended Mennonite and Quaker family, felt they had no choice but to leave

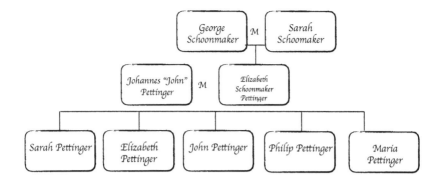

their homeland. They had all survived years of constant and brutal attacks from the French monarchs and individual punishments by Catholic rulers. Shoemaker did not accepted Penn's offer the first time he heard it, but his cousins did. Just three years earlier, he watched them leave for America. They never came back. In fact, for nearly 20 years, Lutherans, Reformers, Mennonites and Quakers from Germany had trickled across the Atlantic seeking freedom and opportunity.

When George heard that Penn was making the offer again, and after the unprecedented harsh winter the year before, George knew they had to go.

George's brothers and cousins were already in Pennsylvania and would help the widow Sarah Shoemaker and her children get established in the new settlement they called Germanopolis, or Germantown. The "Jeffries" arrived on the coast of North America just after the new year in 1686. It was cold, but not as cold as the last winter in Dollendorf, where the Shoemakers were from. The sailing ship didn't carry many passengers for Penn's settlement. It had been one of the last of the 22 vessels with passengers answering his call to come to his new colony.

As it sailed up the Delaware River toward Philadelphia, the passengers were filled with both hope and fear.

When Sarah and her children arrived in Germantown, it was already a successful settlement. The German immigrants were known to be hard-working and peaceful people, pacifists by the theology of the Mennonite and Quaker faiths. By 1689, the settlers of farmers, tradesmen and artisans quickly built many stone houses, small farms and a linen-weaving factory that generated a good deal of business for the town's inhabitants. Other German immigrants and New World settlers wanted to come to the successful settlement.

> "I went through and endured great difficulties, unaccustomed hardships and troubles before I got as far as I am now, but now I am above many, in good shape, and do not consider that I have less of my own than when I left Holland," wrote settler

Shoemaker Family of Cheltenham

First Generation

GEORGE[1] and SARAH SHOEMAKER were married in Heidelberg, Germany, in 1662.* Sarah, widow of George, arrived in Philadelphia 1 mo. 20, 1686, as stated on page 9. Soon after landing she purchased two hundred acres of land in Cheltenham township, located and measured as follows. Extract from deed dated 11 mo. 29, 1686, Philadelphia Recorder's office, Deed Book E, 1, vol. v. p. 515: "For and in consideration of the sum of twenty pounds, lawful silver money of the said Province, paid by the said Sarah Shoemaker, of the said county and Province, widdow, to the said Patrick Robinson. He the said Patrick Robinson, hath given, granted, sold and confirmed to the said Sarah Shoemaker etc. etc. a certain piece of land in the said county, and in a certain tract of land, called Cheltenham Parish. Beginning at a stake near an oak saplin, thence four hundred and eighty Perches south west to a stake by a small black oak marked for a corner, thence sixty six and three quarter perches north west, to a stake upon a hill, near a swamp for another corner, thence four hundred and eighty Perches north east to a stake, about four perches to the northward of a large Poplar tree marked for a corner and thence sixty six and three quarter perches south east to the first mentioned place, containing Two Hundred acres of land bounded on the north east with the lands of Pennapecca Township—on the south west with vacant lands, and on the north west side with William Frampton's lands—and on the south east with the lands of Richard Wall." This land extended entirely across the township from Abington, called in the deed "Pennapecca," on the north, to Bristol township line on the south. More recent surveys show that the actual distance southwest and northeast is five hundred and thirty-six perches, and not four hundred and eighty perches, as named in the original survey. Sarah Shoemaker continued in possession of the land until 1708, when she conveyed one hundred and sixty acres to her son George. Extract from deed (Deed Book E, 5, vol. vii. p. 117, Philadelphia Recorder's office): "This indenture made the twenty eighth of the seventh month, in the seventh year of the reign of our Sovereign, Lady Ann, Queen of Great Britain, and in the year of our

* Richardson L. Wright, family records.

19

PHOTO CREDIT: SARAH BROWNELL, 2017. PAGE 19 OF THE RICHARDSON L. WRIGHT FAMILY RECORDS IN THE HISTORIC SOCIETY OF PENNSYLVANIA.

Daniel Pastorius to his friends in Germany. Pastorius was one of the leaders of Germantown, and was responsible for many of the early actions that helped the settlement become a success. "In all respects, I am very well-to-do. I have here a shop of many kinds of goods and edibles; sometimes I ride out with merchandise and sometimes bring something back, mostly from the Indians, and deal with them in many things. I have no servants except one negro whom I bought. I have no rent or tax or excise to pay. I have a cow which gives plenty of milk, a horse to ride around, my pigs increase rapidly, so that in

191

PHOTO CREDIT: JULIE BOYD COLE, 2017. RECORDS AT THE HISTORIC
SOCIETY OF PENNSYLVANIA.

the summer I had seventeen when at first I had only two. I
have many chickens and geese, and a garden and shall next year
have an orchard if I remain well; so that my wife and I are in
good spirits and are reaching a condition of ease and
prosperity in which we have great hopes. But when we first
came it was pretty hard in many respects.

"The market is supplied with fresh mutton and beef at a
reasonable price, in a way that I would have not thought could
have occurred in so short a time. Sometimes there is a good
supply of partridges for half a stuiver a piece, pigeons, ducks
and teals, and fish in great quantities in their seasons. There are
not many roads yet made in order to receive from and bring to
market, but these things are now beginning to get into order.
In a few years, if it continues in the same way, everything here
will be more plentiful than in other lands. The commerce and
trade are close at the door, to the Barbados, Bermudas and
other West Indian Islands that will bring this country into a
good condition. Time will best show this to be the case.
Nevertheless, I do not advise anyone to come here."

Sarah Shoemaker and her children lived among the settlers and were
awarded more than 200 acres to farm; slowly she fulfilled her dead
husband's quest. One by one, her children grew and married. Sarah joined
the newly formed Plymouth Meeting House of the Society of Friends –
Quakers – where she was eventually buried in 1694. She had less than a
decade in the New World, but in that time she created a productive life for
herself and her children. George may not have lived to see America, but his
dreams were fulfilled, thanks to Sarah.

PHOTO CREDIT: SARAH BROWNELL, 2017. PAGE 20 OF THE RICHARDSON L. WRIGHT FAMILY RECORDS IN THE HISTORIC SOCIETY OF PENNSYLVANIA.

One of Sarah's youngest children was Elizabeth. She was just 20 when her mother died. We believe that she met and married Johannes Pittenger in Germantown. The two were both residents of the tiny settlement, and we know by the baptism record referenced earlier that Elizabeth and John Pittenger lived in Germantown in 1697. It appears that Elizabeth and Johannes Pittenger were part of the Quaker or Mennonite group in Germantown, because the children had not been baptized until 1707. Neither denomination believes in infant baptism, while the Lutherans believe infant baptism was essential.

We looked at all the "Elizabeths" in Germantown at that time, and only Elizabeth Shoemaker was not attached to another family record. Using the process of elimination in the tiny settlement, we believe Elizabeth Pittenger

PHOTO CREDIT: JULIE BOYD COLE, 2017. GERMANTOWN NEIGHBORHOOD IN PHILADELPHIA, PA.

was Sarah Shoemaker's daughter. We knew that Johannes Pettinger arrived in the settlement alone, and left married to Elizabeth.

We also know that Elizabeth Shoemaker, Johannes Pettinger, and Daniel Falckner were all in Germantown together for several years. Elizabeth and Johannes also most likely met Justus Falckner in the small town, as they may have overlapped in Germantown by several months.

We believe that Elizabeth Pettinger was one of the people the Falckner brothers were trying to convert, as historical accounts report they were trying to do in general, and that they succeeded – hence the baptism of Elizabeth's five children in New York City years later by Rev. Justus Falckner.

PHOTO CREDIT: JULIE BOYD COLE, 2017. PART OF LETTER WRITTEN BY NEW YORK GENEALOGICAL RESEARCHER HARRIET STRYKER-RODDA, DATED OCT. 3, 1966, TO THE BLUE BOOK RESEARCH TEAM. HER FOUR-PAGE LETTER IS IN THE BULL STONE HOUSE COLLECTION. WE CAME TO THE SAME CONCLUSION AFTER OUR RESEARCH. MORE OF THIS LETTER IS ON THE NEXT PAGE.

CHAPTER 30
PHILIP WELLS

Philip Wells of Staten Island arrived in America in 1675, or a few years later, with his sister's family. She was Susanna Sarah Wells Merrill, an early settler of Staten Island, and the wife of Richard Merrill. The Merrills became a prominent family of Staten Island, and their descendants are still counted today and have a well-researched family tree. Some of the Merrills are buried in one of the oldest cemeteries in the country, in Edison, NJ, about 10 miles from Staten Island, just over the Arthur Kill that separates the two states.

Susanna was a generation older than Sarah Wells Bull and had many children; all the births were recorded. She, her husband, and her brother were from England, and there is record of their births, marriage, and the births of some of their children there.

The New York record shows Philip Wells worked for the city as a land surveyor, but left the area soon after he was involved in a controversy about a survey he conducted on Staten Island, where he owned land. The record of Philip Wells' work in New York goes silent in 1689. The next record found is the last: his will. Philip Wells recorded his will in Virginia, near Jamestown, and it was proven in December of 1694. He left his estate, including his land on Staten Island, to Susanna on Staten Island, and left her his wedding ring. He makes no mention of a wife or a daughter. If he was Sarah Wells Bull's father, there is no record to explain it. The timing of his death and where he died makes it difficult to line up with Sarah's birthdate and life, though it's not impossible. The Blue Book researchers found the connection improbable. They wrote:

> "It is hard to believe that a wealthy public official's daughter could become an indentured servant and forget to tell her children of her important father or fail to name a son after him."

This we know: the only persons recorded with the last name of "Wells" on Staten Island in the time of Sarah's birth were Philip Wells and his sister, the married Susanna Wells Merrill. The Staten Island Wells family only works as a possible option if we assume that this established, large family had for some unknown reason decided to give up Sarah.

Eliminating Philip Wells then eliminates the last of the known Wells families in the greater New York City area in that time period. There is no record of a Mr. and Mrs. Wells living anywhere then that lines up with an orphan daughter born at the same time as Sarah Wells Bull, despite thousands of historic records reviewed. There are also no records of a traveling minister and wife drowning in the harbor; no record of Christopher and Elizabeth Denne living on Staten Island; no record of them adopting Sarah; no record of Sarah Wells' birth in America or in England. And no records have been found of her and her parents crossing the ocean, despite exhaustive searches through old church records, city and state records, passenger ship records, baptism records and family trees.

Sarah Wells and her mother and father left not one record behind in the Middle Colonies, which only had a population of about 55,000 people. The Bull Family historians, genealogists and sleuths have found dozens of records on everyone else in Sarah's life, including William Bull's baptism record, Christopher and Elizabeth's marriage record, and both of their wills. There are Census records of the area going back to the late 17th and early 18th centuries and volumes of church records. But not only is there nothing on Sarah Wells, there is nothing found on her father and mother. It's been a long-standing mystery for generations of descendants.

HARRIET STRYKER-RODDA
GENEALOGICAL RESEARCH
12 GARDEN PLACE
BROOKLYN, NEW YORK 11201

3 October 1966

Dear Mr. Seaman:

Time runs away so fast when one is working on a problem as
challenging as your Sarah Wells Bull! I am even more fascinated
by it now, after this first period of looking, because it has so
many facets, but only one accurate conclusion. I did more than
the usual five hours of work on the preliminary part of the
search, but I am glad to pass on to you the negative findings
at no cost. It was a pleasure, although frustrating.

I started by reading Eager's account in all its quaint and awful
Victorianism, since that seemed the natural place to start.
In it, you will remember, she is described as "a little orphan
in New Jersey," opposite Staten Island" whom they— who lived with them from her

On the supposition that Philip Wells, surveyor, _might_ have been
the father of Sarah Wells Bull it is going to be necessary to
find out where he went when he left the Province and apparently
died. There is a tradition on Staten Island that there were a
number of Andros' entourage who left there to go to Barbadoes
and Virginia. This was brought to my attention by Loring McMillan,
Director of the Staten Island Historical Society, but he could
not cite a reference on it. If the story of the exodus is true,

ment hypothesis. (or another Wells' wife), but it could ... is no ... proof that she might turn up later

-4-

So here we are right back where we started from: Who _was_
Sarah's father?

It is possible he was a recently migrated Wells of whom no
record remains. It may be that she was truly born in N.J.,
but down in the Cape May –Gloucester area where so many Wells
settled during the migration from Conn. and L.I. I have not
had time to go into this part of the area. It is also
possible that the story told about his grandmother by Sarah's
grandson may have been in error——— memory is a very peculiar
thing when it comes to family names. Therefore it is possible
that her name was not Sarah _Wells_ at all – it might have
been Wills, or Willis, or some other mutation of a name which
when pronounced could easily be mistaken for Wells. There
are so many interesting possibilities...

Thank you for the opportunity to help you on this problem. It
has been most enjoyable, and I regret as much as you do the
fact that in this short time more could not have been found.
However, this will give you a few more negative notes to add
to those you already have, thus clearing away a lot more dead
wood, I hope.

Sincerely,

Harriet Stryker-Rodda

Mrs. K. Stryker-Rodda, C.G.

CHAPTER 31
BIT PLAYERS

The Wawayanda Patent Holders:

Benjamin Aske, a merchant, became a Freeman in 1695 and was sued for having an illegitimate child with an unmarried woman.

Hendrick Teneych, was also known as Nicholas, became a Freeman in 1701 and voted in the New York city elections in 1701 in the West Ward.

Derrick Vanderburgh, also voted in the West Ward in 1701; was a bricklayer and became a Freeman in 1698.

John Cholwell, was a merchant, voted in the West Ward in 1701 and became a Freeman in 1701.

Daniel Honan, was the provincial secretary to the governor and a Freeman in 1695.

Phillip Rookeby, was a surgeon in the militia, according to the Blue Book, but I couldn't find him in any records in New York.

John Merritt, was a major in the militia, a Freeman in 1698, and was appointed justice of Orange County in 1702.

Peter Matthews, was a gentleman and former officer in the militia; became a Freeman in 1695.

Lancaster Symes, was known for having a bad temper. He was a Freeman in 1701, Denne's business partner on the dock, a militia officer and merchant, the Ranger of Orange County. Queen Anne awarded Symes all the Crown's land on Staten Island in 1708. Lancaster also bought a lot on Dock Street in New York from Benjamin Aske.

I could not find **Cornelius Christian**, but the Blue Book says he was listed as a "New Jersey Yeoman." He sold his patent share in 1704. He may have been a Van Horn but used the Dutch naming convention. He could have been John and Gerritt Van Horn's brother or father.

Dr. John Bridges, who died in 1704.

Men and women who bought shares from the original holders:

Daniel Crommelin, voted in the 1701 East Ward election and bought Rookery's, Henrick's and Merritt's shares. (See earlier chapter.)

Adrian Hooghlandt, who was Constable of the East Ward of New York in 1698, bought Cholwell's shares and later, more. He was killed by his slave in 1712. His wife, Anna, kept his shares when he died.

Col. William Merritt, John's father, bought Honan's shares in 1705.

John Van Horn, was the Constable of the Dock Ward of NY in 1697 and bought widow Anne Bridge's shares after John's death.

Anthony Rutgerts, was a Freeman in 1699, bought Col Merritt's shares when he died in 1708.

Some of the other people that are associated with Christopher Denne (Denne also served as an assistant alderman for the New York Common Council for several years until he moved to Orange County):

William Bradford, was New York's only publisher and was a witness to Denne's will. His son, William Bradford Jr., was a benefactor in Elizabeth Denne's will.

Rip Van Dam, was a South Ward Common Council assemblyman and involved in many decisions in New York;

Robert Livingston, of Livingston Manor, was a Hudson River developer well-connected to then-New York Gov. Robert Hunter.

There are thousands of pages of documents to study that note these people. Sometimes their names are spelled incorrectly, but connections can be made fairly easily based on time frames, process of elimination, and even corrected spelling later in the same document. Names that start with "Van" sometimes include a space and sometimes don't. For example: Van Horn, Vanhorn, VanHorne, and so on.

Since the population was small, it was common that every entry of a surname on the Census (which the local government took often to fulfill the Crown's directive) was all from one family.

CHAPTER 32
THE PALATINES REFUGEES

In 1708, a small group of religious refugees, called Palatines, from the Rhine River area of France/Germany were rescued by Rev. Kocherthal, a Lutheran pastor who was on a mission to help those in a desperate situation in that region. Louis XIV was brutalizing Protestants in his realm and along the Rhine River on the border of Germany. Queen Anne and her political partners favored helping any Protestant. She agreed to pay for the fare and one year's worth of expenses to help this group of refugees get to America. They came to the Hudson River and successfully settled Newburgh.

Rev. Kocherthal decided to go back to the region and rescue more of the wandering and terrorized refugees. When he arrived in the Rhine region, more than 3,000 refugees had amassed, and had heard about the Queen's offer. They wanted to go to the "Land of Milk and Honey" as England advertised. Kocherthal led the refugees to Rotterdam and then to London, to the surprise and panic of the Queen. The British did not expect to see such a mass arrival, and were immediately overwhelmed. Queen Anne could not offer the same deal as she had the year before to this massive onslaught because of the expense, so they negotiated a deal with then-New York Gov. Robert Hunter. Hunter and Robert Livingston, who was working to develop the Hudson River and owned thousands of acres, believed the refugees would be an excellent source of labor to begin production of pine tar, used to build Naval ships. They both were concerned about the growing pressure of the French, coming from the north. The refugees from Germany could populate the area as Englishman and secure the land, they thought.

Livingston ultimately offered to sell to New York some of his land that could be used for encampments for the refugees. Hunter agreed to front the money for the settlement. They offered each Palatine family 40 acres each in New York to all who finished their servitude as laborers in what they hoped would become a thriving and successful settlement, where they would manufacture tar from the pine trees. Queen Anne and the Palatines agreed.

Ten ships were commissioned to carry the 3,000 refugees to America in 1709, and left London for what was suppose to be a seven-week trip. However, unlike the first ship of Palatines who settled Newburgh, this expedition was much larger and less resourced for the journey.

There was immediate disaster when the ship, Berkeley Castle, had trouble and returned to port for repairs. Another ship sank before leaving sight of land, and all on board perished.

The rest of the ships also had challenges on the crossing. The weather was stormy. They didn't have enough food for the many on board. Sickness and scurvy ran rampant. In all, more than 400 men, women, and children died during the crossing, and their bodies were tossed overboard.

It took much longer than expected to reach the New World and when they finally made their way into New York Harbor in the summer of 1710, three of the original 10 boats were missing. The Herbert, the ship carrying all their equipment for their new settlements, sank off the coast of Long Island. The citizens of New York, who numbered less than 5,000, were panicked by the number of people on board the ship, assumed they were all infected with disease and protested their deboarding. Hunter, in a hasty move, decided to set up a temporary camp on Nutter's Island (now Governor's Island) for the Palatines, and held them aboard until the settlement could be constructed.

With so many deaths during the journey, there were now dozens of children who were suddenly orphans. Hunter and Livingston came up with a plan to deal with the population of children, as well. At this time in the history of New York, there were no organized orphanages, but there were government procedures to take care of widows and orphans. Mostly, they found families to take them in, since they would otherwise have no way of supporting themselves. Hunter passed an act called the Palatine Children Apprentice act of 1710-1714 that allowed citizens to take in these children as apprentices to be tradesman and housemaids.

Advertisements were placed in the city that anyone could volunteer to take in the children, following a few rules, and the children would be "bound to them" for a number of years: girls until the age of 15, and boys until the age of 17.

And since many couples lost their spouses on the journey, children in those families, many whose mothers were still alive, would also be placed in the program:

> "The New York Common Council: e4 ORDER FOR APPRENTICING THE PALATINE CHILDREN Council 20 June 1710 There haveing beene severall Proposalls made for the takeing many of the Palatine Children for a Terme of Yeares and there being many Orphans who are unable to take care of themselves to work and many who by sickness are Rendered uncapable of doeing any service for some time and in that Condition would be a great expence and there being noe Prospect of Settleing them this siuner by reason its soe much advanced His Excellency does appoint Doctor Staats and Mr Van Dam or either of them to take such Proposalls for Placeing out the Orphans and other Children whose Parents have a numerous ffamily Entring into an Instrument in

Writeing to Cloath Victuall and use them well and to deliver them to the Government when called for It is ordered that an Advertisement be printed Signifying that his Excellency is willing to Dispose of Such Orphans and other children as aforesaid and directing all Persons wao are willing to take any to apply themselves to Doctor Staats or Mr Van Dam or either of them The abore order was amended on 27 July directing that the Boys be bound until the age of 7 and the girls till they reach 15 years For a list of the Children apprenticed under this order."

There were 73 children reported in the program; 43 were true orphans by the time they reached the New World, and 30 had a surviving parent. Of the 73, 41 children were placed in the homes of New Yorkers to learn a trade and be "bound" to their benefactors until they came of age.

All told, of the 41 children apprenticed by Gov.Hunter and bound to a home in New York City, half were documented associates of Christopher and Elizabeth Denne. Dr. Bridges (most likely one of our patent holders) is listed in the letter by Gov. Hunter, as helping him find settlement sights on the Hudson. Dr. Staats and Mr. Van Dam, both known associates of Denne, are listed as the two to find families for the children. Staats became a patent holder of the Wawayanda.

CHAPTER 33
OUR FINAL THOUGHTS ABOUT SARAH'S ORIGIN

It is hard to put down on this blank sheet of paper a final conclusion about Sarah Wells Bull after the 60,000 words that precede this page. We have learned so much more in the last year than we ever knew about our grandmother nine generations removed and that we ever thought we would find out when we started down the path. We went searching for some overlooked piece of data that explained where Sarah Wells came from before she lived with the English couple in New York. We didn't find it. Instead, we found so much more. We found Sarah's voice, thanks to Peter Bull and his Goodwill Notes, thanks to Jesse Booth who put pen to paper in 1796, thanks to so many historians and librarians who store seemingly insignificant documents to collect dust.

Because so many people have recorded, kept, and passed on information in written form, we got to know our ancestor in a new way. The word "amazing" doesn't seem large enough to encompass our opinion about Sarah Wells Bull after this study of her life. Sarah overcame so much in her long life, no matter who her parents were or where she belonged. Maybe, because of where she came from, she was able to meet and overcome life's challenges. She was the first European settler in a wilderness, and thrived.

We have tried to imagine what it must have been like to go from living in a Manhattan townhouse into a hut within one week; maybe only a teenager would be so willing; maybe only a young woman who needed to find a way to get out from under the adults in her life who had let her down. We only know what she said to her grandson Peter; that she was filled with fear, but also hope. It's a sentiment we can all relate to. When hope is lost, life truly does lose its charm, as Sarah said. Thankfully for us and the other 76,000 descendants of this woman, she never lost her faith or gave up. She continued on to the age of 100 and 15 days.

As for her parentage, we do believe that after studying all of this data and so much more we couldn't include in this publication, that Sarah Wells was Sarah Pettinger, daughter of German immigrants Elizabeth Shoemaker and John Pettinger. We believe that Sarah's name was changed by one or all of the three men who were in her life between 1707 and 1712: Rev. Justus Falckner, Johan Viets, and Christopher Denne. These men were instrumental, we believe, in her early life. We believe that Daniel Falckner also played an important role in Sarah's life.

Three of these four men were Germans and knew firsthand the

consequences of prejudice. Viets and the Falckners were known to be kind men who cared deeply about people. We know that Sarah Bull knew Justus Falckner and that alone brings us happiness. After reading so much negative information about Christopher Denne, it was good to know that our beloved Sarah had a man like Justus in her early life in the wilderness.

Here is how we think the narrative went:

John Pettinger left his wife and five young children in Manhattan sometime around 1706 to work on a ship. Elizabeth had a newborn, Maria, and four other children. Sarah, her eldest, was just nine years old when her father went to sea and, most likely, never came back into her life. Elizabeth relied on help from her old friend from Germantown, Daniel Falckner, and his brother, Justus. The brothers were most likely relieved when Elizabeth finally agreed to have her children baptized.

We think she agreed to go against her religious denomination and opt for the baptisms because she wanted her children to be protected by the Lutheran church, both literally and figuratively. As baptized children, their future and eternity would no longer be in jeopardy despite the current hardship. Elizabeth, maybe with the encouragement of the Falckners, decided to move back to Piscataway, where there were Pettinger cousins and support for the now-single mother. Both of Elizabeth's parents were dead and her siblings were now married and involved in the Germantown bureaucracy, where the Falckners were not wanted. She didn't have much support.

We believe that she left behind Sarah and most likely her daughter Elizabeth in indentured service. We don't know what happened to the younger Elizabeth. She might have gotten married or died a servant in Manhattan. But the older Elizabeth lived for more than a decade in New Jersey. She buried two sons there. John was married and age 20 when he died. Philip was just 16. We don't know what happened to Maria, but we suspect she got married. In the meantime, back in Manhattan, Sarah was "bound" by Johan Viets, the orphan master of the Lutheran church, to the Dennes sometime between 1707 and 1710. Viets left Manhattan in 1710, so we believe that he might have arranged for Sarah to work for the Dennes just before he left.

We think that Sarah Pettinger became Sarah Wells because Wells is an English version of the name Pettinger, and the men worried that her German name would cause her or the Dennes some sort of trouble at a time of hysteria in the city about the arriving Palatine refugees.

If our theory is correct, then this is the only missing element of Sarah's origin. We have historic records on all of these people and the whereabouts during Sarah's early life. We even have much of their motivations documented.

However, without the indentured service document, or something similar, we cannot make the connection directly. Only our circumstantial evidence, overlapped with the documented evidence, gives us the basis for our conclusion.

We turned to a problem-solving theory to help us with this problem:

"Occam's razor is a problem-solving principle attributed to William of Ockham (c. 1287–1347), who was an English Franciscan friar, scholastic philosopher, and theologian. His principle states that among competing hypotheses, the one with the fewest assumptions should be selected." (Wikipedia)

We have examined the basic theories that are out there and applied this theory.

But let's first look at what we know:
1. Sarah Wells knew her parents because she told Peter Bull that she did;
2. Sarah Wells was raised in the Middle Colonies, likely New Jersey or Staten Island, because she told Peter Bull this;
3. Sarah Wells had two of her children, number 1 and 7, baptized by the German Lutheran church;
4. Sarah Wells married a German Lutheran, who lived in a close community of Germans;
5. Sarah Wells was not the same religion as William Bull and Christopher Denne;
6. The only Lutheran church in Orange County was experiencing dramatic upheaval during the years of between the births of Sarah's children after 1723 that created holes in the records;
7. There were Episcopal, Presbyterian, and Reformed ministers available to conduct baptisms during the birth years of Sarah's children, yet they were not among those records;
8. Rev. Justus Falckner arrived in the Colonies in 1700 in Germantown, PA, then moved to Manhattan in 1703;
9. Rev. Justus Falckner baptized Sarah Pettinger, and Sarah Wells' son, John;
10. Rev. Justus Falckner's brother, Daniel Falckner, said he picked up the scattered congregations in Newburgh and Montgomery after his brother died;
11. Daniel Falckner knew Elizabeth and John Pettinger in

Germantown and likely in Piscataway;

12. Daniel Falckner was in trouble for a while with the Lutheran leadership and was more or less shunned for ministering to people against the leadership's wishes;

13. Daniel Falckner and his brother were known for trying to convert Quakers and others to the Lutheran faith.

Let's now look at the two basic theories:

1. Sarah Wells was orphaned after her parents, Mr. And Mrs. Wells, died and she was given to the Dennes;

2. Sarah Wells was Elizabeth and John Pettinger's daughter, and was given to the Dennes after her mother went back to New Jersey and her father was believed dead at sea. Her name was translated to English in order to protect her from discrimination.

What assumptions must be made to believe either of these theories?

If the first theory is true, then we must assume that a couple named Wells came to America prior to 1696-1700, settled in New Jersey or Staten Island, where there were only a handful of small settlements, had Sarah, died, and somehow Sarah was turned over to the Manhattan city council? or a church orphan master and bound out to the Dennes.

We must also assume that this couple's names were left off the hundreds of passenger lists, which is possible; that they were left off the various city censuses collected over those years that are still available and complete; that they were more or less anonymous at a time when the settlements were so small that everyone knew everyone else; and that they were never counted in church records, though every church kept some sort of record of births, marriages and deaths.

We would have to believe that all cross-referencing attempts by historians over the years, professional and amateur, produced nothing that shows a Wells family that fits Sarah's known and documented timeline.

We would have to believe that Sarah's indenture to the Dennes was either lost or an unusual handshake deal instead of a written agreement.

We would also have to believe that the Bull family descendants didn't know who Sarah's parents were by the time her great-great-grandson, Prof. Richard Bull, first said that she was of German or Welsh descent, was because she wouldn't tell them for some reason.

What about the second theory? What assumptions must be made in order for that to be true?

Sarah Wells can only be Sarah Pettinger if:

1. Someone changed her last name;

2. Peter Bull and Jesse Booth, who wrote the first genealogy and is the

first record of Sarah's last name, didn't know that Wells was an English translation of the German Pettinger.

What is more plausible in these two assumptions:

That Sarah Wells' family disappeared completely from the record, and that somehow Sarah became a Lutheran at a time when the one Lutheran minister was traveling more than 1,500 miles to serve his congregation?

Or that a group of men decided to change Sarah's name to either spare her expected trouble, like many other Germans did, or because her master, a man running from his debts and empty promises, was worried about himself?

For us, it is much easier to believe the simplest theory with the fewest assumptions: that Sarah was Sarah Pettinger, whose name was changed by people who told her that her original name would bring her pain and trouble. Maybe she didn't talk about it much after that. But we ask those of you who have changed your last names for various reasons: how often do you talk about your original surname?

Until we find a record of someone who fits Sarah's story as written in the Goodwill Notes and the facts surrounding Sarah's life, we believe that we have found our great-great-great-great-great-great-grandmother.

CHAPTER 34
ADDITIONAL ILLUSTRATIONS

PHOTO CREDIT: JULIE BOYD COLE, 2017. THE SPOT ON THE OTTER KILL WHERE SARAH WELLS FIRST SETTLED IN ORANGE COUNTY, NY

PHOTO CREDIT: JULIE BOYD COLE, 2017. LUNCH AT THE SMITHSONIAN MUSEUM OF AMERICAN INDIANS. THIS IS AN EXAMPLE OF NORTHEASTERN WOODLAND FARE. TOP LEFT, POTATO AND PORK STEW, GRILLED SQUASH, GRILLED CORN AND CAKE. THE DRINK IS TEA. SARAH WELLS ATE A SIMILAR MEAL HER SECOND NIGHT IN WAWAYANDA.

ABOVE, PHOTO CREDIT, JULIE BOYD COLE, 2017. BULL STONE HOUSE COLLECTION. SUGAR BOWL FOUND IN THE DIRT AT THE SITE OF SARAH WELL'S FIRST CAMP AT THE OTTER KILL. BELOW, PHOTO CREDIT, SARAH BROWNELL, 2017, BULL STONE HOUSE COLLECTION. ITEMS FOUND IN THE DIRT AT THE STONE HOUSE BY THE FLAG POLE, WHERE THE FIRST BULL HOME IS BELIEVED TO HAVE BEEN BUILT BY THE COUPLE.

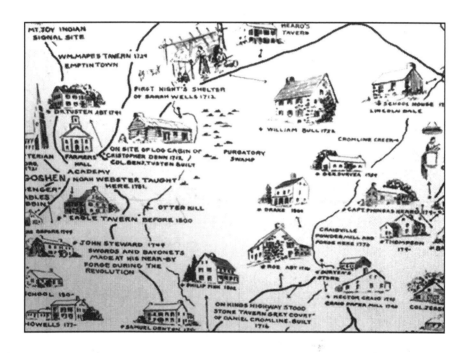

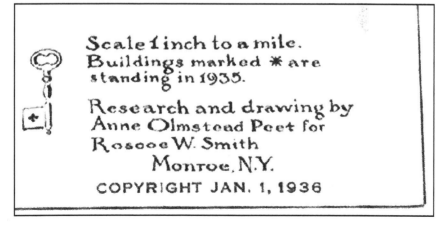

Scale 1 inch to a mile.
Buildings marked * are
standing in 1935.

Research and drawing by
Anne Olmstead Peet for
Roscoe W. Smith
Monroe, N.Y.

COPYRIGHT JAN. 1, 1936

PHOTO CREDIT: JULIE BOYD COLE, 2017. DRAWING OF THE BLOOMING GROVE CHURCH FOUND IN THE CHURCH HISTORIC DOCUMENTS.

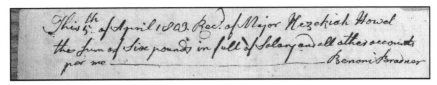

HISTORIC DOCUMENT FROM THE BLOOMING GROVE CHURCH COLLECTION. SHOWS REV. BENONI BRADNER'S SIGNATURE IN 1803.

PHOTO FROM THE VIRGINIA BULL COLLECTION. FROM LEFT, KETURAH
JANE BULL, MARGERY KNIGHT BULL, AND HENRY PIERSON BULL. THEY
ARE THE CHILDREN OF HARRY BULL AND LUCILLE LYNN PIERSON.

Henry Bull, prominent lawyer, dead at 84

By ADELINE GREEN
Editorial Assistant

MIDDLETOWN — Henry P. Bull of
Prospect Avenue, Middletown, prominent
lawyer and longtime Republican city com-
mitteeman, died Wednesday, Aug. 14, at his
home after a long illness. He was 84.

A seventh-generation member of one of
Orange County's founding families, through
the line of John Bull, Thomas Bull and William Bull, he was the son of the late Harry
Bull, former community leader and director and organizer of the Dairymen's League
Cooperative, and Lucille Pierson Bull.

He was born July 28, 1901, in one of the
Bull family homes on the Sarah Wells Trail
in Hamptonburgh and later became treasurer of the Bull Family Association, a
group that is, among other things, responsible for maintaining various family historic
sites.

A graduate of New York University Law
School, he clerked in the New York City law

1938, began practicing law in Middletown
in the office of Charles Taylor.

At the time of his death, he was a senior
partner of the law firm of Bull, Merrvale,
Jackson and Clancy.

In 1938, Mr. Bull was a non-salaried volunteer public defender. In 1952, he was
named special counsel for the City of Middletown in a restricted telephone rate
increase case against the old Orange
County Telephone Co.

He was a 60-year member of the Hamptonburgh Grange No. 850, and a longtime
member of the Excelsior Hook and Ladder
Co., where he served as president for two
terms, and as captain and trustee.

In the late 1930s and early 1940s, Mr.
Bull was one of the founders and developers
of the Wolf Lake Corp. in Sullivan County.
Wolf Lake is a spring-fed pond with a summer home community.

An active Republican, he was a longtime
member and former secretary of the Middletown Republican Committee. He was

also a former member of the board of
directors of the Middletown Chamber of
Commerce, and a member and past president and vice president of the Middletown
Bar Association.

Survivors include his wife of 54 years,
Mary E. Cocks Bull, at home, three daughters, Mary Jane Sorrenti of Middletown,
Martha B. Lounsbury of Phoenix, Ariz., and
Virginia B. Meath of Ithaca; one sister,
Margery Bull Jackson of Middletown; one
brother, H. Culver Bull of Amenia; nine
grandchildren, and two great-grandchil-
dren.

Graveside services will be held at the
convenience of the immediate family at the
Hamptonburgh Cemetery.

A memorial service will be held at 3 p.m.
Saturday at the Hamptonburgh Presbyterian Church, Campbell Hall.

Memorial contributions may be made to
the American Cancer Society and the
Hamptonburgh Presbyterian Church,
Hamptonburgh.

Henry P. Bull

*1985 TIMES HERALD RECORD. HENRY P. BULL, OUR GRANDFATHER, WAS A
GREAT LOSS TO THE FAMILY AND THE COMMUNITY.*

PHOTO CREDIT, JULIE BOYD COLE, 2017. BULL STONE HOUSE COLLECTION OF SPINNING WHEELS USED TO MAKE YARN AND THREAD AND DEVISE USED TO CLEAN FLAX.

Wolverhampton, in the County of Stafford England the *Birthplace* of *William Bull* Esqre of *Hamptonburg* Orange County N.Y. who emigrated to America A.D. 1716 — and the Ancestor of the Bull Family of Orange County ——

The Church on the left with the Square, or Campanile Tower, as seen in the distance in this engraving is the Collegiate Church of Saint Peter said to have been founded nearly nine hundred years ago. It was in this Church that *William Bull* was Baptized on the Second Day of September A.D. 1689. as the following copy of the Certified transcript from the Parish Registers show. ——

1689

"Wm, the Soun of John Bull was bap. September the 2?. —"

I Certify that the above is a true copy of the Baptismal Register of the Parish of Wolverhampton, in the County of Stafford. England — extracted this twenty second day of December in the Year of Our Lord, One thousand, eight hundred and Ninety one, by me

John Thomas Jeffcock
Rector.

[stamp]

PHOTO CREDIT, JULIE BOYD COLE, 2017. BULL STONE HOUSE COLLECTION
CERTIFICATION OF WILLIAM BULL'S BAPTISM RECORD IN ENGLAND.

PART IV
SOURCES

Books:

1.   Emma McWhorter, Dolly Booth, Philip Seaman and other Bull Family members, The History and Genealogy of The William Bull and Sarah Wells Family of Orange County, The Service Press, 1974.

2.   Kenneth Scott, Genealogical Data from Colonial New York Newspaper, A Consolidations of Articles from The New York Genealogical and Biographical Record, Genealogical Publishing Co., Inc., 1977.

3.   Dale Taylor, The Writer's Guide to Everyday Life in Colonial America, Writer's Digest Books, 1997.

4.   David Freeman Hawke, Everyday Life in Early America, Harper & Row, 1988.

5.   Samuel W. Eager, Esq., An Outline History of Orange County, with an Enumeration, etc., 1846-7, Reprinted by Trumbull Printing, 1969.

6.   Teresa Carpenter, New York Diaries 1609 to 2009, Modern Library, 2012.

7.   Philip H. Smith, Legends of the Shawangunk and Its Environs, Syracuse University Press, 1965.

8.   Peter E. Gumaer, A History of Deerpark in Orange County, N.Y., Minisink Valley Historical Society, 1890.

9.   Robert S. Grumet, First Manhattans, A History of the Indians of Greater New York, the University of Oklahoma Press, 2011.

10. Almet S. Moffat, Old Churches of Orange County, New York, Newburgh Printing Company, 1927.

11. Rick Revelle, I am Algonquin, Dundurn, 2013.

12. Denis Boyles with Gregg Stebben, The Lost Lore of a Man's Life, HarperCollins Publishing, 1997.

13. Cemeteries of Town of Hamptonburgh, 1980.

14. Delber Wallace Clark, The World of Justus Falckner, The Muhlenberg Press, 1946.

15. Robert C. Eurich and Robert L. Williams, Old Houses of Hanover, Historic Sites of the Town of Montgomery, Orange County, New York, Published by the Town of Montgomery, 1994.

16. Henry Z. Jones, Jr., The Palatine Families of New York, A study of German Immigrants Who Arrived in Colonial New York in 1710, Volume 1, Picton Press, 1985.

17. Henry Z. Jones, Jr., The Palatine Families of New York, A study of German Immigrants Who Arrived in Colonial New York in 1710, Volume 2, Picton Press, 1985.

18. C. H. Weygant, The Family Record: Devoted for 1897 to the Sackett, the Weygant and the Mapes Families, and to Ancestors of Their Intersecting Lines, 1897.

19. Theodore Weber Bean, History of Montgomery County, Pennsylvania, Volume 1, Unigraphic, 1884.

20. Frank Barkley Copley, The Pioneer Maid of Wawayanda, Outing magazine, Volume 54, 1909.

21. Charles C. Coleman, The Early Records of the First Presbyterian Church at Goshen, New York: 1767 to 1885, Genealogical Publishing Com, 2009.

22. Lou D. MacWethy, The Book of Names, Especially Relating to the Early Palatines and the First Settlers in the Mohawk Valley, Genealogical Publishing Com, 1969.

23. Christopher Morgan, Documentary history of the state of New York, Weed, Parsons & Co, 1849.

24. Lyman Horace Weeks, Prominent Families of New York: Being an Account in Biographical Form of Individuals and Families Distinguished as Representatives of the Social, Professional and Civic Life of New York City, Historical Company, 1898.

25. Charles Frederic Grim, An Essay Towards an Improved Register of Deeds: City and County of New York. To December 31, 1799, Inclusive, Gould, Banks, & Company, 1832.

26. J. Baskett, Acts of Assembly, Passed in the Province of New York, from 1691, to 1718, J. Baskett, printer to the King, 1719.

27. Collections of The New York Historical Society, Volume 27, 1895.

28. Catalogue of Maps and Surveys, in the Offices of the Secretary of State, of the State Engineer and Surveyor, and in the New York State Library, Weed, Parsons, 1851.

29. Archives of the General Convention, Volume 3, Episcopal Church. General Convention. Commission on Archives, J. H. Hobart, Privately printed, 1804.

30. New York (State). Surrogate's Court (New York County), Abstracts of Wills on File in the Surrogate's Office: City of New York, Volume 26, Society, 1895 - Wills.

31. Edward Manning Ruttenber, Catalogue of Manuscripts and Relics in Washington's Headquarters, Newburgh, N.Y.: With Historical Sketch,

Prepared for the Trustees, Under Act of May 11, 1874, E. M. Ruttenber & Son, 1874.

32. Congressional Serial Set, U.S. Government Printing Office, 1843.

33. Jay Campbell, Yeoman of the Revolution: The Untold Story of Joel Campbell 1735-1828, Lulu Press, Inc, Sep 27, 2016.

34. William Henry Egle, Pennsylvania Genealogies: Scotch-Irish and German, L. S. Hart, printer, 1886.

35. Henry Frank Eshleman, Historic Background and Annals of the Swiss and German Pioneer Settlers of Southeastern Pennsylvania, and of Their Remote Ancestors, from the Middle of the Dark Ages, Down to the Time of the Revolutionary War: An Authentic History from Original Sources ... with Particular Reference to the German-Swiss Mennonites Or Anabaptists, the Amish and Other Non Resistant Sects, 1917.

36. Charles E. Stickney, A History of the Minisink Region: Which Includes the Present Towns of Minisink, Deerpark, Mount Hope, Greenville, and Wawayanda in Orange County, New York; from Their Organization and First Settlement to Their Present Time; Also Including a General History of the First Settlement of the County, Coe Finch and I.F. Guiwits, 1867.

37. R. Burnham Moffat, Moffat genealogies, Press of L. Middleditch co., Priv. print., 1910.

38. New York Historical Society Quarterly Bulletin, Volumes 3-4, New York Historical Society, 1920.

39. Alice O'Connor, Poverty in The United States: An Encyclopedia of History, Politics, and Policy, ABC-CLIO, 2004.

40. Documents of the Senate of the State of New York, Volume 6, New York (State). Legislature. Senate 1904.

41. James E. Homans, THE CYCLOPEDIA OF AMERICAN BIOGRAPHY, 1900.

42. Harry Clinton Green, Mary Wolcott Green, The Pioneer Mothers of America: A Record of the More Noble Women of the Early Days, and Particularly of the Colonial and Revolutionary Periods, Volume 1, G. P. Putnam's Sons, 1912.

43. Documents of the Senate of the State of New York, Volume 23, E. Croswell, 1915.

44. J.T. White, The National Cyclopaedia of American Biography, 1907.

45. Stuart Charles Wade, The Wade Genealogy: Being Some Account of the Origin of the Name, and Genealogies of the Families of Wade of Massachusetts and New Jersey. [pt. 1-4] , S. C. Wade, 1900.

46. Minutes of the General Assembly of the Presbyterian Church in the United States: 1840-51, Presbyterian Church in the U.S. General Assembly, 1841.

47. Samuel Whitaker Pennypacker, The Settlement of Germantown, Pennsylvania, and the Beginning of German Emigration to North America…, W. J. Campbell, 1899.

48. Russel Headley, The History of Orange County, New York, Van Deusen and Elms, 1908.

49. Pioneer Families of Orange County, New York, Heritage Books, 2009.

50. Biographical Catalogue of the Chancellors: Professors and Graduates of the Department of Arts and Science of the University of the City of New York …, New York University. Alumni Association Alumni Association, 1894.

51. Who's Who in New York City and State, Volume 6, L.R. Hamersly Company, 1914

52. D. Appleton, The Centennial History of the Protestant Episcopal Church in the Diocese of New York, 1785-1885, 1886.

53. Austin Steward, Twenty-two years a slave, and forty years a freeman: embracing a correspondence of several years, while president of Wilberforce Colony, London, Canada West, W. Alling, 1857.

54. Angus Baxter, In Search of Your German Roots: A Complete Guide to Tracing Your Ancestors in the Germanic Areas of Europe, Genealogical Publishing Com, 2008.

55. E. M. Ruttenbur and L. H. Clark, History of Orange County, New York, Everts & Peck, 1881.

56. Minutes of the Common Council of the City of New York, 1675-1776, Volume 2, Dodd, Mead, 1905.

57. Ralph Weller, The H. Weller Family in America, 1999.

58. Bobbie Kalman, Nations of the Northeast Coast, Crabtree Publishing Company, 2006.

59. Bobbie Kalman, Native Homes, Crabtree Publishing Company, 2001.

60. Dr. John C. Honeyman, History of the Zion Lutheran Church at New Germantown, New Jersey, Vol. 1 Pt. 1, including the years 1715-1774, 2012.

61. Collections of the New York Historical Society for the Year …, Society, 1909.

62. Edward Manning Ruttenber, History of the Indian Tribes of Hudson's River: Their Origin, Manners and Customs, Tribal and Sub-tribal Organizations, Wars, Treaties, Etc., Etc, J. Munsell, 1872.

63. Theodore Frelinghuysen Chambers, The Early Germans of New Jersey: Their History, Churches, and Genealogies, Dover Printing Company, 1895.

64. Don Jordan, Michael Walsh, White Cargo: The Forgotten History of Britain's White Slaves in America, NYU Press, Mar 8, 2008.

65. Justus Falckner: Mystic and Scholar, Devout Pietist in Germany, Hermit on the Wissahickon, Missionary on the Hudson: A Bicentennial Memorial of the First Regular Ordination of an Orthodox Pastor in America, Done November 24, 1703, at Gloria Dei, the Swedish Lutheran Church at Wicaco, Philadelphia, 1903.

66. Edward Manning Ruttenber, History of the Town of Newburgh, E.M. Ruttenber & Company, 1859.

67. Ira Rosenwaike, Population History of New York City, Syracuse University Press, 1972.

68. William Isaac Hull, William Penn and the Dutch Quaker Migration to Pennsylvania, Genealogical Publishing Com, 1970.

69. Collections of the Historical Society of Pennsylvania, Volume 1, J. Pennington, 1853.

70. David Spencer, Historic Germantown, Horace F. McCann, 1908.

71. Robert Francis Seybolt, Apprenticeship & apprenticeship education in colonial New England & New York, Teachers college, Columbia University, 1917.

72. Andrew D. Mellick, The Story of an Old Farm: Or, Life in New Jersey in the Eighteenth Century, Unionist-Gazette, 1889.

73. Martin Grove Brumbaugh, A History of the German Baptist Brethren in Europe and America, Brethren Publishing House, 1899.

74. Colonial Records: Minutes of the Provincial Council of Pennsylvania from the organization to the termination of the proprietary government. v. 11-16 Minutes of the Supreme Executive Council of Pennsylvania from its organization to the termination of the revolution, J, Severns & Company, 1852.

75. Elaine Forman Crane, The Diary of Elizabeth Drinker: The Life Cycle of an Eighteenth-Century Woman, University of Pennsylvania Press, Oct 11, 2011.

76. Julius Friedrich Sachse, The German Pietists of Provincial Pennsylvania: 1694-1708, Page 1, 1895.

77. Lars P. Qualben, The Lutheran Church in Colonial America, Wipf and Stock Publishers, Aug 28, 2008.

78. Justus Falckner: mystic and scholar, devout Pietist in Germany, hermit on the Wissahickon, missionary on the Hudson; a bicentennial memorial of the first regular ordination of an orthodox pastor in America, done November 24, 1703, at Gloria Dei, the Swedish Lutheran church at Wiccaco, Philadelphia, Printed for the author, 1903.

79. Gajus Scheltema, Heleen Westerhuijs, Exploring Historic Dutch New York: New York City * Hudson Valley * New Jersey * Delaware, Courier Corporation, Jul 24, 2013

80. Everyday Nature: Knowledge of the Natural World in Colonial New York, Rutgers University Press.

81. Esther Singleton, Social New York under the Georges, 1714-1776: houses, streets, and country homes, with chapters on fashions, furniture, china, plate, and manners, D. Appleton, 1902.

82. Proceedings to Determine Boundaries of the Wawayanda and Cheesecocks Patents Held in 1785 at Yelverton's Barn, Chester: From Official Record in Orange County Clerk's Office, Goshen, N.Y., Independent Republican Printing Company, 1915.

83. Cuyler Reynolds, Genealogical and Family History of Southern New York and the Hudson River Valley: A Record of the Achievements of Her People in the Making of a Commonwealth and the Building of a Nation, Volume 3, Lewis Historical Publishing Company, 1914.

84. Kim-Eric Williams, The Journey of Justus Falckner, American Lutheran Publicity Bureau, 2003.

85. 50 Years of the Bull Family Picnic, Orange County, New York, Trumbull Publishing, 1973.

Some of the sources we used in this research:

Libraries
- Goshen Public Library
- Newburgh Public Library
- Middletown Thrall Library
- Piscataway Public Library
- Germantown Historical Society
- Historical Society of Pennsylvania
- Bull Stone House Collection

Cemeteries
- Hamptonburgh Cemetery, Hamptonburgh, NY
- Riverside Cemetery, Montgomery, NY
- Hebron Church/Harrison Meeting Cemetery, Montgomery, NY
- Native American/Slave Cemetery, Montgomery, NY
- Edison Historic Cemetery, Edison, NJ
- Crommelin Cemetery, Chester, NY
- Isaac Bull Cemetery, Blooming Grove, NY
- Blooming Grove Church of Christ, NY
- St. Andrews Cemetery, Walden, NY

Churches
- Blooming Grove Church of Christ, Chester, NY
- St. Andrew's Episcopal Church, Walden, NY
- Brick Church, Montgomery, NY

Interviews
- John Pennings, Historian of the Town of Montgomery
- Michael Brown, former Bull Stone House caretaker, President Emeritus of the William Bull and Sarah Wells Bull Stone House Association, former Town of Hamptonburgh historian, Bull family genealogist and historian
- Judy Wood, Bull Family genealogist
- Mary Jane Sorrell, former president of the William Bull and Sarah Wells Bull Stone House Association
- Frank Gillespie, Brick Church historian
- Linda Bull, Blooming Grove Church historian
- Henry Z. Jones, German Palatine genealogist, researcher and author
- Santa Fe College Police handwriting analyst
- Melanie Latimer, former Bull Stone House caretaker
- St. Augustine historic shipwright and clothing experts
- Edward Conner, Village of Goshen historian
- Johanna Yaun, Orange County historian
- Sherry White, historian of the Stockbridge-Munsee Band of Mohican Indians

Places
- Historic St. Augustine, FL
- Historic Germantown, PA
- Piscataway, NJ
- Edison, NJ
- Lake Minnewaska, NY
- Smithsonian National Museum of American Indian, Washington, D.C.
- Historic Society of Pennsylvania, Philadelphia
- Montgomery, NY
- Goshen, NY
- Hamptonburgh, NY
- Sugarloaf, NY
- Walden, NY
- Newburgh, NY
- New Windsor, NY
- Blooming Grove, NY
- And many other New York locations

These are just a few of the hundreds of data points we investigated in researching this book. We spent a lot of time on Google, and are thankful for that search engine and the paths it sent us down.

ABOUT THE AUTHORS

Sarah Brownell and Julie Boyd Cole are first cousins and descendants of Sarah Wells Bull.
They are great-great-great-great-great-granddaughters of John Bull, William Bull and Thomas Bull, three of Sarah's sons.

They grew up in Orange County, NY, and attended dozens of Bull Family Reunions. Their mothers, Mary Jane Sorrell and Virginia Bull Meath, are sisters and the daughters of Henry Pierson Bull. Mary Jane served as the president of the William Bull and Sarah Wells Bull Stone House Association, Inc and Virginia served on the association board.

Sarah Brownell is a published editor, writer, photographer, and researcher. She is named for Sarah Wells Bull, and now lives along the path the early settlers took into Orange County, just as many of her ancestors did.

Julie Boyd Cole is an award-winning journalist and best-selling author. She lives in Orange County as well.

Both are active members of the William Bull and Sarah Wells Stone House Association, Inc.

Made in the USA
Middletown, DE
20 February 2018